KT-368-163

# Eating Out

## Social Differentiation, Consumption and Pleasure

Alan Warde and Lydia Martens

*University of Manchester* and *Stirling University*

CAMBRIDGE
UNIVERSITY PRESS

NORWICH CITY COLLEGE

| | | |
|---|---|---|
| Stock No. | 244 467 | |
| Class | 647. 9509 | |
| Cat. | B7 | Proc 3WL |

CAMBRIDGE UNIVERSITY PRESS
Cambridge, New York, Melbourne, Madrid, Cape Town,
Singapore, São Paulo, Delhi, Tokyo, Mexico City

Cambridge University Press
The Edinburgh Building, Cambridge CB2 8RU, UK

Published in the United States of America by
Cambridge University Press, New York

www.cambridge.org
Information on this title: www.cambridge.org/9780521599696

© Alan Warde and Lydia Martens 2000

This publication is in copyright. Subject to statutory exception
and to the provisions of relevant collective licensing agreements,
no reproduction of any part may take place without the written
permission of Cambridge University Press.

First published 2000

*A catalogue record for this publication is available from the British Library*

*Library of Congress Cataloguing in Publication data*
Warde, Alan.
Eating out: social differentiation, consumption and pleasure / Alan Warde and Lydia Martens.
  p.   cm.
Includes bibliographical references.
ISBN 0 521 59044 2 (hardback). – ISBN 0 521 59969 5 (paperback)
1. Food habits – England.  2. Restaurants – England – Social aspects.  3. Consumer behavior – England.
4. England – Social life and customs. I. Martens, Lydia. II. Title.
GT2853.G7W39   2000
3994.1´2´0941 – dc21                                                       99-36184
                                                                                CIP

ISBN 978-0-521-59044-0 Hardback
ISBN 978-0-521-59969-6 Paperback

Cambridge University Press has no responsibility for the persistence or
accuracy of URLs for external or third-party internet websites referred to in
this publication, and does not guarantee that any content on such websites is,
or will remain, accurate or appropriate. Information regarding prices, travel
timetables, and other factual information given in this work is correct at
the time of first printing but Cambridge University Press does not guarantee
the accuracy of such information thereafter.

# Contents

## Part III    Delivery

## Part IV    Enjoyment: the attractions of eating out

## Part V    Conclusion

# Illustrations

**Figures**

**Boxes**

# Tables

# Acknowledgements

We are grateful to the Economic and Social Research Council for funding the study on which this book is based. The work was part of the ESRC Research Programme, 'The Nation's Diet: the social science of food choice'. We benefited from comments on the work in progress from members of other teams involved in the ESRC Programme and especially from the encouragement of the programme coordinator, Anne Murcott.

We are deeply indebted to Wendy Olsen and Karen Dunleavy, who devised and carried out some of the more complex statistical analysis. We thank Dale Southerton for help with computation, and Caroline Simms, Charlie Bamber and Penny Drinkall for assistance in the transcription and coding of interviews. We are grateful to Stuart Robinson of Public Attitude Surveys for his advice on survey design. We would like especially to thank those who read and commented on drafts of the typescript – Jukka Gronow, David Marshall, Anne Murcott and Dale Southerton.

We much appreciated the stimulation of colleagues at Lancaster University, particularly members of the Sociology of Consumption Group, who discussed with us the research project as it was developing. We learned much from discussions with friends and colleagues at various conferences – particularly from meetings of the European Sociological Association's Working Group on Consumption. We also valued comments on presentations to seminars at various universities including Edinburgh, Helsinki, Keele, Manchester Metropolitan, Reading, Southampton and York.

A period as a visiting scholar at the University of Adelaide and study leave from Lancaster University allowed Alan Warde time for sustained writing, which is very gratefully acknowledged. Thanks are also due to colleagues at Paisley University for agreeing to have Karen Dunleavy work on the statistical analysis and for a relatively light teaching load, making writing possible for Lydia Martens.

In addition, we would also like to acknowledge encouragement, support and informal help from Nick Abercrombie, Hilary Arksey, Chris

Armbruster, Jenny Harris, Kaj Ilmonen, Doug McEachern, Andrew Sayer, Sue Scott, Elizabeth Shove and John Urry.

Lastly, we are grateful to all those who agreed to take part in our research, in particular the Prestonians who liberally gave their time to talk about their domestic food arrangements and eating out experiences.

# 1    Studying eating out

There has been an explosion of social scientific interest in food in the last decade. Nutritionists, social policy advisors, anthropologists, agricultural economists and historians have always studied food habits, though for different reasons. However, before the 1990s general social scientific interest in the practical, social and cultural aspects of food was minimal. For a sociologist, the field consisted of a stuttering debate on the nature of the proper meal and its role in domestic organisation (e.g. Douglas, 1975; Douglas and Nicod, 1974; Murcott, 1983a and 1983b; Charles and Kerr, 1988), a few occasional essays on exceptional behaviour like vegetarianism, health food shopping and children's sweets (Twigg, 1983; Atkinson, 1980; and James, 1990, respectively), and Mennell's (1985) major, largely neglected, historical comparison of the development of food habits in Britain and France. This situation had changed markedly by the time of writing, with the publication of a series of literature surveys and textbooks (e.g. Beardsworth and Kiel, 1997; Bell and Valentine, 1997; Mennell et al., 1992; Wood, 1995) and of research monographs and essays (Caplan, 1997; Fine et al., 1996; Lupton, 1996; Marshall, 1995; Murcott, 1998; Warde, 1997).

One indicator of the growth of interest in food was the Economic and Social Research Council's programme 'The Nation's Diet: the social science of food choice', which began in 1992. We undertook one of the sixteen projects. We designed a survey and undertook semi-structured interviews in order to analyse the contemporary patterns and the symbolic associations of eating out and to relate those patterns to social and demographic characteristics of households. We reasoned that eating out has serious implications for any comprehensive understanding of the nation's diet. Eating out, for instance, throws into sharp relief narrow concerns with food as merely a means of subsistence, for eating out seems to be expanding as a form of entertainment and a means to display taste, status and distinction. Also significant is the willingness of people to swap their private domestic food provisioning arrangements for commercial or communal alternatives. Upon that issue hangs the future of both one of

Britain's largest industries and a major buttress of that troubled institution, the family.

At the outset of this investigation there was almost no systematic social scientific research on the nature and experience of eating out. After the project began the National Food Survey (MAFF, 1995, 39–92) reported for the first time details about eating out in the UK on the basis of its national sample survey. However, it was more concerned with the nutritional than the social aspects of the topic. Previously only highly inaccessible market research reports and occasional historically oriented campaigning books by food connoisseurs (e.g. Driver, 1983) reflected on the practice of eating out. Yet, Britons increasingly consume their food outside the home. As a proportion of food expenditure, that devoted to eating away from home has been increasing since at least the end of the 1950s.

Historical accounts of food provision tend to concentrate either on overall levels of consumption within societies, on questions of poverty and hunger, or on particular foodstuffs, like sugar or tea. Few of the general books on British food habits pay any attention to the commercial provision of meals. Restaurant and café appear very infrequently in the indexes of such works. For example, Burnett (1989) gives a comprehensive overview of changing behaviour in the UK since the Industrial Revolution, showing how differences of class and region influenced types of diet and overall standards of nutrition, and while there are useful short sections on changing patterns of eating out, only a small proportion of a large book is devoted to meals away from home. There is no satisfactory historical account of the catering industry or restaurants, information emerging in passing from Medlik (1972), Mennell (1985), Driver (1983) and Wood (1992b). General histories of food consumption in the USA make more reference to the practice (e.g. Levenstein 1988 and 1993) and, because the habit of buying meals on commercial premises is longer established, America is better served with studies of its historical and geographical diffusion (e.g. Pillsbury, 1990; Zelinsky, 1985). But literature is sparse.

Food and its consumption may be examined at several different levels. Depending upon one's purpose, attention may focus on one or more of the following: nutrients, ingredients, dishes, meals or cuisines. Each poses different kinds of analytic problem and generates different kinds of popular concern. The analytic decomposition of foods into their component nutrients engages biologists, biotechnologists, nutritionists and health professionals. Notions of diets, healthy eating, using food to protect against illness depend on the isolation, measurement and understanding of nutrients. Studies of agricultural production and the economics of the food chain, with concomitant regulations regarding the preservation and the purity of foodstuffs, direct attention to ingredients. Some of the most politically challenging issues about food production arise from examining specific food items, for example sugar (see Mintz, 1985; Fine et al., 1996). Hitherto, most scholarly attention has been paid to nutrients and ingredients. Work on dishes has been primarily practical, as the basis of training in cooking, whether domestic or professional. The stock in trade of a genre of popular literature, food columns in magazines and cookery books, are recipes giving instruction in how to prepare dishes. When people talk of cooking it usually connotes combining and assembling ingredients to create a dish. Levi-Strauss's (1966) observations about the symbolic significance of different techniques for transforming ingredients into foods – of the differences between roasting, boiling and rotting, for instance – has been a major source of social scientific reflection. Also some attention has been paid to recipes and recipe books (Appadurai, 1988; Tomlinson, 1986; Warde, 1997). By comparison there has been far less work on meals, the most clearly sociological topic because a meal presumes social ordering of dishes, rules and rituals of commensality and forms of companionship. Nor has there been much scholarly analysis of cuisine, the realm of general principles governing what is, and what is not acceptable to eat, the bedrock of general meanings attributed to food and eating in different cultural formations (though see Goody, 1982; Mennell, 1985).

Wood (1995: 112) correctly observed that theoretical claims arising from social scientific food research far outreach current empirical knowledge. More focused and detailed analysis of particular practices is essential for our better understanding of the myriad aspects of food provisioning. We therefore concentrate closely upon one level, the meal, and one of its forms, meals taken away from home. This is essentially a book about *meals out*.

Sociologists and anthropologists in the UK have operated with a definition of the meal which was formulated as a curious mix of everyday meanings and structuralist analysis. Nicod (1980, see also Douglas and Nicod, 1974), defined a meal as 'a "structured event", a social occasion organised by rules prescribing time, place and sequence of actions . . . (and which) . . . is strictly rule bound as to permitted combinations and sequences' (quoted in Marshall, 1995: 266). A snack, by contrast, has no structure. Structured eating events in Britain, Douglas and Nicod suggested, contained similar elements, but with different degrees of elaboration. Their sparse definition provided the basis for an elaborated, and arguably stereotyped, model of the 'family' or 'proper' meal, whose properties were identified in the course of interviews with households first in South Wales, then in Yorkshire (Murcott, 1982, 1983a; Charles and Kerr,

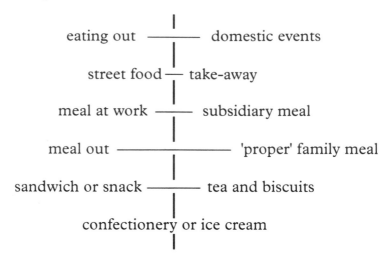

eating out ——— domestic events

street food — take-away

meal at work ——— subsidiary meal

meal out ——————— 'proper' family meal

sandwich or snack ——— tea and biscuits

confectionery or ice cream

1.1  Eating events: at home and away

1988). As many anthropologists and sociologists have noted, family meals are structured food events particularly important in social and cultural reproduction (Douglas, 1975; DeVault, 1991). Unsurprisingly, then, predictions of their erosion before social trends like commercialisation, informalisation and individualisation have given cause for concern.

Determining whether the habit of eating out is eroding the domestic mode of provision depends very much on how eating out is defined. Prima facie it is the taking of food in some location other than one's own place of residence. In that sense there are a great many eating out events; eating a packet of crisps or fish and chips in the street, as well as a sandwich in the office, a barbecue at a friend's house and an elaborate dinner in a restaurant would count, while returning home with a take-away pizza or a made-up dish from the supermarket would not. Figure 1.1 identifies some of the possible variants.

Analyses of contemporary commercial provision of meals out are mostly restricted to estimates of their economic value and prospects for future investment. Many types of organisation provide food in multifarious forms. Restaurants, bistros and cafés specialise in providing food. But for many others food is not their only service or product – hotels, public houses, hospitals and motorway service stations are only partly concerned with food and estimating the proportion of their income derived from food is hazardous. In addition, the catering industries include businesses whose purpose is not to provide meals on the premises; the fish and chip shop has been included in various different categories in official statistics over the years. When the economic and social history of the catering trades comes to be written it will not be helped much by official sources. Some indications of the dimensions and trajectory of the industry can be obtained from market research reports, of which there have been a great many in the last twenty years. But they have well recognised limitations: they are commissioned for the purpose of guiding business decisions, mostly exaggerate short-term trends, are not comparable over time, and are also not easily accessible as public documents (Gofton, 1998). Nevertheless they often offer the only available information on the shape and size of particular sectors.

By contrast there is an interesting and expanding literature on the nature of work in the catering industries. Studies of the labour process are comparatively well developed, with a little on chefs and commercial cooking (see Fine, 1995a; Gabriel, 1988; Chivers, 1973) and a considerable amount on how serving staff manage face-to-face relations with their clientele. Ethnography, observation and interviews have been effectively used to map the variety of work activities in different kinds of establishments which have developed over the years. The work of waiters in traditional restaurant settings is examined by Whyte (1948), Mars and Nicod (1984) and Gabriel (1988). Marshall (1986), Crang (1994), again Gabriel (1988) and Sosteric (1996) offer insights into the experience of waiting on in less formal settings, including pubs and theme restaurants, since the 1980s. In addition, work in fast food places has been subject to intense scrutiny as exemplary of alienated, routinised, 'Fordist' labour in the service industries (see Leidner 1993, Reiter, 1991). However, from these we learn comparatively little about the impact upon consumers. We know much more about what waiting staff think of their customers than vice versa.

That most literature is driven by the concerns of the catering industries rather than consumers is not unique to this field. Social science has typically paid far more attention to production than consumption. Reference to the consumer experience is also mostly in terms of its construction or manipulation by producers. A book by Campbell-Smith, *The Meal Experience* (1967), is often credited with formalising the marketing insight that there are many factors which influence customer satisfaction with commercially provided meals. The restaurant should be not just a provider of food but a site of a theatre performance, in which the atmosphere, appeal to sensual perception and the character of service were all key elements. A text for the aspiring restaurateur, it concentrated on aspects over which an owner might exercise control. The degree of power exercised by the provider is one issue of dispute in studies of dining out. Wood (1995: 199) endorses Finkelstein's controversial extended account in *Dining Out* (1989) which attributes considerable power to restaurateurs. Finkelstein's central thesis is that, in modern restaurants, the decor, service and atmosphere are designed in such a way as to relieve customers of the 'responsibility to shape sociality' (*ibid.*: 5). The regimes of commercial establishments are planned in a way that encourages simulated, rather than genuine, engagement between companions (*ibid.*: 52). Conventional behaviour in restaurants amounts to accepting an 'obligation to give a performance in accord with the normative demands of the circumstances' (*ibid.*: 53). Eating out, she says, is incivil. However, Finkelstein's thesis might be criticised for its scant empirical basis, its construction of customers as passive and misguided, and its indifference to the sub-cultural differences of advanced societies (see further, Martens and Warde, 1997).

Eating out has both practical and symbolic significance. People eat out sometimes out of necessity, sometimes purely for pleasure. Previous research using the British Family Expenditure Survey had suggested that modes of eating out had become a principal form in which social distinction could be expressed through food consumption (see Warde and Tomlinson, 1995). This implied that eating out had considerable social and symbolic significance for some groups, a circumstance making it worthy of study in terms of theoretical debates concerning the expression of social divisions through consumption behaviour and the bases for differential involvement in public and private spheres. Passing reference to eating out in studies of the social division of taste in North America suggest something similar (Erickson, 1991 and 1996; Holt, 1997a). Recent official data and market research reports in the UK indicate that there are social group differences both in the frequency of eating out and with respect to which venues are frequented. Income, age, region, class, gender and household composition all influence access to eating out (e.g. MAFF, 1997). However, there are many sociological questions about variations in practice which could not be answered on the basis of existing materials, hence our empirical study.

## Methods of investigation

The empirical research involved in the project was designed to examine the symbolic significance of eating out and the relationship between public eating and domestic cooking. It aimed to describe contemporary patterns and the symbolic associations of eating out and to relate these to socio-demographic characteristics of households, their domestic provisioning of food, diet and taste. A second and separate field of empirical and theoretical controversy, about domestic organisation of households, was also amenable to scrutiny via the investigation of eating out. It was anticipated not only that the composition of households would influence their eating out behaviour but also that the experience of eating out might influence domestic habits and tastes. Exploration of eating out, besides supplying the first systematic baseline study of a practice accounting for a substantial and increasing part of household food consumption, promised to illuminate many aspects of contemporary social and cultural practice.

Briefly, since methods of data collection and analysis are described in detail in the Appendix, two principal forms of fieldwork were used, semi-structured interviews and a survey. The combination of qualitative and quantitative methods is becoming a more common feature of social scientific inquiry and proved essential for this study (Brannen, 1992). As would be anticipated, the semi-structured interviews provided superior data on the meanings and reasoning associated with eating out. The survey allowed estimation of general patterns among urban populations and the opportunity for statistically based exploration of the association between the social characteristics of respondents and their conduct. The two different techniques proved compatible and the results generally complementary. We use the term 'interviewee' to refer to the people involved at the qualitative stage, and the term 'respondent' to apply to those contacted through the survey.

The research design entailed two phases of data collection. In the first, we conducted interviews with thirty-three principal food providers[1] in thirty households in diverse circumstances living in Preston and the surrounding area during the autumn of 1994. Concentration on Preston, a city in Lancashire in north-west England, with a population of 121,000 in 1991, was opportunistic, but we have no reason to think Preston highly unusual in any respect (see Appendix, p.228).

The personal characteristics and household circumstances of each are indicated in Figure 1.2.[2] Interviewees were asked questions about aspects of eating at home including descriptions of household routines and distribution of food preparation tasks. Questions about eating out included the interviewee's understanding of the term, frequency and reasons for using various places and information details about recent eating out experiences. Discussion was wide-ranging around the key topics and not all interviews addressed each topic in the same depth.

In Phase II, 1,001 people were surveyed, using a questionnaire in three cities in England; London, Bristol and Preston. Respondents were

---

[1] A principal food provider is defined, following the work of DeVault (1991: 22) as 'anyone, man or women, who performed a substantial portion of the feeding work of the household'.

[2] Names of interviewees are pseudonyms, as are the names of all commercial establishments mentioned in the text.

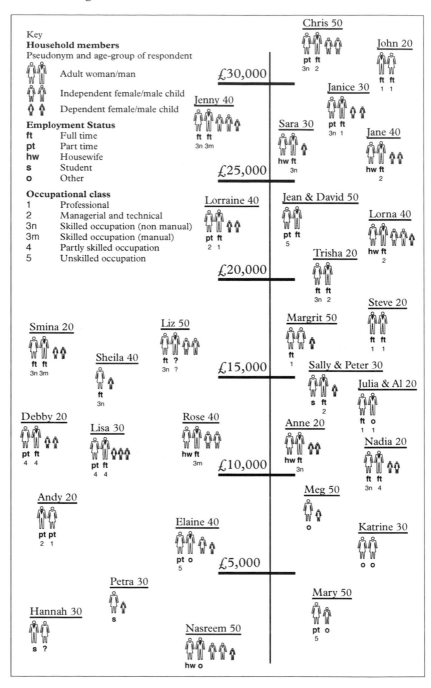

**Key**
**Household members**
Pseudonym and age-group of respondent

Adult woman/man

Independent female/male child

Dependent female/male child

**Employment Status**
ft    Full time
pt    Part time
hw    Housewife
s     Student
o     Other

**Occupational class**
1     Professional
2     Managerial and technical
3n    Skilled occupation (non manual)
3m    Skilled occupation (manual)
4     Partly skilled occupation
5     Unskilled occupation

1.2  Social characteristics of interviewees

engaged face-to-face in their own homes, interviews lasting on average between thirty and thirty-five minutes. Questions were asked to ascertain frequency of eating out, types of outlet visited, attitudes to eating out, extensive detail about the nature of the most recent meal eaten away from home and rudimentary information about domestic routines. Socio-demographic data was also elicited in order to explore variation by class, income, age, gender, education, place of residence, and so forth.[3]

The cities were chosen to offer contrasts of socio-demographic composition and, putatively, cultural ambience. Preston was included partly so that we might compare the survey findings with the evidence of the qualitative interviews, partly as representing a large northern free-standing city without any particularly eccentric characteristics. London was selected in anticipation that its unique features, including its system of supply, would prompt distinctive consumption behaviour, and the two sub-divisions were chosen to illustrate potential differences between central and suburban areas of the metropolis. Bristol was selected as an example of a southern, non-metropolitan city with some claim to be culturally heterogeneous. Since no three cities could be representative of all others in England, these sites were deemed as satisfactory as any. Despite not being a nationally random sample, there is no reason to consider the survey biased in any particular way as a basis for an initial portrait of urban English practice. The survey was undertaken in April 1995 and was administered to a quota sample which matched respondents to the overall population of diverse local sub-areas of the cities by age, sex, ethnicity, class and employment status.

Overall, our estimates of current behaviour, based on what people say they do, are derived from data which are more reliable and representative than those which sustain popular and media speculation about eating out. The use of two different methods gives us extra confidence that we can describe with unprecedented accuracy the range of experience of people eating out in England. Our complex data also give us a fair means to evaluate claims emanating from recent social theory about consumption and consumer culture.

## Theories and themes

### A service provisioning approach to consumption

We approach eating out as a case study of consumption and seek to develop sociological perspectives in the field. Recent sociology of consumption has

---

[3] The data from the survey is lodged at the ESRC Data Archive at Essex University, which holds copies of the questionnaire and the associated technical report from Public Attitudes Survey, who conducted the survey.

focused particularly on the consequences of the intensification of consumer culture and the commodification of services previously supplied by the state or household. Despite some significant theoretical developments like Featherstone's (1991) nuanced incorporation of insights from post-modernist speculation within a cultural studies tradition and Fine and Leopold's (1993) exposition of a 'systems of provision' approach deriving from political economy, there remains a need to develop more fully an integrated understanding of the relationship between consumption and production. Arguably, the further theoretical development of the sociology of consumption requires experimentation with new heuristic frameworks as well as more empirical case studies (Warde, 1996).

We adopt a 'service provisioning' framework because we believe that it is the most effective way to connect analytically processes of production and consumption (Warde, 1992). The essence of the approach, which is elaborated in the introductions to Parts I – IV, is to distinguish between the phases of production – consumption cycles involved in the delivery of services and to identify different modes of service provision. We propose that all items consumed, whether goods or services, incorporate a residue of labour and that the form of the labour affects the meaning and status of the product. The vast majority of goods now arrive as commodities, sold in the market and produced by wage labour. But services are provided from many sources, not just through the market by commercial firms, but also by the state, by household members, and by friends and non-resident kin. Such labour is often unpaid. These different modes of provision entail different relationships between producer and consumer, a proposition that might be supported, for example, by reflection on how complaints are lodged. It is also corroborated by consideration of the social relationships that entitle the consumer to receive such services. Typically, money, citizenship, family obligation and mutual reciprocity govern access to services produced in the different modes. A further key element of service provision is its manner of delivery. As regards eating out, the organisation of service (for example, formal, casual or self-service) and the manner in which interactions between server and served are managed are essential defining aspects of the occasion. The fourth element in a production-consumption cycle concerns the experience of final consumption, the feelings of gratification or discontent which the consumer derives before, during and after the event itself. A phase rarely reflected upon in any detail, we argue that it is central to appreciating the social significance of consumption practices like eating out. This framework permits analysis of key features of any consumption practice and brings to the fore some particularly important contemporary social processes.

Recent sociology has concentrated on the market mode, the commercial provision of items which previously had emanated from the state, communal or domestic modes. Substitution between modes occurs constantly, but the reason for concern about temporal succession is that each has different consequences for social relations. The obligations and bonds associated with feeding friends (communal) or family (domestic) are very different from those entailed in market exchange. For example, DeVault (1991) shows how the family meal acts as a vehicle for the socialisation of children, the reproduction of class and gender relations and the reproduction of the institution of the family itself. The commodification of meal provision might systematically transform these social relations.

*Social divisions*

Modern capitalist societies have always been characterised by powerful social divisions along the lines of gender, class, ethnicity and region which have often been manifest through differentiated patterns of consumption. Precisely how these operate and how they relate to one another is a major issue for sociology, raising both empirical and theoretical questions. For example, perceptions of 'time famine', the normalisation of consumer culture and the consumer attitude, limited employment opportunities for immigrant settlers, the changing social status of women and the levels of married women's participation in the workforce, greater travel and daily spatial mobility, intense mass media attention paid to food, and increasing affluence among the population would all be candidates for a multi-causal explanation of increasing consumption.

Moreover, different types of venue attract different social groups. For instance, French government anxiety about the demise of its culinary traditions is partly generated by the knowledge that young people are increasingly frequenting the fast food outlets of international and national corporate chains (Fantasia, 1995). Other types of establishment also have a clientele concentrated by age group. Previous research has suggested that modes of eating out have become a principal form of class distinction and that the restaurant is a site of strong patriarchal relations (see respectively, Warde and Tomlinson, 1995; Wood, 1990). Moreover, given the way in which domestic food tasks have traditionally been distributed, the benefits and pleasures derived from eating away from home might be expected to accrue more to women than men. Neither would it be surprising if there were some regional differences, nor if the size of a town or city affected the food consumption of their inhabitants.

Regarding all these issues, it seems necessary for social scientific purposes to be more precise about the patterns of eating out than has previously been required by market research or official statistics. This is partly necessary because of the proliferation of claims that social boundaries based upon socio-demographic characteristics are collapsing as social groups become less homogeneous.

Many argue that such divisions are diminishing – though few would claim that they have disappeared. Mennell (1985) argues strongly that social contrasts in food consumption have diminished during the later twentieth century. Contrasts between classes especially, but also between regions, seasons and so forth are, Mennell contends, less prominent. In parallel, market research is abandoning, or at least downgrading, the use of socio-demographic information as a way of identifying and targeting consumer markets, convinced that it is increasingly less effective for the purpose. Such trends challenge traditional sociological orthodoxy which has insisted upon the centrality of class differences in structuring consumption opportunities. The most prominent contemporary expression of such a view is that of Pierre Bourdieu (1984) who argues that styles of life are a primary means of social classification because they express distinctions between classes.

Some arguments about the decline of class see other divisions as becoming more important; for instance Shulze (1992) discerns growing generational differences in consumption. Others, however, foresee merely increasing fragmentation, the disappearance of group identification through consumption. One influential version of this diagnosis predicts greater individualisation. Individualisation may be detected when people cease to behave like other people in a similar social position and with whom they share roots and trajectories. Collective norms are less binding, the claims of other people less obligatory. It refers to a process of social uprooting, suggesting processes either of detachment from the group or of much greater internal differentiation within groups. The social origins of individualisation are usually attributed to institutional developments which make trajectories through life less predictable and hence any one's experience is less similar to those of peers. Beck (1992), for example, sees greater insecurity of employment, the erosion of class alignments, renegotiated relationships between men and women and the instability of marriage as developments requiring individuals to take greater personal responsibility for their own futures and well-being. As it is sometimes put, individuals are now obliged to choose for themselves because the comforting guidance and guaranteed support of other people in their social network is no longer available. Consumption, it is argued, is precisely one of the fields in which decisions are taken to differentiate and distinguish one individual from another. Peer groups and social networks afford neither collective criteria of good taste nor confirmation of appropriate behaviour. With fewer collective constraints conduct becomes less likely to reproduce the sense of belonging or group cohesion.

Individualisation may manifest itself in many aspects of food consumption. It might be demonstrated by a decline of the *family* meal, the reduced likelihood of eating with other family members. Members of the same household might adhere to different diets and have more diverse tastes than before. Individualisation might take the form of refusing highly-valued key items of the groups to which one belongs – for instance men refusing red meat or adolescents refusing to drink Coca Cola and eat fast food. Perhaps its most extreme expression would be the growth of a tendency to prefer to eat alone. Eating out could encourage more resolute individualised conduct by increasing the potential options as regards food items. It might also increase the range of potential companions. But it does not necessarily do either. Nor does it entail the relaxation of ritual practices surrounding food consumption.

The impression that individualisation is a major contemporary trend is much enhanced through the rhetoric of consumer choice. Sovereign consumers are precisely people who can please themselves, choosing what they personally desire without reference to anyone else. Prima facie this is more easily attained when eating out commercially than in any other situation. Only commercial venues generally offer a menu with alternatives from which one can pick a few minutes before eating. It is therefore interesting to explore the extent to which eating out is seen as, or is practised as personal choice, to examine the extent to which individual choice is actually constrained (see Martens and Warde, 1998) and to estimate the effects of group membership on taste.

### Cultural complexity

Culturally, eating is a highly complex activity. The 55 million people in the UK probably each eat about five times per day. There must therefore be approaching 300 million food events per day of which approximately one in ten is away from home (see Table 2.4, below p.33). Viewed in this context, the field might be characterised by widely shared understandings and regularised behaviour. We have few names for meal events and there are comparatively few ways of being fed. Eating is not a field much characterised by eccentricity. On the other hand, eating must fit in with people's daily schedules, material resources, social support, views of food acceptability and so forth. Consequently the practice of eating is inevitably differentiated. This raises difficulties in classifying behaviour, of recognising those features of practices which are socially or symbolically significant, of determining which aspects of difference are worthy of note.

Mennell (1985) claimed that diminishing social differences were symbiotically related to 'increased variety' in the field of food. The immediate contemporary plausibility of a claim to increased variety is attested by inspection of the shelves of supermarkets or consideration of the range of restaurants advertising themselves as specialists in the diverse cuisines of the world. Variety is a primary talisman in the legitimation and celebration of consumer societies. Variety is commonly associated with choice, freedom, personal control and discretion. Yet quite what use individual consumers make of available varied options delivered by the market is less clear. Does everyone pick-and-mix in a random way or are there preferred combinations which convey social messages? Do some people try to experience everything, while others stick to a limited range of items that they know and like? Are some items or tastes considered superior to others or are all sets of preferences of equal worth? Is there any social meaning or status attached to making use of, or knowing about, a broad range of cultural items, or is specialised concentration just as acceptable? Moreover, is the impression of variety an illusion, a way of obscuring standardisation? These are questions which arise from many studies of consumer culture and which will only be satisfactorily answered in the light of case studies of how different goods and services are used and evaluated in everyday life.

The dominant answer to these question in the last decade has been to offer a picture of fragmentation and specialisation, as the boundaries between high and popular cultures dissolve. As a consequence, cultural rules, especially those which implicitly judge aesthetic quality or the appropriateness of particular forms of consumer behaviour, may become less certain. In this respect, the process of informalisation deserves attention. Informalisation refers to a process in which social and cultural rules become less clear and their non-observance less consequential. Though often conflated with individualisation, informalisation does not necessarily refer to the atrophying of social bonds or individuals breaking away from groups and evading group sanctions, for informality can be collective (see Warde, 1997: 186–9). Informalisation implies greater flexibility and discretion, a situation for which casual observation provides evidence. Not only do rules about what to eat appear to be being relaxed, but so are those regarding how to eat. Styles of service, styles of dress, table manners, and various other elements of the interaction situation become less rigid, less bound by rules. Remaining rules are less enforceable. This informalisation of manners and of the regime of service when eating out may mean less embarrassment, greater likelihood of alternative styles of behaviour and perhaps the disppearance of anything that might be considered a hegemonic rule system.

For many, however, a world without rules is dystopian. For instance, Fischler (1980) forecast the steady advance of gastro-anomie, a regrettable condition of widespread anxiety about food choice induced by the absence of authoritative rules of conduct. Indeed, many people seek rules to guide their eating behaviour, as is witnessed by the fascinating government-commissioned report of Symons (1993) on the prospects for, and potential principles underlying, a distinctive Australian cuisine. The problem of meaninglessness might be solved by the construction of new gastronomic principles, or the recovery, reaffirmation or reinvention of older rules which define cuisine. Lack of meaning was probably less of a problem in the past; with less variety and less disposable income diet was often the effect of routinisation of behaviour embedded in a localised 'habitus' – necessity was the mother of convention!

However, the true situation may be less the absence of any regulation, more one which encourages wider interpretation and improvisation upon an older set of shared understandings and rules. Most eating events are characterised by very orderly behaviour, suggesting less anomie and more a shift to a different form of control or discipline which perhaps cannot be prescribed in the manner of a manual of etiquette but which nevertheless imposes social restraint. Notions like courses, their order, the habit of eating the whole meal in the same place and strong rules regarding disapproved behaviour persist.

### Necessity and luxury

Modern capitalist societies have constantly re-defined the boundary between necessities and luxuries. Social and cultural developments have entailed that items once the property of the few and merely the dream of the remainder become commonplace. Economic growth generates higher levels of consumption, higher thresholds of comfort and greater expectations of future satisfaction. So while people still operate with a notion of necessities to which all should have access, that which is necessary is regularly re-defined to include more goods and services. Necessities are also relative to any agent's circumstances: living in a rural area is difficult without private means of transport; making provision for childcare problematic for dual-earner households. Casual conversation provides many reasons for imagining that the imperatives of everyday life modify food habits. Eating away from home and buying 'convenience foods' and so forth are ways of aligning the requirements of regular nourishment and the constraints of daily trajectories through time and space which disperse household members. It is thus worth reflecting to what extent eating out may be accounted for by the circumstantial pressures of other social activities and conditions (like limitations of time or money) as opposed to a desire to engage for its own sake.

The distinction between need and luxury does not coincide perfectly with that between satisfaction and pleasure. Food is a necessity, and people talk of eating until they are satisfied, but it may also be a source of great enjoyment. The circumstances in which people eat – their surroundings, their companions and their schedules – also serve to create distinctive experiences. Context is all-important, perhaps especially when eating out. Hence there is much value to analysing more exactly the experience associated with the different versions of the practice in order to understand better the gratifications in a field which, prima facie, affords opportunities for a form of consumption simultaneously both necessary and pleasurable.

### The organisation of the book

The rest of the volume attempts to account for eating out as a practice. We are unable to tell with any precision how the practice has changed, but can describe in considerable detail its current condition in urban England. The book is divided into four separate parts, as dictated by our service provisioning approach to consumption, with two chapters each on provision, access, delivery and enjoyment. Within each part we report materials, usually together, from both interviews and survey. In chapter 2 we sketch the development of three differentiated systems for producing meals out – the commercial sector, institutional catering and the communal mode. Chapter 3 is concerned with shared understandings of that provision and attitudes to the practice. Chapter 4 analyses the unequal social access to eating out opportunities and chapter 5 explores the ways in which domestic arrangements affect, and are affected by, the spread of eating out. Chapter 6 examines face-to-face relationships, between staff and customers and within groups of companions, identifying the structures of service delivery. Chapter 7 describes the myriad variations in what is eaten, where and when, giving access to the nature of contemporary tastes and the social performances involved. Chapter 8 documents the levels of satisfaction expressed by people dining out and chapter 9 attempts to explain this in terms of the several types of gratification which the experience affords.

*Part I*

# Modes of provision

Eating is quintessentially a domestic activity. Most people still take most of their food at their place of residence. If we consider institutions like hospitals, military bases and religious and educational institutions as places of residence this is even more the case. Eating anywhere else has usually been the consequence of the requirements of travel or work. While the means of preparing meals at these different places of residence are various – upper-class households have servants and institutions have employees – most of the labour associated with the preparation of meals has, in the past, been delivered by household members. Given the prevalence of nuclear family households in the UK since early modern times, most of the labour associated with obtaining (though not growing), preparing, cooking, serving and clearing away food has been in the domestic mode. Familial social relations – personal, gendered, asymmetrical and enveloped in a discourse of care and love – have regulated food provision. Until recently the market mode has governed agricultural production and wholesale and retail distribution of ingredients, but the transformation of ingredients into food was not touched by the logic of economic exchange. However, increasingly with the manufacture of foodstuffs, typically convenience foods, and increasingly with the sale of completely pre-prepared meals by supermarkets, entire dishes have been supplied as commodities, though even these require assembly into meals in the domestic kitchen. The logic of commodification, with its general tendency to corrode personal bonds, invades yet further realms of practice.

The expansion of eating out draws yet other areas of food consumption into the sphere of commodity exchange. This is true not only of provision through commercial retailing establishments like restaurants but also of institutional catering. Some institutional provision has occurred under the auspices of the state throughout the twentieth century, though welfare reform in the UK has increasingly opened this up as an arena of provision governed by market competition, even if not overtly apparent to the consumers who may pay nothing directly, as in hospital, or as part of a package in which food provision is not isolated. Meals also continue to be provided in the workplace by some organisations, and whether produced in-house or by sub-contract the food is usually subsidised for the consumer. The commercial and institutional spheres are growing.

Yet the alternative modes remain surprisingly strong. As we have just argued, the domestic mode remains overwhelmingly dominant in the field of food provision. But the communal mode, supplying private hospitality to kin, friends and associates based on interpersonal relationships with people living in other households, is comparatively strong in this field. Whereas neighbourly aid, community productive activity and informal economic arrangements are of comparatively minor significance in many spheres in Britain (Pahl, 1984), provision of meals for non-household members remains quite extensive and might even be increasing.

One focus of our study is, then, the nature and consequence of shifts of the provision of meals between modes. Assuming that there is a strict limit to the amount of food that any individual can consume and that that limit has already been reached by most of the population of an advanced and prosperous society like Britain, eating out in any guise reduces the amount of domestic provisioning. If there is a current transformation from the domestic to the market mode, the process of commodifying the final service is slow. And though comparisons with the experience of the USA lead us to anticipate an inexorable trend towards more frequent eating out, prospects are complicated by the commercial counter pressure from supermarkets, social processes of familial privatisation and so forth.

In this part of the book we examine provisioning, the first phase in the production-consumption cycle. We describe first the nature and extent of the production of meals supplied outside the household. We then turn to popular understandings of that provisioning process, using evidence from what our interviewees said about eating out and entertaining others in their own homes.

Chapter 2 uses secondary sources to chart the development of the habit of eating out in Britain, by definition a shift from domestic to other modes. We ask questions like, how are those meals which are not eaten in the home provided?; who does the work and under what circumstances?; and how might this have altered in the last thirty or so years? We consider in turn the developments in three spheres, the commercial restaurant and hospitality industries, the institutional catering sector and the communal mode. The most pronounced recent shift has been the growth of the market mode, with a steady increase in the purchasing of meals pre-prepared by commercial establishments of many different types. Though now in decline, provision of cooked meals subsidised by either the state or employers was very much a feature of the twentieth century. The factory canteen and the school dining hall, not to mention the 'British Restaurants' subsidised by the state during the Second World War, were alternative means to get a cooked meal away from home. The communal mode also has had an important part to play in the feeding of the nation, with visits to the homes of family and friends a common means of obtaining a meal. In each case the social relations of provision and access are different and the meaning of the event varies accordingly.

The popular or ordinary meanings of such events are the topic of discussion in chapter 3. Shared understandings are retrieved through the analysis of discussions in the interviews in which people talked about eating out. Their understandings of what was being supplied, in what circumstances and under what conditions was it appropriate to take advantage of opportunities to eat out, are used to throw light on the moment of provision. Interviewees' vocabulary, their everyday means of classifying eating events, was a complex matter, but tacit, shared meanings were extracted. Despite most people being equally familiar with the communal alternatives, the prevalent definition associated the term eating out with its commercial variant. We discuss reasons why people eat in commercial establishments and isolate prevalent attitudes about the activity. We then examine popular understandings of the provision of hospitality: with scant source material available, we examine what interviewees said about both entertaining and being a guest (supported by some survey evidence) to identify the social preconditions sustaining networks of hospitality. From this we create a typology of the characteristics of different modes of supply as composite forms based on the mutual understandings of providers and users. The conditions of production sustained by the co-operative practices of consumers both constitute and differentiate modes of provision.

# 2   The development of the habit of eating out in the UK

This chapter sketches developments in the provision of opportunities to eat out and reflects on the terminology used to describe different venues. It then reviews the available, limited, evidence about the features of three modes of provision – the commercial–retail sector, the institutional catering sector and the communal mode of entertaining kin, friends and acquaintances. This information, derived from secondary sources, is necessary to contextualise the behaviour reported by our interviewees and respondents. Some understanding of provisioning is also required for theoretical reasons, since our analytic approach requires a comprehensive appreciation of all stages in production–consumption cycles.

There are many types of place away from home where currently people may eat a meal in Britain. Some of these are commercial establishments which specialise entirely in the provision of food. Thus we have, among others, cafés, restaurants, steakhouses, diners, brasseries, bistros, pizzerias, kebab-houses, grill rooms, coffee bars, teashops, ice cream parlours, food courts, snack bars, refreshment rooms, transport cafes and service stations, buffets and canteens. There are commercial places to eat which are not primarily devoted to food provision, like the tavern, the pub, the wine bar, the hotel, the in-store restaurant, the boarding house and the motel. There are commercial establishments that provide food to be eaten off the premises – fish and chip shops, lunch counters, sandwich bars and other purveyors of take away or carry out foods. There are, in addition, places which are not solely commercial, such as the canteens, dining halls and refectories of institutions like factories, hospitals, schools, universities, prisons and the armed forces, where the food provided is subsidised or free. Also there are places which are often commercial but not permanently fixed: mobile cafés, catering tents at weddings, race meetings, shows or carnivals. And, of course, one can also eat out at someone else's home, in their kitchen, dining room, living room or banqueting hall, depending upon the social standing of friends or family.

The meanings carried by these different contexts in England are varied and it is difficult to identify a generic term, other than the cumbersome 'eating out place', that describes all of them satisfactorily. 'Restaurant' suggests something elaborate and formal, 'dining room' is redolent of domestic arrangements, 'café' brings to mind something informal and so on. This presents us with some problems of nomenclature, what to call the places where people eat out without prejudging either the type of setting or the occasion. For want of more mellifluous terms we use 'eating out place', 'setting' or 'venue', and sometimes 'establishment' – the last only when referring to commercial places.

The nuances of the terminology applied to eating out places give some insight into the history and development of the catering industries in Britain. Eating away from home must always have occurred when in transit, for economic, military or social purposes. Travel, beyond a certain distance from home, necessitates eating out and most historical accounts of the development of commercial meal provision have concentrated on trends in frequency of travel. Thus Medlik (1972) offers an account of the development of the market for the catering industries which is almost entirely dependent upon the expansion of travel. Increased frequency and intensity of travel is the primary cause of the expansion of commercial facilities for eating out.

There was a network of inns, offering entertainment and accommodation, in England at least as far back as the fifteenth century, and there travellers ate. According to Heal (1990: 203) England had an international reputation for its entertainments, and its banquets in the fifteenth and sixteenth centuries, which were available for travellers who thus no longer were forced to rely on hospitality in private households or monasteries. However, it would seem that availing oneself of a meal provided commercially was restricted to people journeying until sometime at the end of the eighteenth century. Subsequent expansion of services was also dependent upon the extension of commerce and of business travellers. Travelling a distance to work, whether to agricultural markets or commuting to factory or office, where it prevented return home for a midday meal, provided another means by which changed spatial arrangements encouraged eating out. As the habit of taking a vacation, which before the twentieth century was a prerogative of the upper classes, spread to most of the population, a further series of facilities to feed people away from home was generated, especially the seaside hotels, boarding houses and cafés. In all these cases, however, the growth of eating out was associated with, and secondary to, the pursuit of other activities. Now, by contrast, the idea of eating out for its own sake, as a type of entertainment, is predominant in lay understandings of the term.

In England, paying to dine out for pleasure, by preference rather than in situations where no domestic alternative was available, began at the end of the eighteenth century, in the gentleman's club (Chivers, 1973: 643; Mennell, 1985: 155). This remained a largely private occasion, in the sense that one had to be a member of the club. During the nineteenth century hotels increasingly sold meals, but these would be served in people's rooms, rather than in a public dining room, one effect of which was to permit respectable women to eat out. The public dining room, where anyone with sufficient funds could go to eat, in the presence of others, is a creation of the late nineteenth century. The Grand Hotels of the period were the sites where people went to dine out, for its own sake, for pleasure, in public. From the late nineteenth century large hotels had dining rooms open to non-residents where elaborate meals could be eaten, and the restaurant dates from the same period. An aspiring trade journal for restaurateurs, which began publication in August 1909 and ceased in December 1910, tellingly observed, 'the restaurant of today is not merely an annexe to the hotel, in ever-increasing numbers, it has an independent existence of its own, with interests that are not necessarily those of the hotel. These interests *The Restaurant* has been founded to promote and protect' (*The Restaurant*, August 1909:1). The emergence of specialised places to eat out, particularly where there was a choice of food rather than a limited menu, was essentially a commercial innovation of the twentieth century.

It is the gradual evolution of eating out into a leisure activity that characterises the last hundred years. Burnett (1989: 318) records that 'in a recent survey of leisure activities, going out for a meal or entertaining friends to a meal at home were rated as the most popular occupations after watching television.' Eating out has become *popular* entertainment. People say they like going out to eat, and they expect to derive pleasure from it. This is not to say that eating away from home out of necessity has declined, probably the opposite. But the habit of eating out for pleasure has spread to a large proportion of the population.

### The commercial mode

In considering market sector provision it is unclear how best to classify outlets, a necessary precondition for estimating the rate of development and differentiation of the catering industry. Industry statistics are not comparable over time. The complexity of the types of eating out place makes accurate charting of the development of commercial provision very difficult. There is a mosaic of provision, subject to largely arbitrary, though socially intelligible, classification. Provision has become increasingly complex, a function of both the search for profitable commercial opportunities by producers and the changing social circumstances of

Table 2.1 *Number of businesses in catering and allied trades, 1984–1994, by groups of the Standard Industrial Classification (1980)*

|  | 1984 | 1990 | 1994 |
|---|---|---|---|
| Restaurants, snack bars, cafés and other eating places | 41,897 | 48,764 | 42,500 |
| Public houses and bars | 42,010 | 40,155 | 36,591 |
| Night clubs and licensed clubs | 17,786 | 16,806 | 14,740 |
| Canteens and messes | 1,483 | 2,704 | 2,324 |
| Hotel trade | 12,934 | 14,444 | 12,002 |
| Other tourist or short-stay accommodation | 1,605 | 2,027 | 2,038 |
| Total | 117,715 | 124,900 | 110,195 |

*Source:* Business Monitor (1996), *UK Service Sector: catering and allied trades*

potential customers. Some data sources refer primarily to the providers and their organisations, others to consumers.

Precise description of changes in the industrial structure of catering is difficult because official statistics have intermittently altered their way of classifying establishments (for an overview Medlik, 1972: 1–6). The Standard Industrial Classification scheme in 1948 recognised only 'Hotel and Catering', a category that was subsequently sub-divided several times. The frailty of the official data means that most scholars have been forced to rely upon market research reports for their estimates of the scale and scope of the industry. We are no exception.

The main useful source of official information on production is the Business Monitor (1996) for the catering and allied trades. In 1990, it reported 124,900 catering businesses in the UK. This compared with 109,471 in 1980. The figure fell back sharply during the 1990s so that by the time of our fieldwork in 1994 there were only 110,195 businesses. Nevertheless, turnover had risen quite sharply, by 20 per cent in the same five years. The number of businesses in the various sectors is listed in Table 2.1. However, many businesses have more than one outlet and there is no official source of data concerning the number of establishments.

Market research reports give more detailed information about the structure of the industry. In 1995 the commercial market sector had a value of about £24 billion, the institutional sector being worth a further £15 billion. The size of elements of the commercial sector is indicated by Table 2.2. Again, classification of activities is problematic; hotels and

Table 2.2 *UK commercial catering sector: turnover 1995*

| Sub-sectors | Value (£ billion) |
| --- | --- |
| Restaurants | 5.3 |
| Fast food and take-away of which: | 5.9 |
| sandwiches | 1.8 |
| burgers | 1.4 |
| Public houses | 3.1 |
| Hotels | 6.2 |
| Contract catering | 2.3 |
| Other (licensed clubs, holiday camps and caravan sites) | 1.2 |

*Source:* KeyNote, *UK Catering Markets: 1996 market review* (London, Keynote, 1996)

pubs are major sources of meals but have other business too. The fast food and take-away sector is large and of marginally greater value than restaurants and cafés. A KeyNote report(1997:1) recorded that in 1995 only 2 per cent of enterprises had a turnover in excess of £1 million while 84 per cent had less than £250,000.

The sector is characterised by the coexistence of some corporations with high levels of capital concentration and many small family enterprises. As Fine (1995a: 9) points out, competition in some areas of the restaurant trade conforms almost to 'an ideal type of a true free-market system in that capital barriers to entry into the market are relatively modest, large numbers of entrepreneurs compete, and consumers make choices with relatively little pressure'. This sector is thus seriously unstable, as high levels of competition result in frequent failure: Fine (1995a:11) cites estimations suggesting, for restaurants in the USA, that '20 per cent close within a year and that half close within five years'. Moreover the catering trade as a whole is susceptible to economic cycles. Market research reports are prone to estimate short-term prospects for growth directly in terms of upswings and downturns, for people spend less on meals out when times are hard. Larger operators are better able to deal with this instability.

The turnover of the giant corporations in the sector is enormous.[1] Their strength is increasing: as a KeyNote report (1997a: 1) describes the

[1] Reporting for annual periods between 1994–6, Allied Domecq PLC turned over £8.9 billion, Grand Metropolitan £8.0 billion, Scottish and Newcastle PLC £3.0 billion, Whitbread PLC £2.8 billion and Granada Group PLC £2.4 billion (KeyNote, 1996: 12).

trends of the mid-1990s, 'the sector is becoming more concentrated, and the leading players, led by Whitbread, City Centre Restaurants and Bass, are increasing their penetration with a wider range of branded chains covering many of the growing market sectors'.

The catering industries are major employers. The percentage of the workforce in hotel and catering increased from 3.2 per cent in 1971 to 5.6 per cent in 1990 (Euromonitor, 1993:37). In 1990, 1.26 millions were engaged in the commercial sector, and 1.12 millions in the institutional sector. Using figures from the *Labour Market Gazette* for September 1995, a KeyNote report(1997: 16) calculates that there were about 1.3 million persons employed in the hotel and restaurant industry and that 333,000 were in the restaurant sub-sector.[2]

Probably the most striking feature of the changing nature of production besides its increase in volume is the differentiation of the types of establishment. Payne and Payne's (1993) estimate of the number of outlets in the retail meal sector in 1992 gives some indication of the different types. There were approximately 58,000 public houses, 'the great majority' of which now serve food; and 40 per cent had a full restaurant facility. There were also about 1,000 steakhouses, 16,000 mainstream restaurants, 1,500 travel-related and miscellaneous catering outlets, 9,500 sandwich bars, bakery outlets and cafés, 8,000 other fast food/take-aways, 10,000 fish and chip shops, 4,000 burger bars, 4,300 pizza 'outlets' (45 per cent with home delivery), at least 1,000 in-store restaurants, and also no fewer than 15,000 hotels.

Competitiveness encourages differentiation between enterprises. Restaurants sell meanings as well as food (Campbell-Smith, 1967; Finkelstein, 1989). The outcome in recent years has been a rapid expansion in the variety of outlets as businesses try to secure a share of the market. One growth sector is the 'ethnic' specialist restaurants, whose cuisines are increasingly drawn from every corner of the globe. There is no adequate historical source on the growth of restaurants serving foreign cuisine in the UK.[3] Perhaps the most enlightening British account is given by Driver (1983: 74), who maintains that in the early 1950s,

---

[2] The majority of employees were women. Slightly less than half of all employees worked full-time. Of women, almost two in three worked part-time. The commercial and the institutional modes have in common, and indeed are characterised by, the fact that preparation, cooking and serving of food is accomplished by workers who are paid wages. However, the nature of the jobs involved varies considerably depending upon which aspect of the labour process any worker is involved in and upon the type of outlet (see Gabriel, 1988, for a very informative comparison of work experiences in the UK).

[3] The USA is rather better served, as the spread of ethnic cuisine since the colonial era has been described by Gabaccia, 1998, and its commercial outlets mapped for the 1980s by Zelinsky, 1985.

'outside London, the concept of an entire restaurant devoted to a non-European, or even a European, "ethnic" style was almost wholly unfamiliar'. Before then there had been longstanding admiration of French cuisine; ever since the Napoleonic Wars the British elites had enjoyed the services of French chefs and the most prestigious British restaurants offered French dishes, and often complete menus written in French. There is also some evidence of Italian provision from the end of the nineteenth century, though mostly in cafés and through the ice cream parlour. There were also some Chinese cafés in docklands areas, in Cardiff and Liverpool as well as London, and some Jewish outlets in North London. But otherwise catering outlets, and much more so domestic provision, were overwhelmingly British.

Driver (1983) emphasises the rapid expansion of the restaurants offering Chinese, Indian and Middle Eastern cuisine in the period between the mid-1950s and the mid-1970s. He attributes their expansion to patterns of immigration, and to the specific mixture of entrepreneurial ambition among migrants and aptitude of particular cuisines for adaptation to English tastes. Accordingly, Hong Kong Chinese, Indians, Pakistanis and Cypriots were the main instigators for the introduction of the new cuisines that became popular by the 1970s. Other immigrant groups were much less likely to establish catering businesses for a variety of reasons.

A substantial proportion of both the independent restaurants and take-away outlets sells ethnic cuisine, in particular, Indian and Chinese. The extent of such provision is uncertain. Driver (1983) estimated that there were 4,000 Chinese catering businesses in 1970, a mixture of restaurants and take-aways, the shift towards the latter having come in the 1960s. Gabriel (1988: 142) gives figures for establishments in 1983 when there were 'over 12,000 restaurants and cafes providing meals on the premises. Of these, some 3,000 were Chinese, some 2,000 Indian or Pakistani, some 2,000 Italian, some 500 Greek and Turkish, and some 100 French.' The more recent estimate, by Payne and Payne (1993) is that there are about 8,000 ethnic restaurants and rather more than 5,000 take-aways selling 'ethnic' foods.

Historically, this range is unprecedented. As Driver (1983: 89) put it, talking of the opportunities afforded by London: 'An arena where numerous cuisines from different parts of the globe meet and compete in public, importing their own characteristic foodstuffs and making substitutions from what is available locally, and drawing customers from a common pool of "floating eaters", is a new phenomenon of the twentieth century.' Expansion has occurred alongside increasing specialisation of the establishments providing prepared foods. Attempts to capture the diversity of eating out places in typologies have not been particularly effective. Symons (1993) reflecting on Australian provision, distinguishes between restaurant, brasserie, bistro and café, effectively a continuum of price and formality, but only for establishments whose primary purpose is meal provision. Given the widespread use of other sorts of venue his classification is limited. Finkelstein (1989, 68ff.) created a somewhat eccentric typology of seven types of place 'on the basis of their status and cost', with the key dimension of variation being whether places provided for celebrations, simple amusement or convenience. Market research schemes in Britain, which we adapted for our survey, use hybrid criteria of cuisine, function and industrial sector in order to distinguish between cafés, ethnic cuisine restaurants, pubs, hotels and travelling services. While a more coherent taxomony would be useful, the factors involved in differentiating species are numerous. Types of commercial establishment vary in character with respect to at least five criteria: the putative primary requirements of their main clientele, the nature of the service, the elaborateness of cooking, the ostensible pedigree of the cuisine, and whether alcohol is for sale.

One criterion is the primary purpose of the customer. Most obviously, the motorway service station, the railway buffet, the airport lounge, though also the works canteen and the food court in the shopping mall, are classified first and foremost by their functional role. The nature of the customer's trip, often involving a meal being eaten in a restricted period of time and perhaps being subsidiary to another activity like work, travel or shopping, explains the customer's presence. This functional aspect of a venue is reflected partly in its opening hours and partly by its geographical location. The special requirements of customers in such situations mean that these are not commonly the sites of the most elaborate meals, for which there are alternative forms of provision.

The practice of self-service has always characterised some forms of institutional provision, the cafeteria being the generic description of a place where one had to put one's own food on a tray and take it to one's place at a table to eat. Self-service has steadily increased in British commercial outlets, being characteristic of cafés and teashops and becoming increasingly common at bar meals, fast food outlets, transport cafés and buffets (including carveries and salad bars). There are different degrees of self-service. Customers may take a tray, load food and utensils on to it, pay at a check out, and take the food to a free table. One may order food by standing in a queue, and then sit down and have the meal brought to a table, an arrangement for many bar meals, and which lacks many of the rituals of formal service. The setting of a table in advance, with varying quantities of utensils, is usually a sign of a greater degree of formal service. To have one's order taken while seated in an anteroom (with an apéritif, for example) and then to be ushered into a dining room where all table settings are identical and where it is anticipated that the customer will eat several courses, is indication of the highest levels of personal service, though additional degrees of formality are symbolised by the clothing (and the number) of the waiting staff.

A third criterion of differentiation is the elaborateness of food and in particular its style or mode of presentation. Something between a snack and a light meal is sold by teashops. A more substantial plate of food is offered by bar meals, where people mostly eat only one course. A meal with two, and particularly more, courses is likely to be associated with a restaurant. In other words, the length and complexity of the meal typically served is a further criterion for determining how an establishment should be described.

Eating out places are also differentiated by the style in which they cook their food. Most typically this is indicated in terms of its cuisine – vegetarian, wholefood, or 'ethnic', for example, Indian, Italian, English. But some venues are depicted by their tendency to specialise in preparing a particular ingredient, as with steakhouses, by a mode of cooking, as with the carvery, and by a core type of dish, pizza, burger or pancake for example. These are defined not by cuisine, but by the type of dish which dominates the menu.

The extent to which the regulation of the consumption of alcohol has influenced the eating out patterns of north European societies can hardly be overestimated. Legislation licensing the sale of alcoholic drinks has produced distinctive national variations in provision. The current pattern in Britain arises in significant part from the tortuous regulations about the availability of alcohol. Supplying alcohol was itself a specialised activity until recently, with 'public houses' usually selling, at most, snacks. The development of the restaurant trade has also had an intricate relationship with the temperance movement and the licensing laws. One important use of the terms public and private has related to restrictions on who shall be allowed to buy alcohol. A private hotel may serve alcohol to people also staying overnight, but not to other passers-by. Some specialised eating places have 'table licences only', which means that people may drink alcohol only as accompaniment to substantial meals. One way of distinguishing a café from a restaurant used to be that the latter may sell alcohol to diners, or announce 'bring-your-own', while the former will not.

The potential range of ways of combining these various elements (a self-service pizza for the rapid lunch, a quick meal in a place without alcohol, formal oriental banquets requiring sustained concentration, a casual evening meal as an adjunct to drinking in a pub) creates much opportunity for the commercial sector to appear to innovate, promoting novelty, difference and brand distinctiveness to 'thematise' particular meal experiences. Commentators on eating out, particularly market researchers and food journalists, alight excitedly on new trends and fashions. Among the most recent trends gaining publicity in the UK, with both commercial and aesthetic consequences, are: the emergence of food halls in shopping centres (Payne and Payne, 1993); the introduction of other entertainment into restaurants (Crang, 1994); the café bar (KeyNote, 1997); as well as a proliferation of specialisation in the provision of more exotic and authentic ethnic cuisines (Warde, 1998); and growing distinctions between the establishments whose principal function is providing meals, the restaurant and its generic types. Prima facie, variety and options have increased. Such tendencies might lend support to general theories of post-Fordism, the idea that provision becomes increasingly differentiated and flexible to satisfy customers who are more discerning, more concerned with the aesthetic aspects of lifestyle and more likely to demand items tailored to their individual preferences. However, the trends are not so simple.

Counter-trends operate. Capital concentration continues to create chains of outlets, often franchised, which provide a standardised branded product using industrial production techniques redolent of the car assembly plant. McDonalds, in 1997, reputedly had 21,000 restaurants around the world (*Guardian*, 26 June 1997) and 730 in the UK (KeyNote, 1997) dedicated to providing a virtually uniform meal experience. A large segment of the catering industry is oriented towards producing nothing more than acceptable nourishment to people with an immediate need to eat. Many independent outlets have the same suppliers of the same pre-prepared foods which are simply reconstituted at the retail site. The accelerating routinisation of new fashion, transmuting the exotic into the mundane within a few years as successful innovations are rapidly copied, flattens the sense of variety. Thus it is not without grounds that Wood (1994a and 1995), for example, complained about the tendency towards the standardisation, and indifferent quality, of meals out in the UK. The catering industry offers many examples both of mass production and of specialisation and differentiation.

If the evidence concerning the extent and development of the catering trades is sparse and partial, that concerning its customers is no better. Official statistics record frequency and amounts spent on eating outside the home, but little else. Again market research reports provide some means of supplementing the available data, though they often provide insufficient definition of the means of collecting and coding data.

A systematic indication of the changing use of commercial catering facilities can be obtained from official expenditure figures. There are two major annual surveys of the public which allow some appreciation of the changing scale of provision, the National Food Survey (MAFF) and the Family Expenditure Survey (FES).[4]

The National Food Survey only began to examine in detail food eaten away from home during 1994, the year we began fieldwork. Its primary interest was in the nutritional aspect of consumption away from home, which it estimated on the basis of expenditure reported on foods not extracted from 'the household stock'. In both 1994 and 1995 it was shown that 22 per cent of food expenditure was on food taken away from home. However, the level of expenditure reported is considerably less than that in the Family Expenditure Survey and is probably an underestimation. The National Food Survey estimate for 1995 of average spending on food, soft drinks and confectionery away from home was only 78 per cent of that of the Family Expenditure Survey and only 52 per cent of that for alcoholic drinks. The Family Expenditure Survey is probably more accurate in its estimation of overall expenditure of adults, as the National Food Survey (1997: 41) points out. However, the National Food Survey (1997: 42) usefully describes the pattern of expenditure between different kinds of outlet. As Table 2.3 shows, about 10 per cent of expenditure on food away from home is made at work, pubs and restaurants are main sites of expenditure, ethnic restaurants take more money than do the fast food chains, and pubs and wine bars are very popular sources of food.

The National Food Survey also indicates the distribution of expenditure between meals, 'composite' snacks and individual items bought away from home. Of the £3.87 spent per person per week in 1995 on food eaten away from home, £2.01 was spent on meals, 57 pence on composite snacks, which include the products of fast food outlets, and £1.30 was spent on individual items, like sandwiches, ice creams, fruit and so forth (National Food Survey, 1997: 39). That is to say, 52 per cent of food

---

[4] The NFS began during the Second World War as a means to check the effects of rationing on nutrition among the British population. Since then it has been published annually. It is concerned with the size of markets for different products, and nutrient intake and food expenditure of households.

The annual national Family Expenditure Survey began in 1959 and is concerned with total household spending. The data on food expenditure is broken down into food categories: different types of meat, milk products, etc. The number of categories has changed over time; in 1995 there were sixty-three food and twenty-one alcohol categories. A main advantage of the FES is that it contains substantial socio-demographic data on income, social class, region, etc. It has several thousand, randomly selected, respondents in any year.

Table 2.3 *Expenditure on food and drink eaten out by outlet type, 1995*

| | Pence per person per week | | | | |
|---|---|---|---|---|---|
| | Food | Alcoholic drinks | Soft drinks including milk | Confectionery | Total |
| Restaurants, pubs and take-aways | 277.9 | 119.8 | 14.7 | 0.4 | 412.8 |
| of which: | | | | | |
| public houses and wine bars | 56.1 | 103.7 | 6.3 | 0.1 | 166.1 |
| major chain fast food outlets | 21.0 | – | 1.4 | – | 22.4 |
| other take-away outlets | 28.3 | 0.1 | 1.4 | 0.2 | 29.9 |
| ethnic restaurants | 28.3 | 2.3 | 0.3 | – | 31.0 |
| other restaurants and cafés | 144.1 | 13.8 | 5.4 | 0.1 | 163.5 |
| Workplace[a] | 35.0 | 0.9 | 3.4 | 0.9 | 40.2 |
| School[a] | 14.6 | – | 1.7 | 0.6 | 16.9 |
| Other outlets: | 59.8 | 31.6 | 13.8 | 8.2 | 113.5 |
| Retailers in food and drink | 29.6 | 1.8 | 8.5 | 7.1 | 47.1 |
| Mobile vans and street vendors | 5.1 | – | 0.3 | 0.1 | 5.6 |
| Other | 25.1 | 29.8 | 5.0 | 0.9 | 60.9 |
| All outlets | 387.4 | 152.3 | 33.6 | 10.1 | 583.4 |

*Note:*
[a] includes canteens, shops and vending machines. Adults working in schools record expenditure against workplace, not school
*Source:* National Food Survey, 1995: 42, Table 4.5

purchased and eaten away from home was spent on meals, though that figure includes some drinks.[5] The National Food Survey notes differences in expenditure by region (the South-East spends a lot), by household type, by income, by gender (men in 1995 spent more money on food, about a third more than women) and by age group (National

[5] The NFS has typical problems in defining its terms and distinguishing between meals, snacks and other eating events. To quote its glossary (1994: 131): 'a meal is an eating occasion which cannot be described by a single food item code, but which includes a main dish. In addition a meal must be served and consumed on the premises of one of the following types of outlet: respondent's workplace, school, restaurant, public house, catering facilities on trains, buses or aeroplanes, meals on wheels or other catering facilities such as hospitals, football grounds, etc. A meal is distinct from a meal occasion, which is defined as breakfast, mid-day or evening meal or other eating or drinking occasion and may comprise a meal or drink or snack or any combination of these.'

Table 2.4 *Number of meals taken outside the home (per person per week) 1974–1995*

|       | midday meals | other meals out | all meals out |
|-------|--------------|-----------------|---------------|
| 1974  | 1.70         | 1.20            | 2.90          |
| 1979  | 1.81         | 1.39            | 3.20          |
| 1984  | 1.71         | 1.58            | 3.29          |
| 1989  | 1.89         | 1.95            | 3.84          |
|       | basis of time altered in 1990[a] |     |               |
| 1993  | 1.77         | 1.14            | 2.91          |
| 1995  | 1.77         | 1.17            | 2.94          |

*Note:*

[a] Prior to 1990 having a meal of four different types was allowed, reduced to three (breakfast, midday, evening) after 1990. The implication is that a significant proportion of the other meals in the 1970s and 1980s were of an intermediate kind (whatever that may mean).

*Source:* Household Food Consumption and Expenditure (MAFF, HMSO) and National Food Survey (MAFF, HMSO), various years

Food Survey, 1997: 42–6). The 1994 survey showed that slightly more money was spent on food away from home at midday than in the evening; £1.87 as compared to £1.35 per person per week (National Food Survey, 1995: 45) . This suggests that there is still a significant proportion of 'necessary' expenditure associated with work obligations, though it would help to know what proportion of the midday food is actually in the form of a meal rather than snacks or sandwiches.

One other feature of the National Food Survey is that it recorded intermittently the frequency with which respondents ate out and at what time of day. As Table 2.4 shows, the number of meals taken away from home in the middle of the day has remained fairly constant since at least the early 1970s, and other meals increased fairly steadily throughout the period. However, a change in the method of calculation which apparently excluded 'meals' taken mid-morning and mid-afternoon, suggested that even in the 1990s midday remains the main time for eating out. Thus the National Food Survey calculates that during the period of our fieldwork the mean frequency per person (including children) of eating a meal out was about three times per week, but that 60 per cent of those occasions were in the middle of the day.

It is reasonable to assume that a good many of the midday meals consumed were at work. The published Family Expenditure Survey has given explicit information about expenditure on meals at work and on school

Table 2.5 *Expenditure on eating out, 1960–1993 (households per week)*

|                                          | 1960  | 1970  | 1980   | 1990   | 1993   |
|------------------------------------------|-------|-------|--------|--------|--------|
| Total expenditure (£)                    | 16.40 | 28.57 | 102.55 | 236.07 | 276.68 |
| Food expenditure (£)                     | 5.09  | 7.35  | 23.52  | 43.20  | 49.96  |
| Percentage of total                      | 31.0  | 25.7  | 22.9   | 18.3   | 18.0   |
| Eating out (£)                           | 0.50  | 1.00  | 3.95   | 9.04   | 10.43  |
| Percentage of food expenditure           | 9.8   | 13.6  | 16.8   | 20.9   | 20.8   |
| Percentage of total expenditure          | 3.0   | 3.5   | 3.9    | 3.8    | 3.8    |

*Source:* Family Expenditure Survey, various years.

meals since 1994. Previously there was merely a figure for 'meals eaten outside the home' and an (increasingly large) category for 'other foods'. Generally, the Family Expenditure Survey is the more valuable source for estimating change over time for sociological purposes because it contains better socio-demographic data. Table 2.5 shows changes in household expenditure on eating out since 1960. This table shows that eating out has taken a steadily increasing proportion of the household expenditure on food, rising from 10 per cent around 1960 to 21 per cent in 1993. This is evidence of a major shift in the ways that households provide for themselves. However, as a proportion of total household expenditure it has grown very little over the same period, from 3.0 per cent to 3.8 per cent.

The accounting method changed for the 1994–5 Family Expenditure Survey, making eating away from home appear more extensive than before. As Table 2.6 shows, food *obtained* in prepared form (i.e. ready to eat), comprised 27 per cent of all food expenditure. Thirteen per cent was on restaurant and café meals, the principal topic of our analysis, and 4 per cent on meals at school and at work. One of the other categories includes ice cream, soft drinks and confectionery, to the combined value of £1.25, as well as 'hot and cold food' (see Family Expenditure Survey, 1994–5: 110, Table 7.1). If those were excluded from the calculation, along with those take-away meals eaten at home, then probably just under 20 per cent of food expenditure is on main meals and snack meals taken away from home.

Expenditure on meals at work and at school, because relatively cheap, may cover frequent meals and, of course, some of the expenditure on restaurant and café meals would also be meals taken during working time. However, the proportion of food or total expenditure devoted to eating out for entertainment must be less than 13 per cent and 2 per cent respectively.

Table 2.6 *Households in UK, 1994–1995, expenditure per week: in total, on food and on food not from the household stock, pounds sterling and as percentage of expenditure*

| | |
|---|---|
| All expenditure | £283.58 |
| Food expenditure | £50.43 |
| Percentage of total | 17.8 |
| *Food not from household stock (percentage of food expenditure)* | |
| Restaurant and café meals | £6.74 (13.4) |
| Take-away meals at home | £2.06 (4.1) |
| Other take-away food and snack food | £3.07 (6.1) |
| State school meals and meals at work | £1.77 (3.5) |
| Total | £13.64 |
| Percentage of food expenditure | 27.1 |
| Percentage of total expenditure | 4.8 |

*Source:* Family Expenditure Survey, 1994–1995 (HMSO, 1996)

## Institutional catering

Factories, offices, hospitals, schools, prisons and universities all provide refreshment on-site in a canteen or refectory for a clientele restricted by criteria of membership rather than the ability to pay. Of course such meals may be paid for, though rarely by the consumer at a full market rate. This, the industrial and institutional provision of food, 'is generally described as non-commercial or social catering in that it is not principally concerned with making a profit, though the recovery of costs, either in full or in part, is an important consideration' (MINTEL, 1994: 4). This sector of provision only developed after the First World War (Chivers, 1973:641). Members of such organisations, and perhaps their guests, are provided with food of various qualities under modes of provision other than the market.[6]

The number of people eating in this mode has been falling. MINTEL (1994:4) reports, with remarkable detail: 'Over the past decade the industrial and institutional catering market has been in decline, with the number of meals served annually down from 3 billion in 1984 to around 2.5 billion in 1993. The decline is a result of changing government policy on school meals provision; the contraction of heavy manufacturing

---

[6] The private (gentleman's) club is a further example, with the possibility that food is subsidised by income from the organisation's other activities.

industry; and the effects of the present recession.' Nevertheless, there were still 82,605 separate institutional catering sites in 1993, 42 per cent in educational establishments, 31 per cent associated with health and welfare organisations, 22 per cent on business and industrial premises (MINTEL, 1994:86). The value of the sector was estimated at £15 billion per annum in 1995 (KeyNote, 1996: 1). Moreover, the size of this market, looked at from the point of view of producer firms, remains both considerable and lucrative. So-called contract catering is expanding and recent British government policies to sub-contract many activities previously done in-house by state agencies have rendered this a profitable source of investment with highly concentrated ownership. In 1993, when there were 2,457 contract catering firms operating, the three largest (Gardner Merchant, the Compass Group and the Sutcliffe Catering Group) accounted for 52 per cent of the sector by value (MINTEL, 1994:6).

From the point of view of users, however, such outlets rarely deliver highly valued eating experiences. Nobody we talked to when asked about their ideal meal out suggested a school dining room or factory canteen as a venue. These are places which, though giving relief from hunger, would never be conceived as providing entertainment. Yet institutional catering remains a major source of meals out and a reason why in their consumer survey MINTEL (1994: 150–4) found that 51 per cent of respondents claimed to eat out at least once a week. Indeed, 21 per cent of their respondents claimed to eat out 'most days', but when asked about eating out 'in leisure time', this was true of only 3 per cent of respondents. This underlines the importance of the distinction between eating out as entertainment and eating out as necessity.

In institutional settings meal events are symbolically very important. For example, in prisons and hospitals food events punctuate the day so as to define daily routines (see Bell and Valentine, 1997) and the key role of school meals in socialising children into the rules of public commensality has been stressed by Morrison (1996). However, the only institutional setting about which we collected data was the workplace.

For many employees until very recently the workplace was the principal venue in which they would eat out. Workplace cafeterias, together with school meals, still absorb a considerable proportion of expenditure on eating out: according to the Family Expenditure Survey for 1994–5, 13 per cent of all food bought away from home for immediate consumption was spent on state school meals and meals at work. Of our survey sample, 29 per cent claimed to have eaten in their 'workplace canteen or restaurant' in the last 12 months, or 42 per cent of those who had a place of work.[7] For them, mean frequency was 3.5 events per week, a minority of which events were described as main meals. The mean frequency of taking a main meal at work was approximately 1.2 times per week for those who ever did so.

Those who eat most frequently in the workplace are likely to be younger, from households containing more than one full-time worker, to have a higher income, to have no co-resident children and to have an A-level or higher qualification. Listing the times of day at which they would usually eat in a canteen: 78 per cent of those who ever ate at work, usually consumed lunch. Those who ate out several times a week were particularly likely to do so at lunchtime, and the main meals consumed were also most likely to have been lunches. While fewer women than men ever eat in the workplace, those who do have the same patterns of behaviour as men.

Estimating change in the use of workplace canteens and restaurants is problematic because earlier data sources are not directly comparable and are often poor. The most reliable of earlier studies implied that eating at work was a very significant element of eating out. Warren (1958:63–4) asked a sample of 4,557 people in 1955–6 what and where they had eaten on the previous day. Forty per cent of men and 20 per cent of women had eaten a midday meal away from home. Among the men, about 20 per cent had eaten at work, about 12 per cent in a café, restaurant or hotel, and 3 per cent at friends' or relatives'. The comparable figures for women were 8 per cent, 6 per cent and 2 per cent. Warren suggested that 28 per cent of weekday midday meals were eaten away from home, 18 per cent (or two in three) in the workplace.

What might be considered surprising is that our survey of 1995 discovered roughly the same proportion of people eating at midday in their place of work. The fact that ours was not a national random sample might account for this in part; perhaps there are more organisations with workplace facilities in London, Bristol and Preston than in smaller places. But the implication seems to be not so much an erosion of eating in the workplace as the extension of eating in other venues. Nine per cent of our respondents said they had eaten their last main meal on commercial premises between noon and 3 pm on a weekday

In sum, though levels of eating in the workplace may have been falling in recent years, the extent remains very considerable, accounting for the fact that still more meals are eaten out in the middle of the day than in the evening. Some people eat more than once a day at work, about one third of eating events in the workplace canteen are main meals, and the middle of the day is the most popular time for such occasions.

[7]  611 respondents were in paid work and 86 were students.

### The communal mode

The communal mode is defined by its being non-commercial, for though some money may change hands during such transactions this is exceptional and the amount involved is not calculated to reflect the monetary value of the product. The defining feature of the communal mode is its being organised on a principle of reciprocity (whether direct or indirect). One person grants labour services to another in the expectation that this will be returned in some form on another occasion. There is potential for considerable complexity, for the communal mode involves some apparently pure gift-giving, often reciprocity is not immediate, and sometimes it is combined with the commercial mode (as with weddings and christenings where some stages of the event occur in a hotel and others in the home of the person throwing the party). Its principal current form is domestic entertaining, the offering of hospitality in the home of the host(ess) to friends, non-domestic kin or others to whom some obligation is recognised.

If it is difficult to establish the history of the catering industry with any degree of precision it is near to impossible to estimate the changing scope and scale of private hospitality. A brief and sketchy history would suggest that early forms of eating out were governed by communal rules of access. Travellers were treated as guests, and the hospitality due to strangers remains an important aspect of the food rituals of many societies (see Zubaida and Tapper, 1994). However, Medlik (1972: 23) suggests that in the UK as far back as the thirteenth century, the provision of food and lodgings, while occurring in private households or institutions, might be paid for. But nevertheless literary sources would suggest that private hospitality for friends and acquaintances was normal among some sections of the population throughout the last millennium. Until the twentieth century, private hospitality was offered most profusely by the aristocracy and gentry, and subsequently by the commercial and industrial bourgeoisie (Chivers, 1973). Literary and biographical sources attest to that fact and to the elaborate meals that might be offered in such circumstances. Whether entertaining, except for kin, was part of the normal experience of other sections of society is obscure.

Without doubt, ordinary people entertained at annual celebrations, Christmas, seasonal festivals and birthdays, and to mark major life events, like marriages and funerals. The extent to which friends and acquaintances were accommodated must have varied. Some of these events would be restricted to kin and not all necessarily would take place in a domestic environment. But it is possible that entertaining people by giving them a meal was quite rare. Accounts of working class communities in the 1950s and 1960s insisted that scarcely anyone other than kin would ever be invited into the home (e.g. Dennis et al., 1956; Hoggart, 1958; Willmott and Young, 1957) and there is little reason to suppose that the character of working class sociability changed subsequently (see Allan, 1979). There is also little indication that the lower middle class behaved any differently. Even other sections of the middle class may have been infrequent entertainers; after the demise of domestic servants following World War I, it may have taken some time for middle-class women to develop the skills and inclination to prepare dinner parties for their friends. However, the women's magazines of the 1960s were giving advice about entertaining, both buffet style for parties and in the manner of elaborate dinners. That entertaining was part of middle-class life in the 1970s was illustrated in passing by Jerrome's (1984) study of a friendship circle of older women whose regular meetings almost always included provision of refreshments which were often elaborate. However, it seems likely that the habit of inviting friends around to eat a meal was comparatively rare, especially among the working class, until very recently.

Our survey gives a means of estimating the extent of entertaining. We asked respondents whether they 'ever have people from outside your household to eat a *main* meal in your home?' and if so what sort of people and how often. Of our sample, 77 per cent said that they did sometimes have people for a main meal at their home; 62 per cent sometimes invited friends to eat, 60 per cent entertained other family members and 12 per cent sometimes had work colleagues round to their home to eat a main meal. Some respondents entertained very regularly: 5 per cent had guests for a main meal several times a week and a further 14 per cent had people once a week. Entertaining others to dinner is an important aspect of contemporary sociability. Table 2.7 shows respondents' estimates of frequency of entertaining. Other data from the survey imply that they perhaps slightly overestimate the regularity with which they supply meals for guests. Indeed, they probably also slightly exaggerate the frequency with which they are themselves guests. Respondents' estimates of their behaviour over the last year indicated that 43 per cent of meals out were in the communal mode, while reports of the last meal out showed that only 38 per cent were in other people's homes.[8]

While there is little with which to compare our findings, Warren (1958) shows that in the mid-1950s about 2 per cent of people had eaten yesterday's midday meal at the home of friends or relatives, and that about 2 per cent of people had eaten an evening meal or a late supper in such locations. Calculating the annual incidence of such events and comparing it

---

[8] Estimates for the last year showed almost an identical number of events at which respondents had been hosts and guests.

Table 2.7 *Respondents' estimates of how often they had entertained
in the previous year<sup>a</sup> (percentages)*

|  | Percentage |
|---|---|
| Several times a week (60+ times a year) | 5 |
| Once a week (31–60 per year) | 14 |
| Once a fortnight (16–30 per year) | 13 |
| Once a month (8–15 per year) | 22 |
| Once every 3 months (3–7 per year) | 14 |
| Once every six months (2 per year) | 5 |
| Once a year/less often | 2 |
| Never | 23 |
| Don't know/ no answer | 2 |
| Total | 100 |

Note:
[a] How often would you say you have people to a *main* meal in your home?

with estimates from our survey suggest that communal meals occurred 50
per cent more often in 1995 than in 1955. However, the samples are so
different and the estimates so rough that such calculations should not be
considered reliable. One striking aspect of Warren's evidence was the fact
that 'upper'-class men were four times more likely than men of other
classes to have eaten the last evening meal with friends or relatives, there
being no class differences apparent for women.

Our survey shows that the habit of entertaining others by providing them
with a main meal is unevenly dispersed in the English population. The
socio-demographic characteristics which predisposed respondents to
entertain frequently were, in order of strength, extent of educational
qualification (only 12 per cent of people with degrees never entertained,
compared with 36 per cent of those without any qualification), belonging to
professional, managerial and intermediate white-collar occupational
classes, having a higher household income, being female, having a father in
the service class rather than the manual working class, living as a couple and
having more than one person in the household in full-time employment.
Thus, as might have been expected, the communal mode of meal provisioning is most prominent among the educated, affluent, middle classes.

## Provision: a summary

The available evidence indicates the existence of a complex mosaic of provision with each of the three different modes delivering very substantial

numbers of meals every day. Patterns of social use are, however, hard to decipher, making the new data arising from our investigation particularly valuable. Production for profit, in both sectors of the catering industry, retail and institutional, is increasing, as measured by turnover, employment and consumer expenditure. Some of this gain is at the expense of in-house catering by large organizations, which are providing fewer meals than they did fifty years ago. Nevertheless, the number and proportion of meals eaten during work shifts has probably not declined, and continues to account for more than half the expenditure, and therefore a substantial majority of all meals purchased out of the home.

The commercial sector provision of meals primarily for purposes of entertainment and leisure is also expanding, though at an uneven rate, which partly results from its susceptibility to the vagaries of economic cycles. There is evidence of increasing differentiation of provision, as fashions for new forms of delivery and exotic cuisines are introduced. Whether these have the effect of expanding the trade and its variants overall, or simply of replacing defunct businesses is uncertain. Nonetheless, meals for entertainment demonstrate a capacity to appeal to consumers and to absorb an increasing proportion of their food expenditure. At least in terms of household expenditure there are strong indications of changing use of the three alternative modes of provision of meals out.

The most obscure sector, historically and currently, is private hospitality. The extent and the character of this system of provision, where people invite visitors into their homes to eat, is largely unknown. Entertaining at home involving the provision of meals was probably comparatively rare earlier in the century, expanded during the 1960s but has perhaps, as anecdotal evidence suggests, declined since the 1980s. While we can offer no new evidence on trends, both survey and interviews document a vigorous system of reciprocal mutual hospitality in the mid-1990s. How people understand that system, what codes and rules they follow, what adaptations they invent to suit their living and working arrangements is one of the most fascinating topics of this study.

# 3    The meanings of eating out

In *Feeding the Family* (1991), DeVault deploys the concepts of *social organisation* and *shared understandings* in her analysis of why it is women who are recruited into the project of caring for the family.

The concept of social organization explains how women (and others) enter social relations, actively producing their own activities in relation to the activities of others. It points to the importance of shared understandings about particular settings, recognizing that these are subject to change through negotiation, disputation and improvisation, but that they are always relevant to human conduct. (DeVault, 1991: 12)

The notion of social organisation emphasises the significance of individual agency as well as the bearing of larger social relations on this activity. DeVault, who draws on Dorothy Smith's feminist methodology, suggests that the starting point of her analysis is the careful listening and interpretation of accounts of 'everyday lived experience', by which she means 'what happens in people's everyday lives – as well as the processes of interpretation that give meaning to everyday lives' (1991: 11). Individual accounts reveal something about the wider social power relations within which everyday life takes place; 'we find that social organization is "in the talk" and that we can mine the talk for clues to social relations' (DeVault, 1990: 101).

DeVault uses the 'family' as example. 'When we speak about contemporary families', she argues, 'we refer to two kinds of realities, to both experience and institution' (1991: 14). People experience 'family' in diverse ways. But there also exists an institutionalised version, or dominant idea of 'the family' in Western industrial societies. This dominant idea, or ideology of family life, prescribes 'particular ways of doing the work' that produces 'family' (1991: 13). The dominant discourse is one example of a shared understanding about a particular setting (the 'family'), and is evidence of how larger social relations – and their 'legislation' for appropriate conduct – are compelling forces shaping activity at the everyday level.

We use the same framework and techniques as means to understand

Table 3.1 *A working definition of eating out*

| Food is | Consumed outside domestic sphere | Consumed inside domestic sphere |
|---------|----------------------------------|----------------------------------|
| Prepared outside domestic sphere | Eating out (1) | Eating in (3) |
| Prepared inside domestic sphere | Eating out (2) | Eating in (4) |

the nature of the experiences and their interpretation in the field of eating out. We look at how meal provision is understood by consumers in the commercial sector and by providers in the communal mode.

### Shared understandings of eating out

At the beginning of our semi-structured interviews we asked all interviewees first what they understood by the term 'eating out' and then which of a number of eating events might be included. These events were a club barbecue, a restaurant meal, tea or coffee and cake at a neighbour's home, a sandwich in the workplace, Sunday lunch at the home of family, a bar meal in a pub, a snack in a café with friends, and breakfast in a bed and breakfast place when on holiday. All those events would be included as 'eating out' under our initial working definition, the consumption of all foods taking place outside one's own household (see table 3.1). This definition excludes borderline cases like take-away foods; prepared and purchased outside but consumed within the domestic sphere (case 3 in table 3.1). It also excludes foods prepared by non-household members; for instance, caterers at a wedding or birthday party held at home (case 4 in table 3.1). It includes what may be regarded as insignificant instances of eating out, such as the consumption of a packet of crisps or an apple in the street. Differentiating between the consumption of food in household and public settings, this definition emphasises the spatial aspect of where one eats.

Our interviewees' views were more complicated. The twenty-three valid responses to the question 'which of the eating events listed do you consider as eating out?' are presented in table 3.2. The eating events: 'tea, coffee and cake at a neighbour's home' and 'having a sandwich in the workplace' were least likely to be included as eating out. The two events which were most likely to be included as 'eating out' were 'going for a restaurant meal' and 'having a bar meal in a pub', effectively revealing the popular understanding of the activity.

One aspect of the consumers' understanding of eating out is its socio-spatial separation from the domestic setting. Jean's comment: 'eating out

Table 3.2 *'Do you consider this eating event eating out?': aggregated responses from twenty-three interviewees*

|                                           | Yes | No | Don't know/not answered |
|-------------------------------------------|-----|----|-------------------------|
| Restaurant meal                           | 21  | 1  | 1                       |
| Bar meal in pub                           | 20  | 2  | 1                       |
| Snack in café with friends                | 13  | 10 | 0                       |
| Breakfast in B and B on holiday           | 9   | 12 | 2                       |
| Club barbecue                             | 7   | 12 | 4                       |
| Sunday lunch at family's home             | 5   | 11 | 7                       |
| Sandwich in the workplace                 | 2   | 18 | 3                       |
| Tea, coffee and cake at a neighbour's home | 1   | 16 | 6                       |

to me is when you're away from home', was one example. Interviewees who held this notion strongly came closest to our working definition, and tended to call all the events of table 3.2 eating out. Others rejected eating at the home of family, and sometimes even the homes of friends, hotels, and bed and breakfast places because they were too closely associated with 'home'. Janice explained:

Sunday lunch with the family, or breakfast in a bed and breakfast? Yeah I've not really thought about those, but I wouldn't have thought you know, my initial reactions are that's not eating out. But yes you are out of your own home but er it's food within a home if you will . . . again when you are on holiday your bed and breakfast place becomes your home for the period of time that you are staying there. So your breakfast is not away from home as such.

A second aspect of common understanding concerns the work involved. Eating out was, for male and female interviewees, food prepared and served by others. As Sally put it: 'If I haven't cooked it, it's eating out.' Where consideration of the preparation was uppermost, events like takeaways or having someone cook something for you in your own home were classified as eating out.

A third aspect of the meaning of eating out was that it involved payment. John, for example, said, 'er . . . what do I understand by the term eating out? Going out for a paid meal I would consider as eating out.' The dominant view was that eating out occurred on commercial premises, in a pub or restaurant. Steve reasoned aloud about the term:

Usually eating something somebody else has cooked rather than me. I suppose that would include my girlfriend but I don't really suppose that counts, it all depends, she's gone to all the trouble of cooking a meal and setting the table so I suppose that's akin to eating out. But usually when I go eating out it's me and her so she's eating something that somebody else apart from us has cooked, so I suppose that's what I understand by eating out, not having to put any effort in, you don't have to wash the dishes. So I suppose it would include eating some food that somebody I know has cooked as well but like I say it doesn't happen very often, on very rare occasions.

In the end, though, he concluded, 'I suppose a restaurant really is my typical idea of eating out'. The implicit assumption was that eating out happens in commercial outlets, thereby assigning other food events, such as those that take place in the home of family and friends, to another realm. Sheila dismissed eating at someone's home because she associated the activity with commercial enterprise, yet when asked about her workplace canteen invoked a fourth criterion, its social character, as primary:

SHEILA: I wouldn't consider sandwich in a work place (eating out). Even though I'd bought it, I wouldn't consider that eating out.
INTERVIEWER: Why is that?
SHEILA: I don't know. It sounds more like a social activity, eating out, and that's certainly not a social activity. I mean going to work isn't.

Others, like Andy, who especially valued the sociable aspect of eating out, were more inclined to include eating at someone's home.

A fifth, and very important, aspect was that it was special. Meanings of the concept 'special' included references to 'what is eaten', 'how often the event occurs', and 'where'. So, eating events which involved small quantities of food (snacks as opposed to meals), and/or 'lesser qualities' of food, and/or types of food which were eaten regularly or on everyday occasions, and/or in 'non-distinct' or 'everyday' places were likely to be judged not, or less, special. The less 'special' the events listed in table 3.2, the less likely they were considered to be eating out. So, for example, Jenny did not think of the café as a site of eating out 'because we do that every Saturday. When me and my mum go into town we always end up having our dinner in town.' Similarly, Trisha said that because she ate at her parents' home so often, it was instead part of their weekly routine. Typical was Peter's emphasis on place, food quality and quantity: 'Eating chips in a car is eating out! But I think my immediate response to eating out would be erm . . . a special occasion, dining, in a restaurant or a café or something.' Two interviewees of South Asian origin, Smina and Nadia, commented that eating out provided the opportunity to get a 'change from the everyday'. In Smina's case, the emphasis was on getting a change from 'everyday Asian foods'. For Nadia, additional primary factors were getting away from 'everyday places', like the home, and an association of eating out with 'special' occasions and times, like holidays.

Eating out? I would say eating out would mean a special occasion, going to a restaurant. Different atmosphere altogether. You want something different from the everyday ordinary life at home. Breakfast in a B and B – erm . . . yes I would call that eating out, although it's still in the hotel I would call it eating out, because the holiday's a special time as well. You know it's a different sort of food in a Bed and Breakfast as well.

The sixth and final aspect of the lay understanding equates eating out with eating a *meal*, an entity with particular properties. Eating out, according to Lisa, was 'sitting down to a nice big meal', and according to Rose it meant being 'given a menu'. In terms of a structured menu, eating out was thought to involve a meal. We did not explore, nor were we told, of what this meal ought to be made; that is, what its ingredients and methods of cooking would ideally be. However, as is clear from Lisa's comment, meals eaten out are ideally 'big' meals, and they probably will comprise more than one course. Like its domestic equivalents, the 'proper' meal out is not a snack. For this reason a club barbecue or a snack in a café were excluded because of the small quantities of food. Chris, for instance, said that she saw barbecues as 'a little bit of a supper type of thing', whilst a sandwich in the workplace was just 'taking your quick snack'. Related was the idea that eating out meant that the meal was the main purpose of the activity. This was emphasised by Chris: 'A snack in a café with your friends? – no I would probably see that as a shopping trip and maybe nipping in for something to eat.'

One of Charles and Kerr's (1988: 20) respondents alighted on another aspect of the distinction between a meal and a snack:

A proper meal is an occasion, for want of a better word, where everybody will sit down together and take time over eating a meal and do it properly, whereas a snack is something that you could just eat while you were doing something else and on your own, whereas a meal is, I think, an occasion.

When eating out our interviewees commented on the importance of sitting down for the meal, at a table, for some considerable time, during which table manners were adhered to. In terms probably peculiar to eating out, reference was made to dress codes and choice from a menu. Trisha commented: 'I don't usually eat it at the same time as I would have my tea. Really have it a later time because it's the purpose of getting ready and going out for a restaurant meal', suggesting that meals out typically happen later than at home.

In summary, six themes were identified. Eating out is a specific socio-spatial activity, it involves commercial provision, the work involved is done by someone else, it is a social occasion, it is a special occasion, and it involves eating a meal. Interviewees did not mention all these features in their answers, most of them accounting for three or four. These six themes constitute the shared understanding of eating out. The first three – the socio-spatial, commercial and preparation aspects – were particularly prominent in answers to the unprompted question 'what do you understand by eating out?'. These themes may be seen as primary. The other themes, stressing sociability, specialness and meal content aspects, come to mind when further qualification is offered. For instance, people deliberate whether being entertained is also eating out, whether some commercial events are not special enough, or fail to count in terms of occasion or food content. It is important to recognise that this shared understanding – that eating out occurs infrequently, in commercial places, where one goes specially to eat a meal – affects answers to all questions about how often people eat out, when they consider was the last time they ate out and their stated reasons for doing so.

### Reasons to eat out: pleasure, leisure and necessity

The component elements of the definition of the practice identify some reasons why people eat out. But not all are encompassed. Unprompted lay understandings primarily identified reasons for eating in restaurants and pubs, presupposing that reasons for engaging in other events are not necessarily the same. A comparison of reasons for visiting cafés and buying take-aways throws light on the meaning of leisure, pleasure and necessity.

General reasons for eating out included doing or experiencing something different from the everyday, getting a break from cooking and serving, relaxing, having a treat, socialising, celebrating, a liking for food, and preventing hunger. Many of them closely resemble elements of shared understandings of eating out.

Given the emphasis on 'special' in understandings of eating out, it is unsurprising that one reason why our interviewees ate out was related to doing something other than the usual or the everyday. 'Getting a change' included eating different foods, at different times (on holidays and at weekends), in different surroundings (from home or known and tested commercial venues), and in different company (whether acquaintances or strangers). For example, Trisha reasoned: 'Well part of it is wanting to try something different and usually somewhere different. Like if we go to somewhere like Lancaster or something we can also try different pubs and meet different people.' Liz also sought relief from the mundane: 'I like getting dressed up instead of being practical, something practical all the time. I like the aspect of getting washed and changed and dressing up and going and sitting down, having a conversation.' 'Getting a change' referred to both paid work and domestic experiences. Others emphasised the opportunity to relax and wind down from paid work: 'I think it's nice to sit over a meal and have a bottle of wine and coffee and relax. And er, just, it's like a winding down, really I think especially after a week at work.' Phrases like 'getting a treat' or 'getting a reward' were used with reference to both paid and domestic work. Chris cited the busy pace of life and a full schedule of obligations:

And if I've been working on a Friday which I was, we used to have Norman's father for a meal on the Friday evening because he was on his own, his wife had died, so Friday night I was jiggered, Saturday then was spent you know tidying up in the mornings, Saturday afternoon was spent taking my father to see my mother. Saturday evening comes I don't want to be in that kitchen again do I? So I said oh well this is getting silly, I'm too tired to be doing that, so we started either having a take-away or you know going out for a meal.

Whilst some interviewees pointed to the pleasure of being away from home, a break from everyday cooking and serving work was an important aspect, mentioned by all but one of the female interviewees.

Another recurring reason for eating out was to socialise with friends, family, or partner. Socialising with friends was the main reason why Meg ate out in restaurants. Some respondents said that eating out now was the preferred mode of socialising with friends, compared with going to a pub or 'going around town'.[1] Eating out was a means for some others to build and maintain a romantic relationship with a partner, although some married respondents made a point of saying that they no longer ate out only with their partner.

Celebrating special occasions was an often mentioned reason for eating out. For some, like Janice, who had last visited a restaurant to celebrate her wedding anniversary, and who commented: 'usually it's a celebration or something, it's a special occasion', this was the main reason. Particularly among those short of money, eating out was thought indulgent and required a good excuse. Special occasions were seen as good reasons. Interviewees unencumbered by monetary constraints might eat out on special occasions, but sometimes also pointed out that they ate out whenever they fancied it. Thus not all interviewees thought eating out to be extravagant, and this related to their material circumstances.

Two further reasons for eating out stand out because few interviewees mentioned them explicitly. One was a liking for food. Peter and Sally

---

[1]   That pub visits may be less numerous amongst women and older people was corroborated by survey findings. We asked respondents how often they visited pubs for drinks, and regression analysis suggests that the strongest indicators of variation in pub visits are ethnicity, gender and age; men visit pubs more frequently than women, and young people visit pubs more often than older people.

made a point of saying that a liking for food was a good enough reason for eating out, even though money was not abundant in their household.

PETER: I think we eat out obviously because we enjoy eating, . . . I mean I think we do enjoy having a meal prepared for us, and we like the food. And then we'd use somebody's birthday or anniversary as justification for doing it (laughs). Yes, we're going out to eat, we're not needing . . .

INTERVIEWER: . . . an excuse or?

SALLY: I suppose, perhaps everybody feels like we need a legitimate excuse. I was trying to think if there was an excuse for going to Stephanos last time we were there. I am sure we just decided . . . it's such a nice place

Physical need was the other reason, which, when mentioned, was related to travel and being away from home.

One final reason for eating out was social obligation. Lorna, whose case we return to in chapter 9, ate out only when she felt she had to. In the first instance, she was not keen to talk to us because, she said, she and her husband hardly ever ate out. There were two main reasons. Lorna enjoyed only foods which were 'plain' and 'as nature intended it', not those cooked in 'weird and wonderful ways'. She disliked foods cooked in sauces and prepared using alcohol, and she abhorred garlic. Also 'fancy' restaurants were considered a waste of money, because Lorna was unlikely to enjoy the food. However, she conceded that when eating out was the only way to socialise with friends or family, 'a price we'd have to pay would be having a meal', going on to describe visits to 'pub-restaurants' catering for their particular food tastes, at acceptable cost, located nearby, so that afterwards they could easily return home with their companions to socialise further.

Visits to teashops and cafés were part of the social and leisure activities of a number of interviewees. Our impression was that cafés served as an alternative to the workplace canteen for students. Sally, a student, mentioned visiting cafés as a means to meet fellow students, whilst Steve observed that since he stopped being a student and became employed, he visited cafés less frequently.

Café and teashop visits were often part of more extensive social activities; they were done in combination with shopping, with going on trips and with work. Visiting cafés with colleagues, friends, family or a partner was done by both men and women. Even so, a marked difference was apparent in the way men and women talked about their reasons for engaging in such activities. Women who visited cafés and teashops explained these visits in terms of socialising in small groups, with a friend, a sister, a mother or a partner: Jane and Jenny visited cafés with their mothers, Meg would meet one of her daughters in town at least once a week, whilst

Debby and her sister Lisa both commented on going into town together. Men, by contrast, emphasised getting a break or a rest. John said: 'What we do when the work is getting very stressful, there's only one course of events and you go to Marco's [a local café].' Visits to teashops and cafés were commonly seen as part of, or a break from, another activity. No mention was made of special occasions, a love for food, getting a break from cooking. The café has a different social meaning from the restaurant.

Some respondents ate substantial lunches in their workplace canteen every day. This was the case for Steve and Jenny. For Steve, an engineer at Technology International, his workplace lunch was his main meal of the day, so that he avoided preparing food for himself at home. Jenny's reason for treating her 'dinner' as the main meal of the day related to her time restrictions as a full-time employee and mother; by eating a large meal at lunch time, she would use the time that her family sat down to eat in the evening for doing housework. Some interviewees bought their lunch in the workplace, but ate it elsewhere. Others used alternatives, like cafés and teashops, during their lunch breaks. Trisha and her colleagues actively avoided the canteen: 'no we don't bother at all really. Because it's just within this building so if you go there and if your telephone rings you have to go and answer it. So I'd rather go out.' Whilst eating during work time is for some a welcome break, overall interviewees spoke in mainly utilitarian terms, suggesting that workplace canteens offer undistin- guished occasions with little meaning other than to re-fuel the body.

Attitudes towards take-aways were more polarised. Some interviewees were vocal about their reasons for avoiding them, citing four concerns: health, food quality and authenticity, personal tastes and cost. For instance, Andy immediately invoked the discourse of health to explain his infrequent consumption of fish and chips:

take-aways and fish and chips again are rare. I've tried to kind've steer away from the high fat food again. 'Cos when I eat like that I don't actually feel as healthy and maybe I don't know whether it's a placebo effect but I'm aware that if I'm eating kind've chips that have been fried in beef dripping or something like that, I felt the stodge factor cutting in quite a lot, so I, we don't tend to do that.

When asked why he did not use other take-away provision like Chinese or Indian take-aways much, he continued by complaining about the lack of 'quality' and the 'inauthentic' nature of take-away provision. Mary, Elaine and Lorna were also averse to foods served by Chinese, Indian and Italian take-aways. Elaine said that they did not eat Chinese take- aways because her husband 'would never have Chinese', whereas Lorna commented that she hated the smell of garlic and consequently never joined in when her husband and son ate a take-away pizza. Lorna and

Mary were both suspicious of foods that were commercially produced, and according to Mary, home-made foods were 'healthy' foods and commercial foods were 'unhealthy'.

I'm basically eating in the past amn't I? But like I said I don't get stomach upsets or indigestion or ulcers. So maybe, it's not been a bad thing has it? Going back. You know? Eating what me mother made, yes. I mean some can eat too many things, can't they, spicy foods and they finish up with ulcers don't they?

Others valued take-away meals for their relative cheapness, 'convenience' and their use in socialising. The term 'convenience' was only mentioned once, but the ideas of convenience, ease and getting a quick meal without having to expend labour, were implied by respondents commenting on the role of take-aways in their weekly eating routines. Fridays and weekend days appeared to be favourite times for using take-away meals. The reasons given for this by female interviewees related to busy time schedules and the desire for a break from cooking. For instance, Nadia said:

there's an Asian take-away where we can get Asian foods like curries, vegetable curries, meat curries and kebabs and pitta breads. (We do that) . . . mainly on a Friday when I get so sort of fed up. Well I just don't feel like doing anything on a Friday in cooking, that's when we tend to use these, usually a Friday.

Some respondents used take-aways for social occasions. Chris, Jenny and Lisa sometimes bought take-aways when they had friends visiting, and Lisa talked about the place of chips as a weekend treat for her children.

In terms of the desire for a break from cooking and socialising, take-aways fulfil similar purposes as eating in restaurants and bars. Yet, unlike sitting down to a meal in a commercial establishment, which is assumed to take some time, the take-away activity is associated with 'quickness', immediate relief of hunger (as when John buys fish and chips when coming home from playing tennis) and convenience. Moreover, take-aways are not considered 'special', evidenced by the fact that health concerns were a reason for avoiding them. Necessity is foremost.

For those events considered particularly 'special', reasons of pleasure are paramount. Unprompted reasons for eating in restaurants and bars emphasise pleasure and leisure and virtually ignore necessity, hunger and the implications of being away from home. Pleasure is associated especially with getting a change from routine, with socialising and celebrating special occasions and, to a lesser extent, with enjoyment of interesting food. Teashops and cafés also give pleasure, but their use is less likely to be an event in its own right. For less 'special' occasions, necessity is more explicit: when talking about eating in the workplace canteen or buying a take-away, mundane reasoning takes over.

## Attitudes towards eating out

We investigated whether the reasons our interviewees gave for eating out were reflected in the attitudes of a larger population and whether they were shared equally by people of different backgrounds. Current attitudes were explored by inviting survey respondents to agree or disagree, on a five point scale, with a series of twenty-nine statements of opinion.[2] One, for example, was 'I like eating out because it means I do not have to prepare the meal', with which 70 per cent of all respondents agreed. More women than men agreed, 81 per cent, 64 per cent strongly, thus reiterating one principal reason for eating out. This led us to enquire whether some underlying attitudes predisposed people to respond in the same way to the various statements.

A common statistical technique used to explore this is factor analysis. The statements were compiled on an exploratory basis, some reflecting opinions voiced in qualitative interviews and others constructed by us. We used principal component analysis and the details of the resulting nine factors, including which statements loaded onto each factor, are listed in Table 3.3.[3] We discuss each in turn, considering whether and how they reflect our interviewees' reasons for eating out, and consider whether respondents were equally likely to have such attitudes.[4]

Many of the factors correspond with reasons for and against eating out. The attitude 'interested in learning' (factor 1), for instance, reflects a tendency to enjoy trying new foods, and to learn and to talk about them. The 'interested in learning' attitude was strong amongst those with a high household income, with a degree and amongst singles, but was weaker for housewives than for those in paid employment. Not surprisingly, those with an interest in cooking (both routine and for special occasions), doing shopping and using recipes in cooking (see note 10 chapter 5) also held the 'interested in learning' attitude. These respondents ate out more often commercially and at the home of friends, took holidays and visited pubs regularly.

The attitude that 'domestic work is oppressive' (factor 2) reflects the appreciation of release from cooking, eating and being in the domestic sphere. Similar views had been apparent in qualitative interviews, with the desire for a change from everyday routines. Women were more likely

---

[2]  Six answers were available; 'agree strongly', 'agree slightly', 'neither agree nor disagree', 'disagree slightly', 'disagree strongly' and 'don't know'.

[3]  Only factors with eigenvalues greater than one were included.

[4]  The factors were subjected to multiple linear regression analysis with a range of socio-demographic independent variables. The same procedure was repeated to investigate relationships with eating out practices and other leisure activities. We report the strongest statistical associations in our commentary.

to espouse this attitude strongly, as were respondents who frequently bought sandwiches, had children and did not go on holiday. Those eating out less frequently were no more likely than other respondents to hold this attitude.

The tendency to consider home provision as superior and the home atmosphere as generally more congenial for meal purposes was strong amongst those with a 'home is best' attitude (factor 3). Respondents who held this attitude strongly ate out less often in commercial venues and bought fewer ethnic take-aways and fast foods. The attitude was stronger among older respondents, households with a housewife where the partner did not have remunerated work, and 'non-white' respondents. This attitude suggests a population who have not embraced 'the consumer attitude' towards food. The prevalence of this attitude amongst couple households with no-one in remunerated work may suggest pragmatism while among 'non-white' respondents, perhaps, discomfort with some types of public space.

The attitude 'indulgent eater' (factor 4) combines two views: those who generally enjoy indulging in foods and other consumables, and those who believe that everyday food controls, whether they relate to health, food quantity or vegetarianism, may be relaxed on certain occasions. The latter also reflects a desire to escape the everyday; in this case relaxing control of self and body. This attitude was weaker among women, among 'non-white' respondents and Londoners. Those who disagreed with this attitude were more inclined to do fitness training and visit museums, while those who shared it were also frequent users of ethnic take-aways and pubs.

The view that eating out is to be enjoyed was captured by the 'eating out is fun' factor. This attitude echoes the appeal of sociability among the reasons for eating out. It was little differentiated; everyone, it seems can appreciate the fun of eating out. The only significant difference related to social class, with skilled manual workers identifying more strongly, professional and intermediate workers less strongly. Those living in London were less inclined to think 'eating out is fun', as were those who ate frequently at the home of family.

The attitude 'I like what I know' (factor 6) represents the views of those with conservative tastes, and may be associated with the suspicion of commercially produced foods (as expressed by interviewees like Lorna and Mary) and untried foods (as expressed by interviewees like Lisa and Debby). Older and Prestonian respondents were more inclined to have this attitude, whilst those with a degree and A-level were unlikely to. Variations in the measure with which respondents hold this attitude correlated with variations in the frequency of doing certain leisure type

Table 3.3 *Nine attitudes towards eating out*

*Factor 1: 'Interested in learning' attitude*
I have learned about foods through eating out (.81)
I often talk with others about eating out (.73)
I eat things now that I learned about on foreign holiday (.71)
I get excited about going to eat in a new place (.61)

*Factor 2: 'Domestic work is oppressive' attitude*
I like eating out because it gets me out of the house (.74)
I like eating out because it means I do not have to prepare the meal (.72)
I would like to eat out more often than I do now (.48)
I like to eat out because I don't like the meals I have to eat at home (.43)
When I eat out, I like to choose things which I don't eat at home (.42)
When I eat out I like to eat more than I do at home (.32)
I always enjoy myself when I eat out (.31)

*Factor 3: 'Home is best' attitude*
Meals prepared at home are superior in quality (.77)
I prefer the comfort of my own home to eating in public places (.66)
I only eat out on special occasions (.37)
Eating out is poor value for money (.36)
It is the company and conversation I like the best when eating out (.32)

*Factor 4: 'Indulgent eater' attitude*
I am not as concerned about the healthiness of the food served when I eat out (.76)
When I eat out I like to eat more than I do at home (.61)
A vegetarian meal would never be my first choice (.46)

*Factor 5: 'Eating out is fun' attitude*
I always enjoy myself when I eat out (.58)
I feel comfortable in any type of restaurant (.55)
Eating out is poor value for money (−.55)
It is the company and conversation I like the best when eating out (.42)
When I eat out, I feel I am on show a bit (−.39)
I prefer there to be no children around when I eat out (−.35)

*Factor 6: 'I like what I know' attitude*
I am suspicious of foods I do not know (.73)
Quick service is important to me (.66)
When I eat out I like to chose things which I don't normally eat at home (−.41)
A vegetarian meal would never be my first choice (.34)

*Factor 7*
When I eat out I dislike eating alone (.71)
I like to eat out because I don't like the meals I have to eat at home (−.53)
I don't take much notice of the decor (−.35)
When eating out I like my meal to be well presented (.30)

*Factor 8: 'Experienced consumer' attitude*
If I was served an unsatisfactory meal I would complain (.67)
I prefer there to be no children around when I eat out (.51)
When eating out I like my meal to be well presented (.39)
I only eat out on special occasions (−.36)

*Factor 9: 'Informality is desirable' attitude*
I dislike eating out in places that are formal and stuffy (.73)
I like to go to places where the other diners are smartly dressed (−.57)
I don't take much notice of the decor when I eat out (.42)
I feel comfortable in any type of restaurant (−.38)

Note:
*Extraction method: principal component factoring. Rotation method: Varimax with Kaiser normalisation. Variance accounted for: 54.4%.*

activities. That is, those sharing this attitude bought fish and chips and played bingo more frequently but were less inclined to eat at the homes of family, go to theatres and museums, or to attend evening classes.

The seventh factor was difficult to interpret, but suggests the strongly held attitude that eating out is a social activity and should be done in the company of others. Those living alone and in London were less likely to hold such views, whilst women were more inclined to think this way.

The view that commercial provision should be organised and delivered adequately (i.e. without children and well presented), and where it is lacking, complaint is appropriate, suggests an 'experienced consumer' (factor 8). This attitude does not relate to reasons for or against eating out, but to assertions concerning the consumers' right to good service. This attitude was not strongly socially differentiated, with the proviso that semi and unskilled manual workers and those without paid work, as well as those with children under the age of five were less inclined to hold these views. Variations in this attitude were found in relation to the use of services: frequent restaurant users, and those who often buy sandwiches and go to pubs were more inclined to hold this view.

The attitude 'informality is desirable' represents the preference for informal provision; that is provision that allows the diner to relax without the need to be vigilant, for instance, about dress code and behaviour. Like factor 8, it is not an attitude which relates to reasons for eating out, but is instead an attitude about commercial provision preferences. This attitude varied in that the young and skilled manual workers were more inclined to hold it, whilst managers and those with a father in the service class eschewed it. It had no implications for the frequency of engaging in other food or leisure activities.

## Eating out and other leisure activities

Eating out in contemporary Britain derives some of its meaning through its relation to, and comparison with, other leisure activities. Interviewees reflected on its place in their lives among other leisure pursuits. Some preferred it to alternatives: Lisa, Debby and Jenny, for instance, commented that they preferred going out for a meal nowadays rather than going out drinking for a night. Others, like Lorna, preferred going to the theatre. Yet others again sought a balance among favoured leisure pursuits. And although shared understandings define the meal as the main purpose of the occasion, some respondents talked about combining it: Jean and David, who would visit Pizza Galore before going to the cinema, Trisha ate out to celebrate her sister's birthday before moving on to a club, and Sally and Peter visited Stephanos during a day trip to the Lake District.

Table 3.4 *The frequency of engaging in various food and leisure activities (percentages)*

|  | Regularly (weekly +) | Frequently (monthly +) | Occasionally (annually +) | Never |
|---|---|---|---|---|
| Take-aways: |  |  |  |  |
| Fish and Chips | 21 | 32 | 29 | 19 |
| Fast foods | 12 | 27 | 29 | 32 |
| Ethnic | 12 | 34 | 27 | 27 |
| Sandwiches | 27 | 14 | 17 | 43 |
| Sitting down for a main meal in: |  |  |  |  |
| Commercial venue | 21 | 44 | 29 | 7 |
| Home of family | 10 | 29 | 40 | 21 |
| Home of friends | 6 | 25 | 34 | 36 |
| Watching live sport | 13 | 15 | 21 | 52 |
| Playing team sport | 11 | 6 | 8 | 75 |
| Keeping fit | 17 | 7 | 9 | 67 |
| Pub visits | 42 | 26 | 17 | 16 |
| Playing bingo | 4 | 3 | 10 | 84 |
| Theatre visits | 1 | 7 | 41 | 51 |
| Museum visits | 0 | 4 | 42 | 54 |
| Concert-going | 0 | 4 | 38 | 57 |
| Church attendance | 12 | 7 | 30 | 51 |
| Evening class | 5 | 3 | 6 | 86 |
| Meeting of voluntary association | 4 | 6 | 15 | 75 |

Systematic information on how often specific leisure activities are engaged in was collected in the survey. The findings are presented in Table 3.4, which for purposes of comparison includes information on take-aways and sit down meals as well (see chapter 4 for an elaborate discussion on the frequency with which respondents ate out). Eating out in a commercial venue is the most normal of leisure activities, only 7 per cent of respondents never participating.

### Entertaining

Treating people to a meal at home is an important aspect of contemporary social life, with 77 per cent of respondents to the survey reporting that they sometimes 'have people to a main meal at home'. The manner in which people offer hospitality and their understandings of the forms that such events might take were revealed in interviews. We asked people whether they ever entertained and if so in what forms. The question conjured up an image, for some an unpleasant picture, of what it meant to entertain properly. Either explicitly or implicitly, most interviewees drew upon a cultural template of a dinner party against which their own social practices were described. This template betrays some of the social significance and social relations of the activity of offering hospitality. We therefore begin with a discussion of the cultural template, the template of the dinner party, before considering how people accommodated to this 'standard' when entertaining.

The template of proper domestic entertaining has its origins in the middle class dinner party of the pre- and post-war years, the rules of which continue to be rehearsed in etiquette books (e.g. Beyfus, 1992: 177–206). It is a highly structured event which includes an elaborate menu, a prescribed set of rituals, a particularly defined set of companions whose patterns of interaction are set out, and an injunction of exceptional care and attention on the part of the host and gratitude on the part of the guest. Most interviewees were able to recognise elements that together constitute the dominant model of domestic entertaining, regardless of whether they ever enacted it.

Like notions of the proper domestic meal discussed by Charles and Kerr (1988), entertaining means presenting guests with a meal, not snacks like the 'cakes and tea and that sort of thing' which Sheila served her ageing mother, or the 'cheese and crackers and wine' supper which Chris might serve her friends on a Saturday night. Instead, entertaining involves a meal with at least three courses, which might be extended by 'cheese and biscuits, coffee and mints' following a dessert. Entertaining received further meaning through notions of where and how it should be done. Dinner parties were understood to be 'sit down meals' which happened in a dining room and around a dinner table that displayed the household's best tableware. Proper entertaining also only occurred when the right company was present, close kin, very close friends and uninvited guests being excluded. Entertaining was seen to involve a particular set of social relations, some of which mirrored routine domestic cooking. Care in the sense of knowing about and accommodating guests' tastes was a common topic of discussion amongst our interviewees, in the same way that catering for the tastes of individual household members was prominent in the discussions of DeVault's (1991) interviewees. However, the work of entertaining differs significantly from everyday cooking. Entertaining properly was expected to take more time and effort than everyday cooking, dinner parties ideally including various courses and dishes prepared freshly and especially for such occasions. Managing time and sociability were other important concerns for 'doing the job right'. Respondents talked about using the oven and doing a lot of the preparation work prior to the event as ways of managing it in such a way that they were not in the kitchen too often or too long while guests were in the house.

The strange aspect of this shared understanding of entertaining was that it lay at the back of almost everyone's mind when discussing hospitality, yet it was scarcely ever reported as having been implemented or operationalised. If this was an ideal, few people aspired to its achievement. Two interviewees, Jane and Jean, said that they currently gave dinner parties in a full or elaborate form and a few others recorded having provided them in the past. Some others expressed a desire to do so if only they could. But most others showed little inclination to entertain in such a fashion. Some interviewees made a point of arguing that the cooking they did for other people in their own homes was not best described as 'entertaining'. Some quietly improvised on the proper dinner party format without much comment. Others, however, rejected the model vehemently, even while explaining their actual practice in contradistinction to it. The reasons behind wholesale improvisation are diverse and include material constraints, time constraints and particularly a preference for informality.

Evidence suggests social differentiation between those who hosted dinner parties and those who did not. Those from professional, managerial and white collar households in particular were involved in the reciprocity of hosting and being served at proper dinner parties and, with the exception of Andy and Jane, none of them talked about potential material constraints. Margrit (a professional) and Trisha (a white collar worker) expressed the desire to host proper dinner parties, but did not do so at the time of interview because their dining rooms were being redecorated. Instead, they improvised by hosting barbecues and buffets, events which did not require a sit-down meal. Working class interviewees pointed out that lack of space, a dining room or a dining table prevented proper entertaining, even if this was desirable.

Another reason for improvising relates to the care and convenience nexus (Warde, 1997). Several interviewees explicitly talked about the time constraints that shaped their everyday lives. For Liz, time pressures meant that she no longer entertained at home. Jenny, on the other hand, described her entertaining in terms of the 'suppers' she presented to guests. These could include pizza and salad, barbecued ribs, curries, lasagne and garlic bread, and were not of the three course meal variety required by proper dinner party rules. Chris discussed at length the changing pattern of entertaining in her home within the context of increasingly busy weekends. Consequently, rather than hosting a proper dinner party, she now often bought take-aways when friends came around at the weekend or else went with them to eat in a restaurant.

The dinner party is associated with a degree of formality, a view expressed particularly clearly by those who did invite guests home to eat but who denied that this constituted 'entertaining'. Formality was identified by the structure of the meal, by the company present and by the kind of reciprocity that was deemed acceptable. Three-course sit down meals were considered too formal by some, as is clear from Petra's comment:

I'm not really very erm into etiquette or how to conform, it's just a case of, I think of the main dish and if I've got a bowl of fruit handy then that can be the sweet, or you know maybe some, somebody'll have made cake and bring cake along. No I mean it takes me all my time to make the main dish, so I wouldn't fuss or bother over starters or or afters, no, no.

Nadia associated formal dinners eaten at a dining table with discomfort, inhibition and 'Englishness', pointing out that she and her family behaved in a more relaxed fashion that included her extended family eating together around a mat on the floor. Sheila even argued that formal dinner party arrangements, like formal invitations, obstructed the hostess in making guests comfortable and encouraging them to stay as long as they wanted. So she organised her entertainment in such a way that it appeared an impromptu event. Primarily it was an aversion to formality that explained expressions of cultural hostility against the template of the dinner party which seemed to act as a powerful symbol of social distinction based on class differences.

Social distance among the assembled company was an important consideration. Petra pointed out that the meal she was planning for two friends she had not seen in a long while was likely to be more formal than the meals she hosted for more regular friends, while Rose suggested that when her daughters' boyfriends stayed for dinner they had to accept potluck, and Nadia did not consider the times her parents stayed for dinner as entertaining. Social proximity appears to widen the scope for returning favours and to encourage improvisation. Often guests joined in the effort to get a dinner organised. Such participation is not exactly reciprocation, but may reinforce and strengthen interpersonal relationships. John teamed up with his partner and their close friends in getting a dinner organised. In similar fashion, Steve joined in the preparation of the Sunday roast when frequently visiting friends in Manchester, and Anne (see Box 7.2) had no qualms about joining in with the preparations for a barbecue, or in having someone else (friend or family) make food in her kitchen at home. Within the extended families of Nadia and Smina, participation in the kitchen by other family members was perfectly acceptable, indeed even required, because cooking for their large parties was impossible otherwise.

We did not explore further whether collaboration involved male members of the extended family, but other evidence suggests that notions of appropriate gender conduct in the kitchen limit opportunities for sharing. In Katrine's household, for instance, she would cook for her brother, his wife and children, but their contribution was limited to washing up afterwards. Equally, when Jean and David had visited their aunt in Canada, they had been aware of the work created, but sharing it was not seen as an option because, as David explained, 'I mean, you don't expect to go into somebody else's house and cook anyway do you?', to which Jean agreed 'Well, no, no'. They obviously felt inhibited about working in someone else's kitchen.

Inhibitions about entering the kitchen of the hostess may be related to another arrangement whereby the guest brings a dish. This was often done by Jane, who spoke of having to bring a pudding the next time she ate with friends. That this is an uncommon arrangement was evident from the survey, where only 16 out of 351 respondents had supplied a dish.

One final feature of entertaining is that the meal was a gift, the result of a symbolically significant invitation to come to eat elaborately at the home of someone else. But importantly, entertaining was also guided by a strong sense of reciprocity. There was some expectation that the invitation and its associated services would be returned in kind, because a significant obligation had been accepted. The obligation to reciprocity was not assuaged by gifts brought to the meal. Gifts are common, the survey indicating that the most popular item was wine (23 per cent of guests brought this), followed by flowers (7 per cent), chocolates (6 per cent), and other alcoholic drinks (4 per cent).

The extent to which people divert from and improvise upon the template of the dinner party is somewhat difficult to establish, because our survey did not collect detailed information on all of its elements. We have, for instance, no details about whether the last meal was eaten at a dining table, how the table was furnished nor the exact manner of service. We do, however, have information on the menu and course structure, the timing of the meal, the company, frequency of meeting and on expectations of reciprocity. On the basis of this information, it is possible to calculate approximately what proportion of last meals eaten at the home of friends and family could be termed 'proper' dinner parties. A variable was constructed which deemed a 'proper dinner party' to be a meal with three or more courses, where the meal lasted more than two hours, where the people concerned were entertained less frequently than weekly,[5] and

---

[5] Qualitative interviews show that frequent meals at the home of close family or friends are less likely to be seen as proper entertaining.

where reciprocity in kind was anticipated. Dinner parties so defined occurred on only 15 per cent of all occasions of hospitality. The proportion changes if different conditions are set, of course. Relaxing the criteria by allowing all meals with two or more courses lasting an hour or more gives a proportion of 52 per cent. Dinner parties are not the most common manner of entertaining guests. Improvisation on the cultural template is the norm.

Dinner parties occurred overwhelmingly at the home of friends, followed by engagements with kin outside the elementary family. Proper dinner parties were more likely than average to be deemed 'special occasions', although 51 out of 71 were 'just a social occasion' and none were described as a 'convenience or quick' meal. Respondents were more likely to have dressed up and 50 brought gifts, a higher than average proportion for all recipients of hospitality. Guests at such events were more likely to have been older respondents (between 40 and 59), (living as) married, having a father in the service class, a household income greater than £20,000 a year and living in London. The household's own class identification, educational qualifications and gender were not statistically significant, whilst those living with parents, living alone and lone parents were less likely to have been present. If the social background of those hosting such meals is similar to their guests, it seems that improvisation occurs less among older people and married couples. People with more income, living in London and with a service class pedigree may use such occasions for purposes of display or, alternatively, have some affinity for more formal modes of socialising.

It would seem then that there are many different formats for entertaining. The dinner party, as represented in magazines and etiquette books, is a rare occurrence restricted to a small proportion of the middle class. It is interesting that it was those who most disliked the idea of dinner parties who identified most clearly the elements of the template, suggesting the continued social hegemony of a model of middle class entertaining. In practice, however, improvisation was extensive and many of the forms of hospitality were casual and informal occasions about which, in detail, little is known.

### Shared understanding and cultural templates

Eating out is a concept with which people are familiar and which they use in their everyday talk. The people of Preston, for instance, do not use the term dining out.[6] Respondents and interviewees understand and use

---

[6] The term 'dining out' was rarely used by our interviewees.

consistently concepts like restaurant, café, teashop, and take-away. Even so, it is hard to find acceptable words to describe the practice generally; no generic term for places to eat out exists. Nor is there a term other than 'dinner party' to describe offering someone a meal in one's home, even though, as we saw, the label fails to capture the nature of most domestic entertaining. There was a difference in what came easily to mind when our interviewees thought about eating out and entertaining at home. While the idea of the 'dinner party' was inscribed in the mind as a cultural template, no similar firm picture existed for eating out.

The restaurant meal does not seem to have as deeply entrenched an equivalent set of rules or rituals. People know what eating out is – though they have no very strong template for it. This may simply be because there are many alternative varieties of experience. People recognise a set of shared elements which allows them to participate satisfactorily, and to identify which particular activities or events fall into the relevant category, but without any overarching model of how such an occasion should be managed or played out. There is, then, a shared understanding concerning conventions about interaction with strangers in restaurants, how to deal with waiting staff, the order in which to eat dishes, but these are comparatively weakly formulated because the same performance is not called for in all settings. It is more a matter of recognising some negative rules, how not to treat other customers or companions, rather than a set of positive scripted rituals. There is discretion about how to perform in such situations and therefore perhaps less anxiety about infringement of rules.

Arguably, the greater clarity of the cultural template for entertaining arises because most people have experience both of being host and guest, producer and consumer, which focuses their mind more closely than when simply a customer in a restaurant. They do not know and need not possess the skills of the chef and the waiting staff because they never have to perform those roles. Therefore they can be partly indifferent to the precise nature of their treatment. On the other hand, in the systems of reciprocity that characterise hospitality there is need for equivalent performances to be repeated on future occasions, where, indeed, the roles of provider and recipient are reversed. Particularly if these exchanges are supposed to be symmetrical, a clear notion of what is expected or required helps to ensure that the social obligation of equal exchange is achieved.

Contemporary social theory maintains that hegemonic patterns of conduct have (further) fragmented. However, it is important to specify the fields where they have disappeared, where there are now *legitimate* alternatives widely spread and practised, where punishment for deviance has been removed (where 'it really is up to you what you do'). These might be contrasted with fields where alternatives are enacted but not accepted as legitimate and with those where alternative patterns are negotiated. Nevertheless, there are probably also some areas of everyday life where relatively little has changed: where there is no coherent alternative mode of conduct, or way of doing things, where an alternative has not been invented, conceived or formulated. This, arguably, is the case with the dinner party.

The origins of the model are uncertain but its current form is probably a recent invention, emanating from the middle classes in the post-war years, since before the war they would have still employed servants. It is perhaps a much trimmed version of a bourgeois (or perhaps aristocratic country house) model of formal hospitality. It was perhaps secured by the existence of the motor car, which made it possible to attend dinner in the evening at the home of a friend, and by the changed domestic role of middle class women once servants were no longer common. It is probably already disintegrating, the degree of practical improvisation being extensive, making it even more intriguing that the model remains the only one easily available to our interviewees.

There are some practical challenges to its hegemonic role. It is possible to substitute a meal in a restaurant with friends, but that probably implies a change of meaning, no longer a gift but a sharing of the cost. People can also, through a simple telephone call, get a hot meal delivered, so that one can offer the hospitality of home (heat, ambience, drink and sociability) but without the responsibility and labour involved. Alternatively cook-chill meals can be bought, so that there is no problem of culinary expertise, or lengthy preparation, but there is nevertheless the appearance of having added labour and provided the food. Or, there can be compromise over the structure of the meal, offering snacks and drinks rather than a full menu. All these alternatives were mentioned by interviewees in Preston, suggesting that they are becoming increasingly common. The myriad forms and diverse arrangements for hospitality have yet to be catalogued, a potentially difficult task because the diverse arrangements are usually confined to small groups. Where alternative practices were adopted, they seem to have been endorsed and shared by the entire relevant social circle of potential guests; the small size of the circles making negotiation of what is acceptable more easy. Indeed, the creativity and improvisation associated with hospitality contrasts markedly with the restaurant regime. The restaurant offers a specialised service, determined by design and planning, upon which the customer passes judgement by staying or leaving since the format cannot be altered. Among friends, by contrast, particularly because the obligations of reciprocity mean that each member of the circle will be both provider and consumer in turn, an improvised formula is a collective assemblage, achieved by negotiation. Yet despite these modifications of practice (not much reported conduct actually conformed to the ideal), most still judge their behaviour against the hegemonic model of how entertaining ought to be done. They have improvised alternatives but without undermining the hegemonic cultural model. No form of the improvisation has yet been solidified. This can be detected partly by the apologetic tone in which deviant practices are described: it is failing to match up to the ideal, it is less than perfect, it is how *we* do it, it suits us to do it this way, but we wouldn't expect others to copy us. The tone of apology suggests that it is the investment of the labour of care that makes the dinner party particularly socially symbolic, such that to remove that element may downgrade the value of the practice.

In sum, the main differences between understandings of the restaurant and of hospitality might be summarised in terms of the different sources of labour involved which, in turn, sustains one of the defining differences in principles of access, where the mutual reciprocity of the communal mode sets very different parameters from market exchange.

# Part II

# Access

Access to consumption opportunities is controlled by a wide range of different social rules or conventions. Rules of access, which may be enabling or exclusionary, are a defining element of the character of a production–consumption cycle. The nature of the gate-keeping rules conditions the quality of the social relations involved in the delivery and enjoyment of any service and often determines the social and symbolic significance of the activity. Systems of regulating access are highly significant because the range of consumption activities to which one has access are vital aspects of the quality of everyday life, social reproduction and material opportunities. The market is democratic in the sense that it surpasses exclusionary social barriers except wealth, access to goods being open to anyone with sufficient funds to purchase them. Other modes apply more particular criteria. Access may be guaranteed as a right, as with emergency health care in the UK. Access may be by invitation or election, as with membership of private clubs. Sometimes access is strongly influenced by birth or family of origin, as with religious communities and private schooling. And sometimes rules of informal social exchange apply; obligations of reciprocity, often negotiated and not necessarily symmetrical, are the principle of inclusion for dinner parties and celebratory events. These gate-keeping devices mediate the flow of goods and services and are part of a process whereby different people obtain different levels and qualities of consumption.

It follows that consumption levels will be unequal, between individuals and between groups. Particular individuals lack the financial resources, the entitlements and the social networks which might satisfy their needs and wants. The classic demonstration of such a proposition in the field of food is Sen's (1981) analysis of famines, which are almost always a consequence not of crop failure but of unequal social entitlements to the food which is available. Few people in the UK are now threatened by starvation, but the nutritional, and more importantly the social, value of diet is distributed unequally. While we would not deem incapacity to eat out deprivation, participation in particular consumption practices is socially discriminating. To live a 'decent' life requires levels of consumption relative to the general standard of any given society. Standards of comfort, convenience and cleanliness now require access to a range of domestic goods and services which would have constituted absolute luxury in an earlier age. For instance, a majority of the British population surveyed in the mid-1980s by Mack and Lansley (1985: 54) considered having an annual holiday, a hobby and two hot meals a day as necessities. Appropriate levels of social and cultural participation have been added to the definition of minimum standards of existence which constitute citizenship. The sacrifices that poor mothers make to provide their children with suitably branded footwear or with items of food in their dinner boxes which allow them to conform to peer-group norms are evidence of the symbolic importance of appropriate consumption. Belonging to a group often requires access and commitment to particular consumption activities and while increasingly access is facilitated by the market, commitment is often harder to generate. For example, neither of us would feel comfortable, for social, cultural and ethical reasons, at a grouse shoot. But had our biographies been different no doubt blasting shotguns at game birds would have seemed a normal and acceptable, perhaps even obligatory, form of entertainment.

It would be very unusual to be compelled, on threat of serious punishment, to eat out. Everyday language tends to talk of 'choice'. But there are many gradations of experience between freely willing and feeling inescapably obliged to participate in any given social practice (see Warde and Martens, 1998). Eating out is, in important part, discretionary. It is primarily perceived as a leisure activity and a treat, though interviewees recognised that some people were sometimes obliged, because of business reasons, to eat away from home. We consider the most important distinction as between entertainment and obligation. We hesitate to say that it is necessary to eat *meals* out because 'food' is available almost everywhere and hunger rarely requires anyone to sit down to a main meal. But often discretion may be very limited: for instance, a substantial proportion of our respondents claimed to have had no say in whether or not to eat out on the last occasion reported (Warde and Martens, 1998: 136–9).

There are probably some instrumental reasons for seeking to eat out and to eat out in style. Erikson (1996) argues that knowledge of the variety of local restaurants is of instrumental advantage at least to people in positions of authority at work. Effective membership of certain comparatively privileged social groups depends on a level of knowledge and experience of eating out. A capacity to discuss and evaluate food has been shown to be a condition of communicative competence in certain social circles in the USA and at least two scholars have taken eating out as one indicator among many of lifestyle (e.g. Erikson, 1991 and 1996; Bogenhold et al., 1997). Differential access to consumption is both a reflection and a constituent element of contemporary systems of social inequality. Both frequency and quality of opportunities for eating out are germane in understanding social differentiation.

Access is not simply a function of social position, financial circumstances or chosen style of life. The issue of access must also be addressed in the context of available alternatives. Self-evidently, the main option is to eat at home. This alternative is taken by some all of the time and by the rest in the overwhelming proportion of instances. This might suggest tenacious commitment to particular kinds of domestic ideals and, ultimately or potentially, an aversion to dining out. Particularly in the context of common laments of the last two decades about increasing time-pressure and, mostly from women, the unfairness of the distribution of domestic labour, the expansion of eating out might appear surprisingly slow. Certainly these are reasons for anticipating pressure for greater access to commercial or communal alternatives. Such considerations gave rise to hypotheses in the design of the research linking the manner of domestic organisation, including financial arrangements and household division of labour, to the likelihood of eating out. For instance, households containing partners both in paid employment, who thus have less time for domestic tasks and more difficulty in synchronising their daily lives, might have good reason to eat out more often than others. Those households containing a full-time home-maker, by contrast, might be expected to operate very differently.

At the same time, however, there are strong conventional normative contraints which operate to produce comparatively homogeneous responses and ones which predominantly restrain impulses to eat out. In Britain food is still associated primarily with domestic settings. The 'proper' meal is a key motif of family ideology and its provision signifies care and affection of an emotionally highly charged sort. Few people can be entirely immune to the suspicion that being denied the companionship of the domestic table is a mark of deprivation or isolation.

We therefore examined the influence of patterns of household organisation on eating out and considered them in the context of various expressions of family ideology. It was important to recognise that the domestic option is not, even for households of similar composition, identical for all. While size of household, marital status and so forth are suitable preliminary socio-demographic indicators of domestic organisation, and do influence the propensity to eat out, household composition conceals much variation in temper, tenor and tenacity of interpersonal relationships and in normative commitments and social values. Limited participation may not necessarily be a sign of restricted access *per se*, but rather evidence of normative commitment, negotiated adherence or simply routine attachment to domestic provisioning.

Understanding the evolution of a culture of eating out, one which entails familiarity and acceptability of eating outside the home, means that the frequency of its occurrence is a matter of concern. This is addressed in chapter 4. So too is the question of whether the various ways of getting a meal without someone having cooked it at home are substitutes for each other, or whether there is a cumulative effect, with the same individuals consuming more take-aways, more restaurant meals and more meals as guests. We enquire whether socio-demographic characteristics serve to allocate people between the many different alternative ways of getting a meal outside the home, exploring commercial eating out and eating with family and friends. Even more interesting, from a cultural point of view, is the use of competing outlets of the increasingly differentiated catering industry. Thus we look at the social characteristics of people who eat in restaurants characterised by particular types of menu or tariff. Chapter 4 also explores the role of space and time in determining patterns of access.

In chapter 5 we look at the relationship between domestic organisation, family ideologies and the use of commercial provisioning services. Thus we examine the organisation of domestic work amongst our survey respondents and investigate especially whether couple households with different patterns of paid work organise domestic food preparation differently. We enquire how readily people incorporate commercial alternatives, and eating out specifically, into their everyday dietary practices, and how important is the factor of 'saving time'. Then, in an effort to examine the ways in which the restaurant may be influencing domestic organisation, particularly the proper meal and its familial social relations of consumption, we look at the way in which shared understanding of the domestic meals and meals eaten out are related. We argue that such shared understandings operate as compelling forces for appropriate conduct regarding decisions about the use of different meal options. Finally, we present evidence on the prominence of the proper meal, and compare domestic meals and meals eaten out on the basis of their social relations of consumption. This chapter complements chapter 4 by offering a detailed analysis of widely shared conceptions that the domestic sphere is the primary context of food consumption where family obligations and responsibilities, with their associated roles and emotional investments, are negotiated and redeemed.

# 4    Patterns of eating out

There are many different types of place to eat. One important question is who uses different places and how often they go. As sociologists we are initially very interested in the social and cultural characteristics of people who behave differently. Such characteristics indicate the financial, social, practical and cultural forces, systematically distributed across the population, which constrain or encourage people to engage in particular ways of eating out.

It would be surprising if the very poor spent the same on eating out as the rich. However, sociologically it would be very unusual if income were the only relevant feature of differences. Earlier commentaries have identified other factors which affect eating out. For example, it has been maintained that women are discouraged from eating out (Wood, 1990; Finkelstein, 1989). Eating out also has class connotations. It was a practice severely restricted by social class until at least the middle of the twentieth century. It has generally been thought that the significance of class declined thereafter. Thus, for instance, Burnett (1989: 264, 318) says that it was only in the inter-war period that the lower middle classes began to eat out and that it was some time after the Second World War that the practice became more or less universal. Also, it is the principal thesis of Mennell (1985) that social differences in food consumption behaviour have been in long-term decline: the 'diminishing contrasts' of age, region and season, but particularly of class, have accompanied increased variety of available foodstuffs. That class should have mattered was less a result of differences in income, more one of the exhibition of style, taste and distinction. Cultural capital[1] generates a capacity to behave properly and knowledgeably in public, to exercise discriminating taste when selecting

---

[1] Bourdieu's concept of cultural capital is complex, not necessarily quantifiable on any single scale, and involves not only formal cultural resources but also informal, dispositions and cultural affinities inherited from family of origin – including posture, accent, taste and disposition. It is most usually operationalised in terms of educational qualification and experience, but can also be estimated by relevant socio-demographic characteristics of parents responsible for socialisation.

places to go and things to eat, and to facilitate conversation about and evaluation of culinary matters. There are cultural, as well as economic, aspects of class distinction which are associated with educational and occupational experience.

There are also practical constraints encouraging or restricting the ability to eat out. Care for young children constitutes a potential negative constraint making it difficult to get out in the evening. Conversely, people living alone often reason that there is little justification for expending effort on cooking an elaborate meal just for one. However, while they might therefore be inclined to eat out more frequently, there is also a general reluctance to dine out alone. In our survey, 76 per cent of respondents positively endorsed the statement 'I dislike eating alone.' Variations by life-course stage indicate the existence of practical constraints, though the consequences for activity are often complex. For example, care for small children can be evaded occasionally, and if eating out were an important leisure activity it may well attract parents as a treat. In some households, typically ones shared by young people, the routine of cooking for one may be particularly inconvenient and unappealing.

To the extent that eating meals is defined primarily as a *social* activity, one which is not to be done alone if alternatives exist, then relationships among household members will be powerful determinants of eating out. So too will be the availability of companions. Ease of access to family and friends is important. Some people have few of either, which will tend to reduce their opportunities for eating out. If kin live nearby people may take meals with them as an alternative to eating solo. More generally, the spatial proximity of commercial outlets matters, with, most obviously, sparsely populated areas offering fewer options than central cities.

Finally, different cultural attitudes towards food and eating also impinge. Although social circumstances affect attitudes, there are often variations within social groups regarding tastes and preferences. These complicate the analysis of access, for as other studies of discretionary consumption have observed it is dangerous to assume that abstention is always a consequence of social or material condition. So although a majority of respondents in Mack and Lansley's (1985: 54) survey on poverty asserted that eating meat or fish every other day and a roast joint once a week were necessities rather than luxuries, there were clearly also some vegetarians who abstained on ethical rather than financial grounds. Similar behaviours may not all be motivated by the same reasons. Students may eat out just as often as rich middle-class couples without family responsibilities, but for entirely different reasons. Such matters can be explored partly using survey data, but only properly understood through examination of people's practical reasoning.

### The forming of a habit?

We asked respondents how often they ate out under different circumstances (see Table 3.4 for results). Excluding holidays and eating at the
workplace, on average the respondents to the survey ate a main meal out
on commercial premises about once every three weeks. 21 per cent ate
out at least once a week, a further 44 per cent at least monthly and only 7
per cent claimed never to eat out. Mean frequency of eating at someone
else's home was about the same, but a much larger proportion of people
(20 per cent) never did so. 20 per cent of respondents claimed never to eat
in the home of other family members, and about one third never at the
home of friends. Very regular eating out with either kin or friends was not
very prevalent, but being a guest to a main meal in someone else's home is
a part of the experience of a large majority of the population.

Reasons why frequency of eating out varies are in part obvious, but the
overall pattern is complex and not just a consequence of income or time-
pressure. The cross-tabulations reported in Table 4.1 give some indication of the factors which increase and reduce frequency of eating out in
three different locations – commercial establishments, homes of family
and homes of friends. Frequency of eating on commercial premises is
particularly strongly associated with the socio-demographic position of
respondents. Higher income, more education, younger age, being in full-
time employment, not having children, city of residence, being single,
male and higher occupational class are all significantly positively associated with eating out frequently. So too is the frequency of family meals
at home – the less regular the domestic meal, the more often people eat
out. There is also some positive association between eating out commercially and eating out as a guest. However, the likelihood of being invited to
eat frequently with other family members is very weakly related to the
respondents' social characteristics. Students, and young people more
generally, are the most likely guests of non-resident kin; being female and
being employed are also predisposing factors; but neither income nor
class makes any difference to these practices mediated by kinship. Eating
out at a friend's house, on the other hand, is quite strongly related to
income and class, including father's class: being in the professional and
managerial classes, or having a father from such classes increases the frequency of receiving hospitality. So too, very strongly, does education,
measured both by level of qualification and type of secondary school
attended. Having children and living with a partner reduces frequency.
Finally, there is a strong positive association between being a guest of
friends, guest of family and commercial eating out. Opportunities to eat
out are cumulative, particularly eating out commercially and with friends.

Table 4.1 *The frequency of eating out in a restaurant, at the home of a family member and at the home of a friend. Associations with socio-demographic characteristics of respondents. Cross-tabulations*

| | Frequency of commercial meals | Frequency of meals with non-resident kin | Frequency of meals with friends |
|---|---|---|---|
| Frequency of family meal | −.16** | − | − |
| Frequency of commercial meals | 1.00*** | .18*** | .37*** |
| Frequency with non-resident kin | .18*** | 1.00*** | .45*** |
| Frequency of meals with friends | .36*** | .44*** | 1.00*** |
| Respondent's income | .29*** | − | .21*** |
| Household income | .27*** | .08* | .17*** |
| Employment status | −.26*** | −.01** | −.06* |
| Father's social class | −.13*** | −.07* | −.22*** |
| City of residence | .11*** | −.06* | .09** |
| Gender (+ = female) | −.14*** | .11** | .08* |
| Age | −.20*** | −.15*** | −.19*** |
| White | −.11 | − | − |
| Number of full-time wage earners | .18*** | − | − |
| Household size | −.06* | − | − |
| Children under 16 | −.26*** | − | −.18*** |
| Educational qualifications | .29*** | .16*** | .37*** |
| Type of secondary school | −.14*** | − | −.23*** |
| Marital status | −.25*** | −.07 | −.30*** |
| Unemployed | −.18* | − | − |
| Student | .29*** | .25*** | .39*** |
| Retired | −.37*** | −.15* | −.29** |
| Occupational class | .19*** | − | .12*** |

*Note:*
Measure of association, gamma; significance, z statistic *** $<.001$; ** $<.01$; * $<.05$.

We examined use of commercial outlets more closely by applying linear multiple regression techniques to the survey data. We were able to explain 17 per cent of the variance in frequency of eating out using a standard set of socio-demographic variables, corroborating and refining the findings. It transpired that the factors most strongly predisposing high frequency of access were, in order of importance, being young, size of household income, having a degree, not being a housewife and not having children under sixteen at home. Slightly more of the variance could be explained simply in terms of the attitudes of our respondents. Thus when we used the nine attitudes isolated in factor analysis (see chapter 3), we were able

to explain 20 per cent of the variance. The factors with the greatest pre-
dictive power were those which clustered around enthusiasm for novel
eating, an 'experienced consumer' approach to eating out and the denial
that home is best. Also significant were the factors indicating a preference
for informality and the desire for relief from the domestic mode and its
associated labour. Frequency of eating out is, then, more or less equally
strongly related to social characteristics and to attitudes. If we consider
both sets of independent variables in the same analysis we improve the
statistical prediction, so that 27 per cent of the variance is accounted for, a
substantial proportion. The strongest independent effects come from the
first three attitudinal factors mentioned above, with age and household
income the next most powerful influences.

Hence, there are social constraints on the frequency of eating out. Age,
household income, educational experience and the presence of children
all have influence. Interestingly, being in full-time employment, social
class, marital status and city of residence are insignificant. However, attitudes indicating a positive interest in learning about different foods and
attitudes towards eating meals at home were more important than social
characteristics.

The findings concerning the socio-demographic effects on frequency
of eating out were corroborated by our interviewees, the richer, younger
and better educated tending to eat out more frequently. We also asked
both interviewees and respondents 'would you like to eat out more often
than you do now?' In the survey, 59 per cent answered affirmatively. Our
interviewees were more or less evenly split between 'yes' and 'no', their
reasoning sometimes complex, with money being one of four prominent
themes, the others being competing leisure activities, domestic constraints, and anticipation of pleasure.

Many interviewees mentioned money as a constraint which reduced
their frequency. 'Yes, I would love to be able to eat out more often. It's
more a case of being able to afford it than anything else,' said Steve; 'Yes.
Yeah . . . It's economics, that more than anything else I would say' (Liz);
'We would go out more often if we had more money' (Sally). But other
respondents commented that money did not play a major role. Lorna
could afford it: 'as you get older then you're not as financially restrained
as a young couple struggling with a big mortgage and a small family and
as you get a bit older it gets a bit easier so there's no reason at all why we
couldn't eat out more if we wanted to; we just choose not to.' Another type
of response acknowledged that there now exist many alternatives varying
by cost. As Trisha said, 'I think you can eat out quite inexpensively, if you
want to.' Jenny made the same point:

I don't know, depends where you go. I mean if you are talking about going to a restaurant if you go to a good restaurant, and me and Jim have been out for a pub lunch on a Sunday dinner and had a really good pub lunch for me, him and Eddie and it's been like under £12. But then Jim and I have been out for a meal at night and it's cost us about £60 just for the two of us. So it depends where you go and what you eat really. You can make it as expensive as you want or as cheap as you want can't you?

This option did however depend on the interviewee's culinary standards. Jane, for instance, identified money as a constraint because she thought only expensive places were worth visiting, since unless the food was exceptional she would rather cook at home.

As we will see below, the specifically socio-demographic features affecting the practice of eating out are of more importance in explaining variations in taste than in explaining its frequency. Evidence concerning the commercial mode suggests that besides the constraints of limited income, young people are more habituated to paying for meals out than their elders. We cannot determine whether this is solely an effect of life-course stage, such that today's young adults will abandon restaurants for the home as their responsibilities alter, or a generational effect, whereby the habits learned in youth are continued throughout a lifetime. Probably there is some truth to both propositions. But maybe more important is the way in which frequency is related to aspects of people's overall organisation of their everyday lives. For some, visiting restaurants is clearly a significant leisure pursuit in its own right, for others more an obligation, considered either inferior to the domestic alternative or less amusing than other pastimes.

### Commercial venues: who visits where?

To be seen in the right places and in attractive company, or at least to let others know that we are familiar with the most exciting or rewarding of experiences, is part of a process of display and performance which contributes to reputation. Early sociologists examining consumption were particularly interested in the claiming and attributing of status through exhibitions of a prestigious style of life (e.g. Weber, 1968 ; Veblen, 1925). They were particularly concerned with the ways in which individuals established reputations for refinement, superiority and distinction. Consumption patterns reflected social standing, and particularly class position. Eating out is a potential means for such display, through the use and avoidance of different venues.

Whether there is any longer one simple and linear hierarchy of prestigious consumption behaviour is much contested. The current balance of opinion avows that late modern societies are characterised by a plurality of criteria or standards of reputation such that no cultural attainments would be universally recognised as meriting applause (e.g. Bauman, 1991). But others disagree. Bourdieu (1984) continues to maintain that aesthetic preferences are a function of class habits and an indicator of an individual's level of cultural capital. Some recent empirical research supports Bourdieu, having identified considerable persistence of class-based distinction (Savage et al., 1992; Erikson, 1996; Warde and Tomlinson, 1995; Warde, 1997) and shown that status judgements concentrate along a small number of dimensions (Lamont, 1992). This issue of status is more general than the pursuit of a specialised reputation as gourmet or bon viveur, which is appropriate only to food enthusiasts. Rather, the more generalised ability to display knowledge, experience and judgement about cuisine as a cultural and aesthetic matter is potentially a key marker of social discriminations. The survey evidence offers some insight into the socially differentiated use of different types of restaurant which, providing that at least some convey differential social meaning, may make it possible to detect claims to distinction.

The degree of differentiation of the clientele of different kinds of restaurant is a topic worth investigating. If there is a concentration of people with particular socio-demographic characteristics in a certain type of outlet then we might reasonably assume that all are not socially equivalent. There is probably no other basis for determining equivalence, since judgements about whether the food served in one place is distinguishable from that in the next is not amenable to reliable, systematic estimate. We therefore examined answers to a survey question regarding whether people had eaten a main meal in any of a list of nineteen nominated restaurant types during the previous twelve months. Table 4.2 lists simple percentage responses and compares them with those of a nation-wide market research survey from 1992. The list of options was derived partly from common sense, partly from previous market research reports and was pre-tested at the pilot stage to ensure that respondents would recognise the labels.[2] This permits some grip on preferences and aversions to certain sorts of venue.

---

[2] We are aware that the labels are imprecise and open to the objection that the classification lacks rigour. The taxonomy is problematic because it indiscriminately mixes types defined by cuisine, e.g. Italian, by manner of delivery, e.g. bar meal, and by function, e.g. roadside diner. Nevertheless, labels caused respondents no perceptible difficulties of comprehension. We took some comfort from the apparent lack of difficulty faced by respondents in answering these questions (the response rate to this battery of questions was over 99 per cent for all types except 'other British', where about 5 per cent failed to record a response), partly from the fact that in the qualitative interviews similar categories were used spontaneously by interviewees.

Table 4.2 *Two classifications of type of restaurant eaten in during last twelve months (with percentage of respondents who had eaten in such a restaurant at least once)*

| Payne and Payne (1993) | % | Our sample (1995) | % |
|---|---|---|---|
| Pizza | 24 | Specialist pizza house | 41 |
| | | Fast food restaurant /burger bar | 49 |
| Fish and chip | 23 | Fish and chip (eat in) | 18 |
| Wine bar | 8 | Wine bar | 17 |
| Roadside diner | 28 | Roadside diner or service station | 31 |
| | | In-store restaurant or food court | 31 |
| | | Café or teashop | 52 |
| Steakhouse | 21 | Traditional steakhouse | 19 |
| Pub | 60 | | |
| | | Pub (bar food area) | 49 |
| | | Pub (restaurant) | 41 |
| Hotel | 31 | Hotel restaurant | 25 |
| Other British restaurant | 16 | Other British style restaurant | 6 |
| Indian | 24 | Indian restaurant | 33 |
| Chinese | 29 | Chinese/Thai restaurant | 29 |
| Italian | 16 | Italian restaurant | 31 |
| American-style | 16 | American-style restaurant/ diner | 12 |
| French | 7 | | |
| Greek | 7 | | |
| | | Other ethnic restaurant | 21 |
| Vegetarian | 4 | Vegetarian restaurant | 9 |
| Other | 6 | Any other establishment | 1 |
| None of these/don't know | 13 | None | 7 |

As can be seen, pubs, fast food places and teashops were familiar to more people than were wine bars, vegetarian and ethnic restaurants. The pattern of who goes where is complex. We undertook a good deal of complex statistical analysis of respondents' familiarity with different types of venue which cannot be displayed here for reasons of space (see especially Olsen, Warde and Martens, 1998). For present purposes we report on some of the conclusions.

All types of venue are to some degree socially differentiated in their custom; there is usually some statistically significant association with age, education and income, though not always in the same direction. For example, those independent variables which predict the likelihood of having eaten in a Chinese restaurant in the last twelve months are significantly different from those for fast food. For Chinese and Thai restaurants, high income, higher educational credentials, higher social class background and city of residence are important predisposing factors. For fast food places where meals are eaten on the premises (like McDonalds or Kentucky Fried Chicken), income, class and city make little difference, while being younger is very strongly positively associated.

The role of age is often highly significant. There is a general tendency for people to eat out less as they get older, though this is crosscut by a tendency for people in their thirties and forties to make use of particular kinds of outlet. But there are some exceptions to the trend, with the pub restaurant and motorway service station being more appealing to older than younger Britons. Age effects probably reflect both generational and life-course factors. However, it seems probable that those young people who have developed a taste for fast foods and pizza will continue to eat such fare in later years, even while they add new tastes to their culinary repertoires.

Asking people whether they ate in a particular type of restaurant in the last twelve months is some measure of the acceptability of cuisine or particular kind of ambience. That is not, however, the same thing as popularity. Popularity is better estimated by generalising on the basis of asking people where they last visited, a proxy for frequency of visits to places of a particular type. Given that the average respondent ate around eighteen main meals in a commercial outlet in the previous year, never to have eaten in a pub or in any ethnic restaurant makes it probable that abstention implies an aversion to public houses or 'foreign' food. People have favourite types of food and might generally be expected to select those more frequently. We can address this question because we asked people, in addition, at what sort of an establishment they ate their last main meal away from home. A measure of popularity is obtained by counting what proportions of the sampled population had used different venues most recently.

Table 4.3 shows that of the 576 people whose last meal out was in an identified commercial establishment of some kind, 80 had eaten in the bar of a public house and 92 in a restaurant attached to a pub. 30 per cent, in other words, had eaten last in a pub. The next most popular venues were Italian restaurants at 8 per cent; 'other' ethnic restaurants (including Greek, French, Turkish, etc.) also at 8 per cent; specialist pizza houses and Indian restaurants, 7 per cent each; and hotel restaurants and traditional steak houses, each 6 per cent.

There was, however, significant variation from city to city. Most notably the pub venues were most popular in Bristol, where 42 per cent of people reported them as their last visit; the proportion was also high in Preston, 37 per cent; but the figure for London was a mere 10 per cent. In London, ethnic restaurants were much more popular. Considering all five

Table 4.3 *Type of commercial establishment visited for the last main meal out*

|  | Frequency | Per cent |
|---|---|---|
| Specialist pizza house | 39 | 6.7 |
| Fast food restaurant | 21 | 3.6 |
| Fish and chip, eat in | 13 | 2.2 |
| Wine bar | 9 | 1.5 |
| Motorway service station | 2 | 0.3 |
| In-store shop/restaurant | 11 | 1.9 |
| Café or teashop | 18 | 3.1 |
| Traditional steakhouse | 34 | 5.8 |
| Bar food area of pub | 80 | 13.7 |
| Restaurant attached to pub | 92 | 15.7 |
| Hotel restaurant | 37 | 6.3 |
| Other British style | 28 | 4.8 |
| Indian restaurant | 39 | 6.7 |
| Chinese/Thai restaurant | 32 | 5.5 |
| Italian restaurant | 46 | 7.9 |
| American style restaurant | 6 | 1.0 |
| Other ethnic restaurant | 45 | 7.7 |
| Vegetarian restaurant | 1 | 0.2 |
| Any other establishment | 23 | 3.9 |
| Don't know / not answered | 9 | 1.5 |
| Total | 585 | 100.0 |

categories of ethnic restaurant, overall 49 per cent of Londoners said they had last eaten in one such establishment. The comparable figure for Preston was 24 per cent, and for Bristol 14 per cent. In London, 'other' ethnic restaurants accounted for 17 per cent of last outings, and both Chinese and Italian exceeded 10 per cent. In Preston, Italian was the most popular (11 per cent) followed by Indian (10 per cent). In Bristol no type of ethnic cuisine was recorded by more than 4 per cent of respondents.

One of the most remarkable features of the late modern affluent societies is the range of different commodities and services which are available (see Warde, 1997). Such an observation is particularly apposite in the field of food where, as Mennell (1985) maintained, 'increasing variety' is a major trend of the twentieth century. Compared not only with the monotonous diets of the European peasantry in early modern times, but even with the diet of ordinary people in the first half of the twentieth century, the variety of different ingredients, meals, menus and cuisines now available is stupendous. This has potentially considerable consequence for processes of social classification and aesthetic judgement. It is often claimed that people today use consumption to signify who they are to other people from whom they hope for approval and esteem for their 'style'. Prima facie, extensive variety makes this increasingly difficult because it permits greater differentiation of cultures and sub-cultures and threatens effective communication between groups, for the same icon may easily have different meanings according to the company or audience (e.g. DiMaggio, 1987). It is argued that a new kind of cultural strategy has emerged, dubbed 'omnivorousness' (Petersen, 1992), one which comes to value variety for its own sake, equating knowledge and experience of the widest possible range of alternatives with cultural sophistication. This strategy gives those involved both a means of selecting among goods and activities when faced with bewildering variety in circumstances where they no longer have the capacity or guidance to make 'reliable' aesthetic judgements. It is also a means to communicate with as large a number of other groups as possible, hence increasing the chances of being recognised as being a socially competent person of style and good taste. Thus command of variety becomes a key form of social and symbolic capital. It is unclear, however, whether omnivorousness is a solution to the anxiety associated with an ambivalent modernity, an expression of greater cultural tolerance, or a particular form of social distinction in its own right (see further Warde, Martens and Olsen, 1999; Warde, forthcoming).

People's use of different types of eating out place is one possible avenue for examining these propositions. Notwithstanding the gripes of commentators, like Wood, who insist that they are mostly equivalent, there is a wide range of options. True, the spread of themed chains is significant, but they primarily reduce regional variation by making the range of options similar from town to town. Also there is much simple repetition and replication of services by independent operators in close proximity, such that pizza places and Indian take-aways tend, even on the same high street, to offer similar products. But nonetheless there has been a major differentiation of provision – of cuisine type, quality of food and nature of restaurant regime – in recent years. The options are sufficiently multiplied to be able to distinguish between people who adopt an 'omnivorous' approach and more conservative persons who use few of the alternative facilities available. Hence we ask which, if any, people use a wide range of options, and how this reflects on issues related to distinction and status.

The evidence suggests that in practice the pursuit of variety is influenced to a significant degree by socio-demographic characteristics. We constructed a simple index of variety. We calculated how many of the 19 types of commercial place on our list respondents had visited in the last year. This was constructed as a simple arithmetic scale which was then condensed into those who had never eaten out, those using few (1–3) types, those with a moderate level of exposure (4–7 types) and those who had the widest experience of alternative venues (8–19 types).[3]

The 'variety index' was then used in linear multiple regression analysis. The final regression equation (see Table 4.4, column a) explained 26 per cent of the variance (adjusted R-square) on the index, a moderate but acceptable level given the nature of the independent variables and the heterogeneous character of the components of the index. It indicates that breadth of exposure can be predicted best by high household income, having a university degree, being in the middle of the age range (thirty to forty-nine), and being currently in a white-collar occupation, especially being an employer or manager. Being a student, having a high personal income and holding educational credentials below degree level were also significant and positive. This is prima facie evidence that a distinct and comparatively privileged section of the population achieves greatest variety of experience. The independent significance of income, occupation and educational credentials suggests that social class is a principal factor explaining differential experience; in Bourdieu's (1984) terms, a combination of economic and personal cultural capital influence behaviour. Moreover, it supports Erickson's (1996) observation that people in positions of authority in the workplace are likely to have the broadest cultural experience. Employers and managers are the socio-economic group with the greatest tendency to score highly on the index.

It will be appreciated that people with these characteristics are also those who eat out most frequently and the likelihood of experiencing a wide variety of types is, unsurprisingly, increased with greater opportunity. It is therefore important to note that an equivalent attempt to predict the frequency with which respondents ate out was statistically much less successful. The directly comparable linear multiple regression analysis, using the same independent variables, explained only 15 per cent of the variance (see Table 4.6, column b).[4] Exposure to variety is not simply a consequence of frequency of eating out; their correlation is low ($R^2 = .31$), the variety index being more strongly determined by socio-demographic characteristics, suggesting that it bears some social and symbolic significance. However, the amount of variance explained by socio-demographic factors for use of ethnic restaurants was significantly higher than for either the index of variety or for frequency of eating out on commercial premises.

[3] We used the collapsed scale because we sought to compare its statistical explanation with that of other scales whose maximum ranges were 0 to 4.

[4] The different $R^2$ ratios for this and the earlier regression equation (15 and 17 per cent respectively) is explained by differences in the dependent and independent variables used.

Table 4.4 *Standardised regression co-efficients for each dependent variable: three models of eating out*

| | Dependent variable (see text for definitions) | | |
| --- | --- | --- | --- |
| | a<br>Variety | b<br>Frequency | c<br>Curiosity |
| Independent variable: | | | |
| Household income | .23*** | .16*** | .23*** |
| Personal income | .08* | .10** | .07* |
| Degree | .22*** | .13*** | .23*** |
| GCSE | .08** | | |
| A-Level | .08** | .08* | .05 |
| Ethnicity | −.12*** | −.09** | −.05 |
| Student | .10*** | | |
| Part-time worker | .05 | | |
| Household size >2 | | −.06* | −.08** |
| Housewife | | .09** | −.09** |
| Preston | .09* | .08** | |
| London | .24*** | | |
| Father service class | | | .08** |
| Professional | .05 | | .06* |
| Employer | .10** | | .07* |
| Intermediate | .09** | | |
| Supervisory | .06* | | |
| Age | −.547** | .359* | |
| Age squared | −.175*** | .341 | −.502** |
| Adjusted R-squared | 26% | 15% | 34% |
| n | 1001 | 976 | 1001 |
| F-statistic | 28.5*** | 18.8*** | 38.6*** |

*Note:*
Significance levels *** = .001 or better; ** = .01; * = .05. Variables with significance lower than .10 have been excluded from each model.

The term 'ethnic', when applied to food, is inherently problematic. In a country like England, where foodstuffs have been imported in large quantity for centuries and which is increasingly affected by the international economy and global culture, purity or authenticity of cuisine is hard to identify (Cook and Crang, 1996; Narayan, 1995). A potential technical difficulty therefore arises, how to decide what should count as, for instance, an Indian or an Italian restaurant. Should a pizza and pasta place be deemed Italian; is a certain level of authenticity to Italian regional cuisine required, since many will serve English dishes too? Our study left the respondents to decide, offering a list of types of eating out place which included Italian, Chinese/Thai, American, Indian and 'other ethnic'. The last, we assume, will be mainly French, Greek and Turkish restaurants – because although Nepalese, Indonesian and Mongolian restaurants can be found in Britain their numbers are few. Because we recorded respondents' answers to a list offered by the interviewer, we cannot be sure that the establishments supplying meals would see themselves in the same way.

Factors which encourage use of one type of specialist ethnic restaurant increase the likelihood of eating at each of the others. Probably the clientele of Chinese and 'other' ethnic restaurants are the most socially distinctive, and American-style restaurants the least. But overall the same cluster of variables affects all these types, which is not the case for many other kinds of venues.[5] Precise delineation of the factors influencing familiarity with ethnic restaurants was obtained by constructing a 'curiosity index', a scale which recorded the number of different types of ethnic restaurant a respondent had visited in the last year. The scale included four types, Indian, Italian, Chinese/Thai, and 'other ethnic' restaurants, thus permitting scores from zero to four. The index exhibited levels of statistical association greater than for other forms of eating out. As table 4.4 column c indicates, 34 per cent of the variance was explained by the socio-demographic characteristics of our respondents. Involvement is more pronounced among those with higher income, those living in London and those holding a degree-level qualification. Household income was very important, personal income less so, though still significant. London residence was very important, reflecting in part the superior supply of the metropolis, which has a long history (Bowden, 1975; Driver, 1983). Restaurants with different specialisations are unevenly distributed throughout the country; for example, Preston has a greater than average number of Italian and Indian restaurants and living in Preston was, compared with the third city, Bristol, also likely to enhance familiarity with meals in ethnic restaurants. Again, being a housewife and living in a large household reduced familiarity. But particularly interesting is the effect of social and occupational class. There was a significant association with the social class of the respondent's father when the respondent was aged sixteen, a variable which had no independent impact in almost any other statistical test we have attempted. Having a father who held a service class position enhanced curiosity, implying a process of inter-generational transmission of cultural capital. Association

---

[5] These findings were confirmed by use of logistic regression analysis (see Olsen, Warde and Martens, 1998).

with measures of class based on the socio-economic group of the respondent's household were also significant with respect to professional and managerial occupations. Prima facie, attendance at a wide range of ethnic restaurants indicates possession of high levels of both economic and cultural capital. This strongly suggests that social distinction is being maintained in at least one corner of the vast field of food provision.

Wider access to foreign cuisine has been thought to increase a sense of cosmopolitanism and appreciation of cultural diversity. The movement of different culinary traditions has accelerated in recent decades, not only through migration, but as a consequence of tourism, broadcasting and writing about food, the globalisation of culture industries, and greater opportunity to eat out. Van der Berghe (1984:396) has argued that, unlike some expressions of ethnicity, an association with food is potentially constructive:

ethnic cuisine represents ethnicity at its best, because at its most sharable. It does not take much effort to learn to like foods, even exotic ones. Ethnic cuisine is the easiest and most pleasant way to cross ethnic boundaries. As eating together is perhaps the most basic expression of human sociality, ethnic cuisine could well be the ultimate reconciliation between a diversity we cherish and a common humanity we must recognise if we are to live amicably together.

He may be somewhat optimistic in postulating that shared culinary taste is an effective source of social harmony and inter-ethnic co-operation, but it may encourage greater tolerance of cultural difference. If so, the positive associations and negative connotations of ethnic foodstuffs and the aversions and involvements of different social groups in eating foreign foods may be socially significant. The extent of the incorporation of the tastes of the multitude of international cuisines into the British food culture is also some measure of cosmopolitanism and conservatism.

If learned acceptability of ethnic food, or its frequent consumption, is an indicator, multiculturalism is still limited. Only 20 per cent of people had experience of three or more different cuisines (on our curiosity scale), while 48 per cent had never eaten in an ethnic restaurant in the last twelve months. Some of this avoidance may, of course, have been due to an aversion to restaurants *per se*, for there are other sources of ethnic cuisine: culinary knowledge may be extended by the use of cook-chill meals from supermarkets or the large number of ethnic take-away outlets.

Since the product is most often taken back home to eat, the take-away does not fulfil the criterion of 'eating out'. However, its prevalence is worth considering briefly with respect to matters of changing British taste. About a quarter of the population (27 per cent) claim never to buy ethnic take away-foods, while 14 per cent recorded it as a weekly, or more frequent, event. Ethnic fast food was particularly popular with those in full-time employment and with students. Age was also significant: abstainers were disproportionately likely to be over the age of fifty and disproportionately the most frequent users of take-away ethnic food were people between sixteen and twenty-nine. The impression is that this is a comparatively cheap and appealing source of supplementary or alternative meals for young people living at home with their parents and also a form of generational distinction. It would seem that it does have some cultural or style connotations, insofar as the association with measures of convenience, while significant, are comparatively weak. Thus, numbers of earners in the household, distance travelled to work, being in full-time employment, do matter, but probably less than for some other forms of take-away foods. There is also a moderately strong class dimension: working-class individuals were generally abstainers, but those who did engage were quite likely to be frequent users. Income is important but less determinant than for many forms of purchasing of food and there are intimations that it is those classes who pursue variety who take these foods. Education is even more significant, suggesting again that some cultural capital is involved.

The tendency to be experimental, having a positive attitude to novel foods, is also associated with the tendency to buy ethnic cuisine. When we also took into account our measured attitudes towards eating out, the ability to predict scores on the curiosity index improved considerably. The factor 'interested learners' proved the most powerful predictor of 'curiosity' in a multiple regression analysis.[6] London residence, holding a degree and higher household income were the next most powerful inde-

[6]  Table n4.1 *Curiosity index: multiple regression analysis results* *

|                                        | B         | Beta  | Sig T |
|----------------------------------------|-----------|-------|-------|
| Factor 1 'interested learner'          | .34       | −.25  | ***   |
| Resident in London                     | .69       | .23   | ***   |
| Degree qualification                   | .68       | .21   | ***   |
| Houshold income                        | 1.73E-05  | .17   | ***   |
| Factor 3 'home is best'                | −.20      | .15   | ***   |
| Factor 6 'I like what I know'          | −.18      | .13   | ***   |
| Factor 8 'experienced consumer'        | −.14      | .10   | ***   |
| Resident of Preston                    | .26       | .09   | **    |
| Respondent female                      | −.01      | −.07  | **    |
| Student                                | .35       | .07   | *     |
| Father in service class                | .26       | .06   | *     |
| Respondent a housewife                 | −.25      | −.06  | *     |

*Notes:*
* Independent variables included both socio-demographic variables and factor scores

pendent variables. Two other attitude factors were also important – denial that 'home is best' and that 'I like what I know'. A very substantial proportion (43 per cent) of variance was statistically explained by the equation, indicating a convergence of positive attitudes towards the commercial provision of exotic food and social characteristics of the educated, metropolitan middle class.

Equally important in the patterns described is the popularity of the pub as a venue. In many ways a principal symbolic site of English recreation, it is a place where a majority of people have been to eat during the last year and much the most frequently chosen location for the last trip out by our respondents. By extension, if the pub is the quintessential English institution, and use of commercial eating places is a means of reproducing ethnic identity, then we might conclude that despite a considerable appreciation of foreign cuisine which, it is argued, induces social tolerance, the most popular form remains the one peculiar to the dominant culture. It was, however, shunned by many of the respondents from ethnic minority groups.[7]

In our survey 108 respondents, in response to a question about ethnic affiliation, 'To which of these groups do you consider you belong?', selected a category other than 'white'. There were eight further alternatives (those of the 1991 Census).[8] Taken together the respondents who classified themselves as other than white were particularly likely never to eat out. Whereas only 5 per cent of white people never ate out, 17 per cent of ethnic minority respondents never did. There were strong indications of differences in preferences between the ethnic minority groups, but the numbers involved from each were small, making generalisation hazardous and interpretation of tastes and practices difficult. There were two clear differences between the white and the 'non-white' groups. A very low rate of attendance at pub venues for all the minority groups separately, as well as all together, does indicate a fairly pervasive aversion. The reasons for this cannot be derived from our study, but they might include fear of greater racism there than elsewhere, the lack of appeal of the types of food being served, abstention from alcohol, or the manner of service. As regards eating with family and friends, there are also large differences between minority groups. At the homes of friends, whites are guests more than once every two week in 11 per cent of cases compared with 4 per cent for African-Caribbeans, 35 per cent for Pakistanis, 24 per cent for 'others'. Patterns of being a guest are roughly paralleled by those for

---

[7] To some extent, since there were more ethnic minority respondents in London than elsewhere, these features may be partly complementary.

[8] White; Black Caribbean; Black African, Black Other; Indian; Pakistani; Bangladeshi; Chinese; Other.

entertaining. The overall picture is that friendship and kinship networks among Pakistani and other ethnic groups operate around gifts of food more than average in England.

It is not possible a priori, nor on the basis of existing evidence, to determine what meanings of the contemporary obsession with variety in food are most widely held among Western populaces. However, attention to the social differentiation of the use of ethnic restaurants gives some preliminary clues. We cannot be sure whether customers of ethnic restaurants value variety for its own sake, whether they see familiarity with foreign cuisine as a statement of cosmopolitan tolerance, or whether they believe that social prestige derives from acquaintance with multiple foreign cuisines (see further Warde, 1998). Nevertheless, it is clear that a process of social closure operates, with a particular section of the educated middle class distinguishing itself in this respect. It is also clear that a significant proportion of the populations of three big English cities are not availing themselves of substantial parts of the full range of available culinary experience. Not everyone is in eager pursuit of variety. If learned acceptability of ethnic food or its frequent consumption are indicators of multiculturalism, then its extent is still limited, suggesting continued conservatism in taste among the English population. There is a sufficiently high level of abstention from foreign foods and, as the survey also showed, an enduring popularity of the English public house especially in the provinces, to suggest that the ecumenical effects of learning exotic tastes, anticipated by van der Berghe (1984), are still far from thoroughly diffused among the British population. Indeed, given that some ethnic foods are both cheap and easily accessible, many seem resistant to such variety.

## On being a guest

In the communal mode, reciprocity is the norm of exchange between friends and between family members, though the manner of returning a meal at someone's home varied. It primarily involved providing a meal in return, but joining in the work involved bringing gifts, and providing a service other than a meal were also recorded. The outcome depended on social distance, gender and generation.

The overwhelming way of repaying the debt of receiving food, service and company is to host a food event in return. A resounding majority of respondents who ate at the home of friends or family the last time they ate out (351 in total) said that they would invite the host/hostess back to their home for a main meal. Nearly 75 per cent were convinced that they would return the favour, whilst a further 12 per cent thought that they probably would. The remainder, 14 per cent, thought that they 'probably' would not return the favour. There was no significant difference in the likelihood of this form of return between different types of host/hostess, although sons and daughters were somewhat more likely to be unsure whether they would invite their parents back, or to decline to do so. Whether this suggests a degree of uneven reciprocity is uncertain.[9] The respondents most likely to shirk this form of reciprocity were single men (or men living alone), lone parents, or someone for whom the relevant meal had constituted a single course.[10]

Respondents who ate at the home of a friend were more likely to bring a gift than respondents who ate at the home of family, again suggesting that social distance is related to gift giving. The likelihood of giving a gift increased with the age of the respondent (excluding our oldest respondents, people in their sixties) and the household income of the respondent. It was higher for meals eaten by a respondent in the service or intermediate class, by Londoners, or when the occasion was a special one, suggesting that gift-giving is somewhat middle class and metropolitan. Possibly, people who know that they cannot host an event in return (maybe because they cannot, or do not have the resources to cook for guests) might bring a gift instead, but in fact there was no trade-off between the giving of gifts and the likelihood of returning the favour of entertaining. Bearing gifts does not adequately satisfy the obligation of reciprocating in kind. A final manner of returning the favour of a meal is to exchange it for another type of service. Interviews revealed examples, as in reports that a sister cooked a meal for her brother who cut the grass in exchange, but the survey did not enquire about this, making it difficult to say with certainty that the respondents who were not planning to return a dinner invitation rejected the norm of reciprocity outright.[11]

Access to private hospitality depends upon a personal invitation, and what can be gleaned from the quantitative data is the uneven social distribution of such invitations. Table 4.1 outlined the socio-demographic features which dispose people to frequent visits to restaurants, the homes of kin and the homes of friends. Different social factors operate. One of the sharpest differences is in the role that income plays; while insignificant in

---

[9] Finch and Mason (1993) have argued that parents tend to give more than their children, making interpersonal exchanges between them asymmetrical. That study, however, looked at these relations in the long term, including various sorts of favours and services, whereas in our study we explored reciprocity solely at the level of food work. There were examples in our interviews where food services rendered by parents to grown up sons and daughters were not returned.

[10] Cross-tabulation findings were often unreliable here because the numbers who declined were low, resulting in high ratios of low minimum expected frequencies.

[11] It may well be that there are more single men out there who do not return a dinner invitation, but who, like Sheila's brother who cuts her grass, do something else in return.

determining whether one is a guest of kin, it is of some appreciable importance with respect to friends. Since the social definition of the dinner
party concerns primarily exchange with friends, the discussion will concentrate entirely upon the frequency of being a guest of friends.

Probably because the comparatively well-off are better able to entertain, they are the most frequent recipients of invitations to eat with
friends. Resources are needed to reciprocate adequately (Kempson,
1996). Hence, income permits the development of friendships of one of
the most intimate kinds – eating with friends in private. However, students especially, and the unemployed, eat frequently with friends,
whereas housewives and full-time employees do less. There is a telling
and very strong relationship with the father's social class; a white collar
(service and intermediate class) father means high levels of visiting; a
working class background means little. This is one of the strongest examples of generational continuity in cultural capital.[12] People in London rely
on friends, those in Preston do not. Gender is not quite statistically
significant at the .95 threshold, but women are more frequent visitors
than men. Age is monotonically significant: the younger the respondent
the more frequent their visits to friends. Having children deters visiting,
while living alone much enhances frequency. Households with an uncon-
ventional domestic division of labour are frequent visitors and are less
likely never to visit friends. Education is a very strong predictor, with
higher educational qualifications particularly associated with frequent
visiting of friends. Qualifications are more important than the school a
respondent attended, although there is a significant private sector effect.
A service class occupation, especially a professional job, increases visiting
considerably, while manual workers, by contrast, are infrequent visitors.

## Metropolitan and provincial patterns

Evidence suggests systematic differences in patterns of eating out
between the capital and the two provincial cities. Overall, Londoners
exhibited more varied tastes. Avoiding pubs and hotels, they spread their
custom widely across all types of establishment. No doubt this partly
reflects more widespread and varied provision; but equally probably
experience of variety creates more catholic tastes, which in turn support
diversity. The difference between London and the other two cities is
perhaps greater than might have been anticipated.

---

[12] Father's class is a variable that generally explains relatively little of the variations in behaviour indicated by our survey, though this may partly be because it is not very robust. For
various reasons, 27 per cent of respondents did not record the occupation of their father
when they were aged sixteen.

Residents of London were less involved with kin, and the distance travelled to see them was much greater. Conversely, provincial respondents used commercial venues rather less, but were prepared to travel further to a restaurant and were less likely there to meet friends rather than family. We suggest that these constitute different modes of social organisation and that the behaviour is partly explained in terms of simple necessity: the frequency with which the population of London eats out commercially is a function not just of taste and available opportunity, but also of necessity. Larger commuting distances, dispersion of friends across a much larger metropolitan area and absence of kin living locally make for a different general pattern of association. Frequency of commercial eating out, the opportunities seized to eat more variously, the distances travelled and the patterns of companionship all suggest a distinctive metropolitan mode. To some extent, however, the metropolitan mode is a function of the differences in the social composition of its population.

## The concentration of inequality

We described above some differences in the social preconditions which affect access to different kinds of provision. The frequency of invitations to eat with non-resident kin is not restricted by the same social constraints as frequency of eating in restaurants or with friends. Theoretically, this is of considerable importance because it illuminates the relationship between different modes of provision. Preparation and consumption of the meal have proved bastions against the secular trends towards total commodification, where everything is purchased and meaning potentially reduced to monetary values.

One aspect of inequality is the extent to which opportunities to eat out concentrate. We noted that there was a positive relationship between commercial eating out, and being a guest in the home of kin and friends. There are, of course, other ways of obtaining commercially prepared food, take-away outlets having a substantial role, for example. We asked respondents how often they purchased different types of take-away food, distinguishing between ethnic, fast food, fish and chips and sandwiches. There is a positive association between frequency of consuming all of these and the eating of main meals away from home. Eating out and purchasing other forms of commercially prepared ready-to-eat foods go together. This is not to deny the social differentiation of the clientele of these different sources of food. Indeed, for most of the take-away foods, except fish and chips, age is much the strongest determinant of usage with the younger people the primary market (see Dunleavy and Martens, 1997). Reliance on cooked dishes and meals provided as commodities concentrates among particular sections of the population.

The range of factors influencing both frequency of eating out and selection of venue are complex. Financial, practical, social and cultural constraints all operate with considerable force. As regards most activities, income is, on aggregate, a significant consideration. The poor make less use not only of commercial facilities, but are also less likely to be involved in the exchange of hospitality between friends. Practical constraints – of household and family type, work schedules, distance between home and commercial facilities – all affect behaviour to some degree, as do socio-demographic characteristics of individuals and the social distribution of cultural tastes.

Frequency of eating out is rather less determined by social and cultural characteristics than is choice of venue. Frequency of eating away from home is more a matter of financial and practical constraint than of social and cultural characteristics. The choice of where to go is, according to our statistical analysis, more powerfully determined by social position and cultural taste. Thus, whether to eat in an Indian restaurant or at the bar in a pub is a decision much more powerfully associated with age, class, ethnic affiliation and education than the original determination to eat out. Almost all types of restaurant have a particular clientele. This is more a matter of the relative preponderance of people in different social catego-ries than of systematic exclusion. No social characteristic prohibits atten-dance. Nevertheless, significant social selection operates to make the customer base of pizza houses, hotel dining rooms and Chinese restau-rants substantially different.

The power of educational qualifications in predicting statistically who goes where is an indication of the importance of variation in cultural tastes. Cultural capital consists of much more than qualifications, but the independent statistical effect of credentials suggests that particularly the experience of having been a student in higher education alters a person's approach to eating out. It seems likely that both the habit of eating out and the preparedness to try different types of venue is learned during student days. The expansion of numbers in higher education in recent years may thus further stimulate the taste for variety of experience.

Our statistical analysis demonstrated that those with experience of a wide range of venues were a particular fraction of the population. If this is a measure of cultural 'omnivorousness', then omnivores concentrate within the upper echelons of the middle classes. High scores on our variety index were recorded by those with high household income, having a university degree, being in the middle of the age range (thirty to forty-nine), and being currently in a white-collar occupation, especially being an employer or manager. Furthermore, these social attributes proved to be even more powerful as predictors of familiarity with the range of different types of ethnic restaurant. In addition, the father's social class, as well as London residence, became a significant predictor of involvement, suggesting that, above all, distinction in the realm of eating out was most closely associated with the use of restaurants specialising in foreign cuisine. Our data thus corroborate claims that a privileged section of the middle classes, endowed with high levels of cultural capital, appreciates, and hence cultivates, an impression of cosmopolitanism (see for example, Holt, 1997a, for the USA and Savage et al., 1992 for the UK). Distinction is entailed in the taste for foreign cuisine.

Social distinction is also associated with the habit of exchanging domestic hospitality with friends. While being a guest of non-resident kin is socially undistinguished, eating at the home of friends is socially exclusive, indeed more so than eating out commercially. This again, while partly a function of financial and practical circumstances, is more importantly an effect of social position. So though being young, single and rich increases the likelihood of belonging within a circle of friends exchanging hospitality, being highly educated is more significant.

# 5    Domestic organisation, family meals and eating out

In this chapter, we consider how eating out is related to domestic organisation and speculate whether this relationship has changed over time. Two debates are relevant. The first is the so-called re-negotiation debate, regarding the implications for unpaid domestic work in situations where paid work takes up a substantial part of the time available to couples in households. The second concerns the implications for family life and social cohesion of commercialisation in the food field.

Recent analyses of change and continuity in domestic organisation and housework, without exception, take women's increased employment participation as their starting point. The growth of dual-earner and dual-career households, where both partners are full-time employed, potentially poses a great challenge to traditional arrangements. In such relatively well-to-do households *time* rather than *money* may have become the greatest constraining factor in life. This, of course, is not to ignore the simultaneous growth in the number of households where the opposite must be true and lack of money continues to be the primary constraint. Also, in Britain, implications may be limited because 40 per cent of economically active women work only part-time, a popular 'strategy' for combining paid and domestic work, but one with less impact on the dominant pattern of household division of labour.

If an increasing number of households now suffer from 'new' time constraints (see Gofton, 1990 and 1995, Schor, 1992, Hewitt, 1993), the question is how such households organise their unpaid work? Whether domestic organisation is changing has in the first instance been mainly addressed by asking if households are re-negotiating the gendered division of domestic work (see e.g. the British studies of Morris, 1990; Wheelock, 1990; Gregson and Lowe, 1993; and Gershuny et al., 1994; and the American study of Hochschild, 1989).[1] The general view of these studies is that re-negotiation has so far not been prominent. Symbolised

---

[1] In a way, this is not surprising, since this debate is directly related to the concurrent attempt to broaden the concept of work to include all types of work, including housework (e.g. Oakley, 1974 and Pahl, 1984).

in concepts such as 'stalled revolution' (Hochschild) and 'lagged adaptation' (Gershuny, 1992), changing the social organisation of domestic work is portrayed to be at best a very slow process.[2]

Related, but distinct from the literature on renegotiation is research conducted into the specific area of domestic food work. Feeding work is argued to be a 'female preserve' and, possibly for that reason, studies have not concentrated so much on change as on the subtle gendering processes involved, being concerned with the (re)production of families and other social relations of everyday life, and also with health and body image (see, respectively: Murcott, 1982 and 1983b; Charles and Kerr, 1988; Lupton, 1996; Caplan, 1997; and especially DeVault, 1991). While the renegotiation debate treats the household primarily as a unit of production, the domestic food literature pays more attention to the interplay between production and consumption. The importance of viewing households not just as social units where work occurs but also as units where consumption happens is clear when considering another possible solution contemporary households may engage in to cope with 'new' time constraints – shifting from domestic service towards commercialised provision. The use of nannies or private nurseries by working parents is one example of such a trend. Food options provided through commercial channels are widening, and households may now select ways to make food work more or less time consuming. In other words, households may seek to re-define and re-organise (rather than, or as well as, re-allocate) domestic work and make it more time-efficient by adopting commercial alternatives.

Much everyday food preparation and consumption happens within a domestic mode of provision, with its distinct methods of production and rules of access. Yet, such provision increasingly intersects with the market mode through, for instance, shopping for foodstuffs and the acquisition of mass-produced machinery for the kitchen – microwaves, food processors and dishwashers. At times preparation is entirely replaced by the market mode, as when household members eat out in commercial venues. As a result, speculation occurs – on the part of moralists as well as scholars – about the extent, causes and implications of the presence of marketised options in everyday food provision and consumption.

Whilst some scholars have recognised the complexity of the issues involved, many arguments assume the encroachment of market provision necessarily to have negative consequences for the 'cement' that 'holds'

---

[2] Similar conclusions arise from studies of household decision-making regarding finances: see Pahl (1989, 1990); Vogler (1994); Hertz (1992). This research asks different theoretical questions than those posed in the re-negotiation literature (e.g. who has control over money expenditure, and how is access to household money organised; see also Vogler, 1994: 251).

society together. Britons, for instance, receive regular warnings that the increased use of marketised food provisioning leads to the breakdown of family life, and therefore also to moral decline in society (see e.g. Dennis and Erdos, 1993; Hardyment, 1995; Health Education Authority, 1996; James, 1990). However, negative consequences may not follow all forms of marketised food provision, and certainly not all equally. Some which intermediate with the domestic mode of provision may be more harmful than those which replace it entirely.[3]

Eating out is potentially threatening to the family domestic meal in a number of regards. First, eating out enhances the opportunity for each family member to eat a hot meal independently of every other member, thereby avoiding the beneficial aspects of the mutual communication facilitated by co-presence at the dining table. Second, eating out makes public what is usually portrayed as a private, intimate, relaxed and partic-ipatory event – the family meal. In a sense, a key family function has been exported into the light of public scrutiny and surveillance. If, then, people mostly ate out, some aspects of the privacy of family life would be jeopar-dised. Third, the symbolic significance of mother's cooking, which is central to the achievement of emotional security, a token of care and love, as well as a basis for the maintenance of dominant gender and genera-tional relations, is by definition excluded when eating on commercial premises (Lupton, 1996). The work is done by a professional; the respon-sibility for provision, and appropriate gratitude, is given to someone else. Hence the restaurant might undermine the proper meal and its familial social relations of consumption. Nevertheless, eating out in a restaurant may be less 'detrimental' to family life than the transformation of domes-tic provisioning facilitated by microwaves and ready meals.

## The organisation of domestic food work

Three major studies on the gendered organisation of food work and domestic food consumption in the home argue that women still do much of the work involved in feeding the family (DeVault, 1991; Charles and Kerr 1988; Murcott 1983a and 1983b). Food work, as pointed out by DeVault, is a complex combination of tasks which neither starts nor stops with the cooking of the main meal of the day, but also includes shopping, planning, preparing ingredients, serving and washing dishes, as well as

---

[3] A much discussed example is the incidence of 'snacking'. Snacking suggests that the intermediation of the market mode of provision in the arena of domestic cooking greatly changes the character of the domestic organisation of feeding. So, microwave ovens and ready meals make it possible for household members to serve themselves quickly when-ever they want food, potentially displacing the family meal which is cooked by mum and eaten together.

organising subsidiary meals like breakfast. Both phases of our research explored the multi-task character of domestic food work.[4] In this section, we compare our survey results with earlier findings about gendered food work, and we investigate the relationship between the employment status of partners in couple households and their relative contribution towards the work involved in making main meals.

Following the emphasis in the domestic organisation literature on heterosexual couple households, we concentrate on food work in couple households. In 599 households the respondent was part of a couple. Table 5.1 shows the proportions of women and men *recorded* as having done various food-related tasks the last time these were done. With the exception of table clearing and dish-washing, these tasks were reported as having been done predominantly (over 50 per cent) by women alone. In the cases of planning, cooking and serving the last main meal, women had done each task in three quarters of cases. Sharing in these three tasks was negligible. Recorded sharing was higher with regard to shopping, clearing the table and washing dishes. Men were reported to have done the last two tasks in 32 and 39 per cent of the cases respectively. Most of the other persons involved in table-setting, table-clearing and dish-washing were children. 115 men were recorded as having cooked the last main meal.

These findings support the claims of DeVault and others (e.g. Charles and Kerr 1988; Warde and Hetherington, 1993; and Warde and Hetherington, 1994), that food work remains predominantly women's work, even though male and female contributions vary across these tasks. However, it is important to know if levels vary by socio-demographic characteristics of households, and particularly by the employment status of partners. To provide clarity about these issues, we constructed a 'male contribution index'. The male contribution index for food work was constructed by aggregating information on who had last done the seven tasks. If a man was recorded as having done the task last time alone, or if the task was 'shared' with a partner, households were given one point.[5] Taking the male contribution index as a proxy for actual food work patterns, the

---

[4] During the in-depth interviews, there was some discussion on who generally did specific feeding tasks and who had done them on the last occasion, but interviewees also talked in a general way about their involvement, and that of other household members, in domestic food work. The survey questionnaire contains systematic recording on who did a variety of feeding tasks; doing the main food shopping, planning the main meal of the day, cooking the main meal, table-setting, food-serving, table-clearing and dish-washing, on the last occasion these were done.

[5] Given that there were seven tasks, the male contribution index scores range from 0 to 7; zero for households where the male partner had been recorded as contributing towards none of the seven tasks and seven for households where the male partner had been recorded as contributing towards all seven tasks.

Table 5.1 *Who did various feeding tasks the last time they were done? Couple households only (percentages)*

|  | Woman | Man | Both | Other | n |
|---|---|---|---|---|---|
| Shopping | 56 | 14 | 27 | 3 | 599 |
| Planning | 75 | 15 | 7 | 3 | 599 |
| Cooking | 75 | 19 | 3 | 3 | 598 |
| Table-setting | 55 | 23 | 4 | 18 | 591 |
| Food-serving | 75 | 17 | 5 | 4 | 598 |
| Table-clearing | 44 | 32 | 13 | 12 | 593 |
| Dish-washing | 40 | 39 | 11 | 9 | 599 |

*Note:*
With the exception of shopping (which refers to the main food shopping) all these tasks refer to the work involved in the main meal of the day.

higher the score, the greater is the contribution of male partners in that work.

The male contribution index was subjected to multiple linear regression analysis with a range of socio-demographic variables.[6] The findings are presented in table 5.2. The adjusted $R^2$ indicates that 31 per cent of the variance in the male contribution index was explained. Respondent's sex was the strongest explanatory variable in the equation; male contributions were greater when estimated by male than by female respondents. This corroborates earlier findings that interviews conducted with the female partner of couple households systematically result in lower estimations of male contribution than interviews conducted with male partners (see Warde et al., 1989; Martens, 1997), even when asked who had done this task the *last time* it was done and the option to say that the particular task is shared was readily available. Nevertheless, the regression equation provides additional information.

Households with three or more residents, for instance, recorded lower levels of male contribution in the household's food work than households with two residents (i.e. couple-only households). This was attributable to men contributing less in households with children between the ages of five and fifteen. In households with children younger than five male contribution was greater than in other households. However, if we distinguish between the *central* tasks of planning, cooking and serving the main meal

[6] In addition to the socio-demographic indicators used in our discussion in chapter 4, the list of independent variables included information on the character of financial management in the household, on respondents' views about their contributions towards the household's feeding work, and on respondents' general interest in food.

Table 5.2 *The male contribution index: multiple linear regression results*

| Independent variables | B | Beta | t | |
|---|---|---|---|---|
| Respondent female | −1.60 | −0.40 | −9.877 | *** |
| Household size | −1.12 | −0.27 | −7.054 | *** |
| 'Do less than fair share' | −1.19 | −0.20 | −5.419 | *** |
| Interest in food | 0.07 | 0.16 | 4.463 | *** |
| Degree qualification | 0.63 | 0.14 | 3.970 | *** |
| Presence of children under 5 | 0.57 | 0.13 | 3.201 | ** |
| Full-time/housewife partners[a] | −0.61 | −0.12 | −3.260 | ** |
| 'Do more than fair share' | −0.46 | −0.11 | −2.823 | ** |
| Housewife/other households[a] | −0.79 | −0.09 | −2.662 | ** |
| City of residence | 0.33 | 0.08 | 2.208 | * |
| Financial management system | 0.42 | 0.08 | 2.075 | * |
| Constant | 3.75 | | 22.72 | *** |

*Notes:*
$R^2 = 30.6\%$, $F = 24.978$***
(3 outliers)
*$p < .05.$**$p < .01.$***$p < .001$
[a] Household employment included combinations of the four options: full-time employed, part-time employed, housewife and other. The regression equation measured systematic differences in male contribution recordings between the variety of household employment types and households where both partners were full-time employed.

and the *ancillary* tasks of table setting, clearing up and washing dishes, a similar regression analysis shows that the presence of children under five only resulted in a greater male contribution to the ancillary tasks.

Another significant variable explaining the male contribution index was an evaluation of perceived contribution. Immediately after being asked about the seven tasks, respondents were asked to evaluate their contribution. Three options were available: 'I do my fair share', 'I do more than my fair share' and 'I do less than my fair share'. Overall, the majority of respondents chose the first option; 58 per cent thought they did a fair share. A further 29 per cent of respondents thought that they did more than their share, whilst 13 per cent thought that they did less than a fair share.[7] Respondents' judgements about their own contribution ('do

[7] These answers varied significantly with respect to respondents' sex. Female respondents were less likely to say that they did just their fair share (51 per cent versus 64 per cent for male respondents). In contrast, women were much more likely to feel that they did more than their fair share (45 per cent as opposed to 12 per cent for male respondents). The majority of those who felt that they did less than their fair share were male (24 per cent versus 4 per cent for female respondents).

less than fair share' and 'do more than fair share' in table 5.2)[8] were significantly related to scores on the male contribution index. Where the score was low, respondents were more inclined to be discontented (i.e. they were more inclined either to say that they did more or less than their fair share). This indicates that when the male contribution index is high, respondents, whether male or female, are more likely to be content with their own contribution.[9]

Also important was a measure to indicate interest in food and food tasks. An index was constructed on the basis of questions about interest in cooking (both routine and for special occasions), doing shopping and using recipes in cooking. Identified as 'interest in food' in Table 5.2, it too resulted in higher male contributions.[10] However, further analysis on split samples of male and female respondents showed that this effect occurred *only* if male respondents had a self-professed high level of interest in food. The male contribution index was not sensitive to variations in women's enthusiasm about food: a woman's contribution does not vary with respect to her general interest in food. This strongly supports the notion that the 'norm' still is that food remains a woman's responsibility and if men become involved they do so out of choice. If a man cooks, it is something he enjoys and is not equivalent to mundane work. Such men use this attitude to 'explain' their involvement, and why they are different from other men.

Respondents with a degree qualification also recorded higher male contribution levels compared with those without qualification. Further analysis, however, suggested that this effect too was only significant amongst male respondents. The educational qualifications of women did not impact on the male contribution index. These findings are supported by the four Preston men who did cooking; all had university qualifications

---

[8] In the regression equations discussed here, 'doing my fair share' was used as the option against which 'doing more than my fair share' and 'doing less than my fair share' were measured.

[9] Differences in attitudes between male and female respondents were clarified by doing a further regression on split samples of male and female respondents. Male respondents with a low score on the male contribution index were more inclined to think they did less than their fair share, while female respondents in households with a low male contribution index score tended to think they did more than their fair share.

[10] An index of 'interest in food' was constructed by aggregating responses respondents gave to questions about their relative interest in routine cooking, cooking for a special occasion, shopping for food and using recipes from cookbooks and other sources. Five possible answers ranged from 'very interested' to 'not at all interested'. High index scores attest to a high degree of interest in these four domestic feeding work tasks. Women were more likely to score highly on this index. Of those 'very interested' in domestic food and feeding, 66 per cent were female and 35 per cent were male. Of those not at all interested in domestic food and feeding, 70 per cent were male and 30 per cent were female.

and three of them talked about their university days as a time when they consciously explored food and started to learn to cook.

Of lesser significance in determining divisions of domestic labour were employment status, city of residence and financial management in the household. Households containing a full-time employee and a housewife, and those with a housewife and someone involved in other activities (i.e. student, retired or unemployed) recorded significantly lower male contribution rates than full-time dual-earner households. There was, however, no difference between full-time dual-earner households and those which included one partner in part-time employment. The low level of association of employment status in this regression corroborates earlier crosstabulations that household employment status was not statistically significant for *all* feeding tasks. Further analysis did, however, show that employment status is more prominent in explaining variation in male contributions towards the ancillary feeding tasks. For the central feeding tasks, meal planning, meal cooking and meal serving, employment status is not important.

In households where time is scarce, as when both partners are employed full-time, there is potential pressure on men to contribute towards the work of feeding their family. Overall, this analysis suggests that if men share in the food work, they are more inclined to be involved in those tasks least tied up with their gender identities. Recorded male contributions were higher in households with two full-time employees than in households with a full-time housewife, but only for the *ancillary* feeding tasks. The *central* feeding tasks were not sensitive to household employment status. The presence of young children had a similar effect, men contributing more to ancillary tasks but not to cooking main meals. (Whether men in households where time is scarce pull more weight in other kinds of domestic work was not explored.)

Men do cook meals; 115 men out of 598 couple households were recorded as having cooked the last main meal alone. Men with degrees cooked the last meal most frequently, those with no qualifications least often. When men cook meals they do so not so much because they feel pressurised into doing so, but rather because they are more interested than other men in food; 36 per cent of men who had cooked the last main meal claimed to be very interested in food compared with 19 per cent of all men in couple households.

### Commercial alternatives: substitution, time and money

Equal allocation of everyday domestic food tasks even in households susceptible to time famine is rare, raising the question whether they make more use of commercialised alternatives. We therefore examined the relationship between the division of labour around food in couple households and the frequency of eating out in commercial venues. Only the ancillary tasks, and more particularly washing dishes by the male partner, proved relevant. Indeed, in explaining the frequency of eating out amongst 'couple only' households, the male partner having washed the dishes the last time was the second strongest influence, after household income. Commercial food alternatives are diverse in kind and eating out constitutes only one of them. We reflect on the substitutability of eating main meals in commercial venues (eating out), the consumption of take-aways, and the consumption of ready meals and convenience foods.

In chapter 3 we discussed the reasons why people engage in the different commercial food options available to them. Eating a meal in a commercial venue, for instance, may be done because of a special occasion, because it is a suitable leisure activity to meet with friends and socialise, because it offers an opportunity to do something different from the everyday, or because of a liking for new and well-prepared foods. Time-saving may be an issue (although this did not feature in the reasons given for why our interviewees ate out), but eating a meal out often takes up considerable time and is therefore not necessarily an effective 'time-saving' strategy (see chapter 7 for details on the length of meals eaten out). Whether time is actually saved also depends on with whom one eats out and what alternatives exist. So, for instance, time may be saved when the alternative to eating a meal out with a group of friends is that they all come to eat in your home, and you are left with the responsibility to prepare it. Moreover, the idea that eating a meal in a commercial venue does not necessarily 'save' time is highlighted when interviewees explained it as an opportunity for the temporary release of time controls offered by eating out. Feelings of having been overburdened or having gone through a particularly busy patch in paid work, generate the desire to be treated by the 'time-extravagance' that constitutes eating out. This was expressed, for instance, by Andy.

when we've had a particularly hard time er, or rough time or stressful time where we've both been working flat out . . . the time before last when we ate out, we'd both been working very hard like three weeks with hardly seeing each other so we thought, right now we'll go out and we'll *make a night of it* and *take our time* about things. (our emphasis)

This link was not solely related to paid work. For Chris, time pressure resulted mainly from a full schedule of weekend engagements associated with family caring. So, eating out was seen as relaxation when one can 'take one's time' in juxtaposition to a generally hurried lifestyle. It seems, therefore, that saving time is not an overriding concern for those who eat main meals in commercial venues, but that, as a leisure time activity, it *is* directly contrasted with the bustle of everyday life.

Substitution also involves monetary considerations. Households may suffer time constraints but not necessarily have much disposable income. This may be because their initial income is not great, or because other expenditure takes priority over food expenditure. In such instances, eating out may be regarded as unduly expensive – particularly when compared to cheaper commercial options.

In principle, take-away meals may be considered a better solution to saving time on cooking. People who are tired after a heavy week may prefer to eat a take-away at home rather than to eat a meal out, since the latter may involve exertions like dressing up and travelling. Our qualitative research supported the view that take-aways are often sought at the end of the working week, when people are tired, and/or when food cupboards are empty. Tiredness was the overwhelming reason for Nadia regularly to want a take-away on Fridays. Janice, on the other hand, commented that buying fish and chips depended on how organised she had been during the day.

Janice suggested that take-aways may offer a more *flexible* commercial food alternative to eating out for households who, by necessity, cannot leave the domestic sphere at short notice: households with young children, for instance, are usually faced with 'extra' exertions and costs when they want to eat out. Take-aways may also provide a more cost-effective solution compared with eating out in a commercial venue, although some interviewees explicitly pronounced them too expensive to buy often (for frequency of use see Table 3.4). However, our qualitative material warned against the view that the consumption of take-aways is always related to necessities of this kind; pleasure was an important reason for some. Thus, take-aways may be regarded as better means to save time and money than eating out. For the gourmet, the reverse might be the case; take-aways might be avoided because the food or the experience is deemed of inferior quality. Take-aways would probably also not be experienced so much a treat.

We did not systematically investigate the use of ready meals and other 'convenience' foods. There is, however, no doubt that 'convenience' foods had been incorporated into the everyday food practices of interviewees, and that this was by some directly related to time experiences. Trisha, for instance, had been used to eating ready meals, whilst time-pressured Nadia would like to eat more frozen foods and ready meals if only her husband would allow it and join in. Both worked full-time and Nadia also had children to cook for.

Alternative commercial food options have diverse implications for 'time-saving' and monetary expense. Consumers use commercial services for many reasons and 'saving time' is not always primary. Sitting down for a meal in a restaurant may be neither cheap nor likely to 'save time'. Indeed, rather the contrary; a leisurely pace is often one of the appeals of eating out. Experiences of time do affect the organisation of food consumption by households, but the causal connections are neither simple nor straightforward. We continue by digging deeper into the social relations that underly this complexity.

### Shared understandings of the meal and the regulation of eating out

The relationship between everyday domestic organisation around food and eating out is best uncovered from our in-depth interviews. The essence of this relationship can be traced back to the definitions, or *shared understandings*, of meals (see chapter 3).

One example of the presence of 'shared understandings about a particular setting' is the family meal (DeVault, 1991: 236). Discourses of the 'family meal' stipulate particular ways of doing meals. This can be readily recognised in the description of the 'proper' meal which Charles and Kerr (1988: 18–24) formulated from lay understandings, voiced by their British respondents, which prescribe *what* should be eaten, *how* the meal should be eaten and *who* should prepare it. Similarly, lay understandings of eating out may also be read as a *shared understanding*, which stipulates 'particular ways of doing' such meals. Particularly relevant was the notion that eating out is 'special'. By ranking eating events in terms of 'degrees of specialness', interviewees clarified what was appropriate to eat when eating out, how often it was appropriate to eat out and what places were the appropriate ones for the eating event to count as 'eating out' (see Dunleavy and Martens, 1997 for a more elaborate discussion).

Understandings of eating out and eating in are interdependent. They inform each other. Lay definitions of eating out construct and reflect not only its attributed cultural meanings, but also those attached to eating in. Shared understandings of meals are 'prescriptions' as to *how often* specific food/meal occasions should occur; *where* they should happen; *what* it is appropriate to eat during these occasions; *what circumstances* are appropriate; and *how* the performance should be conducted. Such prescriptions for eating in and eating out are summarised in table 5.3. Whereas shared understandings about family eating emphasise some features, shared understandings of eating out may remain quite silent on those prescriptions, and vice versa. For instance, understandings of eating out

Table 5.3 *Understandings of eating out and eating in*

|  | Eating out | Eating in |
|---|---|---|
| How often? | infrequently; weekly, monthly or less often | regularly; daily |
| Where? | away from 'home'; in a significant commercial venue | around the domestic dinner table |
| What to eat? | meal, but large quantities, 'good quality' food, food which is different from the everyday, many courses | meal, but everyday food |
| What circumstances? When? | special occasions, like birthdays, weddings (anniversaries), christenings, Christmas and weekends | everyday, weekdays |
| How it should be done | being served and cooked for; mannered rituals including time, dress, menu | cooked and served by women for husbands and children; mannered rituals |
| With whom | acquaintances, not strangers | immediate family members |

make explicit reference to *how often* it should be done, whereas it is more implicitly understood that 'proper' domestic meals are eaten on an everyday basis. The latter is important, because it stipulates that the 'norm' remains daily domestic meals with their associated relations of provision.

Shared understandings entail that eating out should not occur too frequently. To the extent that such understandings operate as compelling forces in everyday decision-making this notion is likely to influence behaviour.

A common explanation for interviewees replying 'no' to the question whether they wanted to eat out more than they currently did, was that the frequency of eating out and the pleasure expected were inversely related. So interviewees (particularly those for whom money was not considered a constraint) who answered 'no', believed that the frequency with which they ate out needed to be controlled to maintain the 'specialness' of the event. Sheila said: 'it is more of an event if you don't do it too regularly, yeah. Although sometimes if I do go out to Giovanni's I think, yes, I should come in here once a week for my tea, you know, and treat myself, but, yeah, maybe less frequently would, it makes it more fun if you do it less frequently, yeah.' Her opinion was shared by a number of other interviewees, and suggests that self-regulation of the use of marketised food services is not uncommon.

Lay definitions of eating out also included the idea that the labour was shifted from the domestic worker to the commercial service provider. Getting a break from cooking, being served and not having to clean up afterwards featured strongly in the reasons given by female interviewees as to why they ate out, as well as in expressions of pleasure received from eating out. Jane exemplified comments of other female interviewees. 'It's nice to try some food somebody else has made, somebody else is going to clear up and after you just relax. . . . You know having a choice there to choose what you'd like that somebody else is going to cook.' Other interviewees spoke in terms like 'gives you a change from cooking', 'it saves you cooking', and 'it's a break from doing something yourself'. We want to draw attention to the language used. These expressions suggest temporary release from feeding work that eating out offers. They indicate an expectation that release from feeding work may be achieved every so often, but certainly not on a regular day-to-day basis. By talking about eating out in this way, our female interviewees consented to an ideal of 'proper' eating out by denying that it is the norm. Nowhere was there any indication that eating out was thought of as providing the potential to refrain *for ever* or even *mostly* from domestic provisioning.

Shared understandings about eating out are not the only influences which induce people to regulate their use of commercial services. Understandings about 'proper' family life, and related to it 'proper' family eating, can also operate as compelling forces in decisions to use commercial food services. This was illustrated rather well in the discussion with one interviewee, Jenny.

Jenny talked extensively about the contradictions of modern living. On the one hand, she aspired to comply with the demands voiced by images of 'proper' families and 'good' motherhood. She was, on the other hand, very aware of the commercial services available to make the feeding work of busy women easier. And, as a full-time employee and mother of three children – all of whom still required her care and attention (even though two were in their twenties) – Jenny's time schedule was very tight. Jenny's partner did do some of the feeding work, but Jenny thought that this was really her responsibility. Consequently, Jenny had introduced a number of time-saving devices into her daily feeding work, always using frozen vegetables, for instance. Yet she believed that she was inadequate in her role as mother and carer, because her employment did not enable her to do her mothering job in the 'proper' way: keeping up with the ironing, using fresh vegetables and the superior cooking skills of a friend all came up in discussion.

In response to the question whether she would like to eat out more often, Jenny could not make up her mind: 'I don't know really, yeah I would, yeah I would. No I mean, I don't know.' She was caught between the desire to do so, and the fear that commercial feeding services lowered the 'quality' of her family life, reflecting badly on her as a mother and woman. She avowed that eating out without her children too frequently was not acceptable because it replaced the 'proper' family meal. Being away from home and her children, spending time on things other than 'proper' family meals, and the implication that eating out would entail that no 'proper' meal was being cooked at home, contradicted Jenny's notion of 'proper' domestic family eating. Having said that, Jenny was also acutely aware that traditional notions of 'proper' family eating were not valued so highly by her grown-up children.

There are a number of ways in which the desires of the domestic worker, and those she cares for, can clash. Nadia worked full-time and had two children and did most of the household's feeding work, helped by her mother. She wanted to eat out more often, or alternatively, wanted to have a freezer filled with ready-made foods, so that she could get release, at times, from the demands made on her regarding feeding work.

INTERVIEWER: So you said if it was up to you you would eat out more?
NADIA: Eat out more often or otherwise have more things in the freezer.
INTERVIEWER: And why is that?
NADIA: You have something different to make every day, you get sort of sick of making the same sort of foods more or less. Can't decide what to make. It's a lot easier when you've got something to take out of the freezer. When you are not feeling well that's one time that er you do miss a freezer. If I don't make a meal. But yes, if it was up to me.

But it was not up to Nadia. In her discussion, Nadia explained that her husband's wishes were rather the opposite. He was suspicious of ready-meals and frozen foods. Consequently, frozen foods were not often consumed in the household, and if they were, Nadia was still expected to make her husband something different, defeating the purpose of serving those foods in the first place.

## About family meals and moral panics

Shared understandings, in their totality, embody the persisting cultural dominance of domestic meals and their associated relations of provision. It is the institution of the family meal which people refer to, use and reflect upon in view of their own food activities and desires. Shared understandings of meals are internalised discourses of appropriate conduct, and they operate as a force that make individuals limit their use of eating out services. Given this, it is somewhat peculiar that the 1980s saw the re-emergence of moral concern about the decline of the family meal in the UK. As Hardyment (1995:199) put it, 'rumours of a nation eating on the streets led to many panic-stricken claims that the family meal was on the way out, taking family values with it'. How can the validity of such worries be examined in relation to the use of restaurants, pubs and other commercial places where people primarily go to eat meals? This is possible, we argue here, by returning to Charles and Kerr's (1988: 18–24) definition of the 'proper meal'. They defined the key characteristics of a proper meal when developing an analytic construct to make sense of the responses of their interviewees in Northern England in the early 1980s. 'For the majority of women a proper meal was clearly taken to be a meal made up of meat (sometimes fish), potatoes and vegetables . . . the term "proper meal" was never used to refer to anything but the main meal of the day, the cooked dinner.' It was 'often defined in opposition to a "snack" or "snack-type" meal which usually constituted the non-main meal of the day'. 'In contrast to a snack a proper meal is often seen as a social occasion: a chance for all the family to sit down and eat a meal together.' Moreover, 'for most of our families eating a proper meal involved eating at a table', and 'Table manners were also considered to be important to a family meal.' '[I]t is also a meal cooked by the woman in the household for herself, her partner and her children.' The proper meal, then, assumes the coincidence of four elements – structured menu, mannered rituals, nuclear family companionship and housewifely provision. For the purpose of our analysis here, it is further possible to see the first two elements in their definition as describing a structured eating event; the second two as the social relations of consumption associated with a family meal – appropriate companions and a particular relationship between provider and consumers, namely service by a housewife.

Our survey data make it possible to compare domestic meals and meals eaten out in terms of the social relations of their consumption. Arguably, much of the moral panic about the decline of the family meal is not about the transformation of the elements in the structural dimension of the eating event, though the changing menu of French meals does worry the French commentator Fischler (1980). Rather, it is the demise of the context for the playing out of the social relations of consumption, which are considered positive for the maintenance of existing norms of family organisation, that worries British conservatives. Below, we examine what proportion of domestic meals corresponds with the appropriate social relations of consumption as stipulated by notions of the proper meal. We then compare this with evidence on the social relations of consumption of meals eaten out.

In the vast majority of households surveyed (82 per cent), a main meal was cooked every day.[11] There are, then, for most households frequent opportunities for members to eat together at least once a day. Let us concentrate here on the evening meal, which is now the main meal for most people of working age and is the one at which family members will eat together most often. Looking at all respondents in households with two or more people in them (i.e. excluding the 155 single-person households in our sample), 19 per cent had eaten yesterday's evening meal alone. Of course, our respondents lived in diverse households, and given that concern for the family meal is primarily around households which contain partners and children, let us consider the rate of main meal participation in those. The proportion of households where *every* member was present at the main meal on the previous day was 73 per cent. There was some variation between households of different size, with larger households in general having greater difficulty in gathering all members together for meal times.

By knowing how many of the residents in each household had eaten an evening meal with the respondent the previous day, and who had cooked that meal (see table 5.1), we were able to estimate the proportion of households consuming a proper meal on the previous day, as defined by its social relations of consumption. Amongst the 598 couple households in the sample, 152 (25 per cent) households had failed to receive a proper meal because such a dinner had not been cooked solely by a female partner. A further 126 (21 per cent) failed because not all household members were present, though the meal had been cooked by the female partner. This means that 54 per cent of all couple households had eaten a proper meal the previous day. Whether there were children living in the household made no difference to this proportion.

When interpreting these findings it should be remembered that the question we asked was about yesterday only. The absence of one member of a household on one particular day in no way undermines the principle of the proper meal. We have also applied quite stringent criteria for identifying a proper meal (the female partner must have done the work without help from other family members, and all other members of the household must be present, even though some might be adult children or very young children). Given this, we may conclude that the notion of a 'family' meal remains prevalent among couple households, that it is certainly not on the verge of extinction and that many children will consequently gain extensive experience of such events.

[11] Another 15 per cent of households cooked a main meal several times a week, whilst only 2.2 per cent did so once a week. The proportion of households in which main meals were cooked less often than weekly was negligible.

Eating out is more convivial than eating at home. Only 2 per cent of respondents said that they were alone on the last occasion they ate out, whilst nearly 70 per cent of respondents claimed not to have eaten out alone in the twelve months prior to the interview. As we noted above, 19 per cent of the sample (excluding single-person households) did not eat an evening meal in the company of any other household member on the day prior to the interview,[12] and although it is difficult to know the extent, it is likely that at least some of the 155 respondents living alone also ate by themselves. Hence, it is almost certain that eating alone occurs much more often in a domestic setting than in a public one.

More important in terms of the social relations of consumption is the finding that people are as likely to be in the company of family members when they eat out as they are when they eat at home. We have just seen that in 73 per cent of couple households everyone living in the household had been present for the last meal. In 87 per cent of those cases, at least one other household member was present. Last time they ate out 72 per cent of people reported being with partner and/or family. Amongst respondents living with a partner, 86 per cent had eaten out in the presence of family. Though this figure includes non-resident kin, by way of compensation, not every co-resident person counted as present at the last domestic meal will necessarily be kin or quasi-kin. Hence the ironic fact that the chances of the last main meal being taken with kin is roughly the same whether people were eating at home or eating out.

In terms of the overall stability of the family, our endeavours here have been rather artificial, since people still eat out comparatively infrequently. Therefore in absolute terms eating with kin much more commonly occurs at home. However, at the same time, this evidence refutes any suggestion that eating out endangers family eating together or reduces channels of family communication. Currently, the meal out is, in the majority of cases, a family occasion of some kind, and hence does not deprive people of family company.

### Domestic organisation, families and commodification

Domestic organisation is a broad concept which may direct attention to the organisation of domestic work, the connections between the organisation of paid work, domestic work and consumption, or to domestic power relations more generally. In this chapter we have engaged with all of these in some way, even though our discussion was limited to the food field. There exists an implicit assumption that commercialisation in the food

---

[12] Of course not all of these would actually be eating by themselves; some will have been in restaurants with other people, and some will have been guests of kin.

field has increased in the context of a rise in the hours household members spend in paid work, leaving relatively less time for unpaid domestic work and generating more disposable income to buy such services on the market. That the causal pattern may not be so simple was borne out by our failure to find a clear statistical relationship between paid work, domestic food work and the use of commercial meal options. It calls to mind Gofton's (1996) observation that contemporary usage of 'convenience' foods does not relate in a simple way to 'saving time', but that it is intricately bound up with the social relations that shape domestic organisation around food in contemporary households.

Shared cultural understandings of meals point to these social relations, including the designation of who should do the unpaid work involved. Our findings corroborate existing evidence that domestic food work is predominantly done by women, and that this manner of organisation is resilient to pressures for change. We might, for instance, have expected greater collaboration and sharing of this work in households where, because of paid work or other reasons, time is scarce. Yet this is not the reason for men to get involved in the more time-consuming aspects of this work, although there was evidence of men in these households helping more with the more 'ancillary' food tasks.

Inflexibility in the allocation of food work in households might encourage greater commercialisation in the field. Yet, our findings show that social barriers exist against unlimited recourse to eating out. More specifically, shared definitions stipulate that eating out should be infrequent, in contrast with the mundane domestic norm. This was evident in language such as 'getting a break from cooking' and understandings of eating out as a treat. 'Saving time' did not feature in the reasons Prestonian interviewees gave for why they eat out, and if anything, eating out is not about 'time saving' but about 'time indulgence'.

It is a matter of judgement whether one considers the frequency with which family members eat together at home as becoming insufficient and thereby evidence of a decline in domestic cooking and family life. Whatever the view, it is dubious whether eating out has had much impact on continuities in family life, not least because eating out is not (yet) part of everyday food routines in the great majority of households. This is, of course, not to deny that the number of meals eaten out has increased nor that most people eat out sometimes.

Perhaps ironically, restaurants and other food venues may in fact provide the possibility for qualitatively better familial relationships than are achieved around the dinner table at home. First, eating out, whether in restaurants or private houses, is often done in the company of family members. Second, if Finkelstein (1989) is correct that 'civilised' conduct is only possible in contexts where everyone involved has a similar degree of power, then domestic meals are unlikely to provide a context for democratic interaction. The provider of the meal is present both as servant, but also as the person to whom others are beholden for a precious gift, and the routines of turn-taking in dinner-table conversation are likely to reflect the more general hierarchy of power and authority in the household, thus disempowering younger and female members. Compared to domestic dining, restaurants increase the choices available to the weak, in control over what is eaten, for instance, and eliminate the servile aspects of domestic provision. Relief from domestic chores – which is an important part of the appeal of eating out, as well as expectations of pleasure – may improve mood and communication within family groups. Finally, restaurants offer, probably more emphatically than the domestic sphere, the opportunity for mannered eating. If one aspect of the idealised proper meal is that it requires people to sit at a table, appropriately set up with drapery and implements, exhibit table manners, concentrate primarily on eating while engaging in conversation with fellow diners, then the restaurant probably offers an even more conducive environment. In such ways, the family might potentially be better served by eating out together than by dining at home.

However, it is not clear that commercialisation, as currently constructed, liberates women at all. The market mode of provision has some potential, because it is organised on different principles and requires different practices. However, the experience of eating out has had limited effects on dominant understandings of the gendered organisation of food preparation. Shared understandings of eating out currently tend to articulate dominant power relations in the field.

Another question arises: do women want to be 'freed' from domestic work? Or, to put it differently, do women and other household (family) members want to escape from a number of common domestic arrangements, like domestic meals and domestic childcare, in favour of commercial alternatives? In relation to this, DeVault and others have pointed to a number of dilemmas, addressed within feminist thinking, about 'alternatives' to current modes of social organisation. Firstly, caring work, such as food provision, at least as currently organised, may play an important role in the generation and reproduction of gender inequalities, but it is also activity imbued with value and importance. Caring for people can be burdensome, but caring about people is often associated with high levels of satisfaction. Should such activity be relinquished to the market, or is it possible to change the ways in which it is currently domestically organised, for instance, by a greater input of men in such tasks? Secondly, it has been pointed out that commercial alternatives often do not challenge, but rather reinforce, the gendered character of such work (Cockburn and Ormrod, 1993; Gregson and Lowe, 1994; DeVault, 1991). Gregson and Lowe, for instance, point out that the employment of child-minders or cleaners takes away the need to re-organise this work amongst household members. Equally, DeVault has hinted, and our research corroborates, that rather than changing the organisation of domestic food work, eating out at best offers an occasional break or treat for busy women.

*Part III*

# Delivery

The process through which a consumer actually receives a good or service, and how that reception is managed, is a defining element of almost all consumption events. Even the most fleeting and simple of transactions, the activity of transferring money to someone else in exchange for goods, can be evaluated in terms of the quality of its delivery. Whether a shop assistant was pleasant, whether the mail order form was appropriate, whether the despatch of goods was quick are criteria influencing customer satisfaction. Consumption episodes which involve more elaborate and extensive servicing work are more susceptible to judgements of this kind. A meal in a restaurant may take several hours and involve repeated communication with staff; taking a holiday in a hotel may last a couple of weeks; a course of educational instruction may take years and involve sustained interaction; a relationship with a general practitioner may last decades. When the process of consumption is protracted, and where the level of personal interaction between provider and recipient is extensive or sensitive, then the nature of the setting and the human relationships involved become especially important. The nature of the experience, and hence the perceived quality of the episode, depend upon how the presentation and transaction of the service is managed.

The environment of delivery in the commercial mode is largely determined by the producer. This is the fundamental truth of Finkelstein's (1989) observation about the already given character of the restaurant as a setting. Explicit examination of the consumer experience in the catering industry was pioneered in the academic literature by Campbell-Smith (1967). He observed that pleasure in eating out was not achieved simply through the provision of adequately cooked acceptable food in sufficient quantity, but was affected by the decor, the atmosphere, the presentation of the food, the conduciveness of the service, the attractiveness of the serving staff, the opening and closing of the visit and so forth. These features, which we call the restaurant regime, constitute an inescapable backcloth which provides a structuring framework for the customer's experience of the event. Though settings are important, most analytic attention has been paid to the human interaction involved in the serving of food, with different modes and timbres of service being seen as particularly critical in attracting or upsetting customers. The proliferation of customer satisfaction questionnaires designed to evaluate, and implicitly applaud, the quality of service – in hotels, airports, hospitals and universities – symbolises the appreciation by the public relations departments of producer organisations that consumers' perceptions of their treatment are an important economic matter. For the producers it is seen as a major factor affecting competitive position in the commercial sector or, in the public sector, levels of future funding.

However, customers also play an important, if neglected, part in the definition of the setting. Into this context diners bring their own particular projects, their definition of the occasion, their expectations about the way the particular meal will be conducted. People plan, with varying degrees of sophistication, different sorts of events in the, apparently justifiable, expectation that different kinds of experience will be furnished in different venues. As part of this process they make different forms of preparation for their visit: what time of day they venture out, whether they dress up, or make a long journey, are elements that they contribute in anticipation of achievement of a desired outcome. Their subsequent conduct is constitutive of the dramatic scene and the overall atmosphere, a contribution which they make for free yet without which few restaurants would be considered appealing. It may be helpful to conceive the conduct of the diners as a social performance, which begins some time before entering an eating place and may not yet be finished at the point of departure.

In chapter 6 we look closely at the interaction between diners and providers. The experience of receiving commercial service by paid waiting staff is examined, for the experience will be strongly defined, and its quality affected, by the nature of the service provided. Incontrovertibly, one of the foremost differences between eating in a hamburger bar and in a smart restaurant is the nature of the service system, both practically and because of the texture of interaction with staff. Eating out involves not just food, but many other components of service. Appreciation of service is examined through people's talk about the merits and defects of service that they have received as customers in restaurants. Their perceptions are partly clarified through the contrast made between eating out commercially and being recipients of hospitality in the homes of friends and kin. The latter also has its specific mode of delivery; a dominant normative regime being implied in definitions of the dinner party.

Chapter 7 gives some detailed description of the nature of the experience for customers in commercial establishments and for guests in private situations, concentrating on what the consumer brings to the event. It is concerned with two aspects of the experience of eating out. First, we examine the selection of dishes and courses, whether from a menu in a restaurant or by allocation at home, looking at the social patterning of types of meal considered appropriate to particular places, occasions and groups of companions. This gives some insight into contemporary food tastes and permits comparison of communal and commercial settings. We also examine the wider social performance of customers on the last occasion they ate out. We include information about the extended nature of the episode, for the dining out experience has its own planning and preparation stage for the consumer whose expectations will be to some degree disclosed by that planning and preparation.

Although not a topic receiving a great deal of scholarly attention, several commentators have regarded the restaurant and the hotel dining room as sites of social control and discipline. Mostly this has been a matter of the strategies that staff or management use to obtain maximum desired compliance from clientele, it being not enough for customers to spend money, for they must also behave in an acceptable fashion. Contrary to any presumption of consumer sovereignty, some accounts (especially Whyte, 1948; Mars and Nicod, 1984) suggest that waiters are adept at manipulating their customers, and that there are some unpleasant punishments for those who resist. Finkelstein (1989) implies that control is built into the design of a restaurant, such that its 'diorama', or ambience, serves to prescribe customer behaviour. Wood (1994b), probably more sanguine than Finkelstein, observes that there is a genuine problem of appropriate interaction between providers and consumers of commercial hospitality services, and seeks to isolate some of the ritual rules involved and to explore how these have developed over time, such that behaviour in dining rooms is, for the most part, orderly and predictable. However, he notes elsewhere (Wood, 1990) that the restaurant is a masculine environment, implying that male diners (and managers) exercise some degree of power and control over women.

This chapter explores these propositions regarding the operation of power, examining whether people feel restrained, constrained and repressed; if so by what or by whom. This may indicate some features and trends of the nature of public behaviour in places of entertainment, particularly trends of informalisation and domestication. Is there a trend for restaurant meals to become more like domestic ones? Is there a process of informalisation? What do these activities indicate about attitudes to strangers and decorous behaviour in public places?

The precise nature of the parallel process of delivery in situations of private entertaining is less easy to analyse. The arrangements of the restaurant regime provide comparatively clear guidance for managing the situational and interpersonal aspects of the meal experience; service is standardised and regularised to whichever of the different formats the establishment has adopted. Entertaining at home also involves orchestration of an event, including putting guests at ease, co-ordinating courses, delivering food to table and so forth. As reference to etiquette books or women's magazines describing how best to entertain guests will reveal, there are some rules about appropriate procedures and conventions for dealing with these matters. However, there is almost no scholarly literature on the topic. Nor did our research uncover much about the ways in which private guests received, or reflected upon, service delivery. What little information we gleaned was as a result of respondents comparing being a guest with eating in restaurants, which tended to revolve around notions of familiarity, formality and relaxation.

Scholars interested in services have been particularly fascinated by the potential importance of the intervention of face-to-face relations in the delivery process (Urry, 1990; Hochschild, 1983; Leidner, 1993). This sometimes means that employees have to be accommodating in their manner and demeanour (by offering good advice, encouragement and flattery, pleasantness, or by exuding efficiency). By complete contrast, many people pronounce themselves discouraged from spending their money when there are staff in attendance lest they apply pressure to buy, give insufficient time for reflection and so forth. Sometimes vendors play a co-active part in the process; Abu-Lughod (1991) reports the irritation of vendors in North Africa with Westerners who refuse to barter, even refusing to sell a product because their own asking price is too high. It is said that in Taiwan customers require to feel the goods and to meet the vendor as part of the system of trust and guarantee. Interestingly, in the UK consumer concern about the quality of goods and the trustworthiness of vendors has in many sectors become impersonalised through corporate and state guarantees of recompense for shoddy or inappropriate produce, an important development in retailing.

More specifically in the delivery of services the appropriate level of intervention by staff is contextual and contested. A customer might, or might not, expect or welcome an exchange of pleasantries and opinions with the person behind the bar or the driver of a taxi. The same uncertainty holds for waiting staff who are intermittent co-actors, are certainly co-present, and about whom customers have certain expectations and can discern inappropriate behaviour.

Many different values might be emphasised regarding the nature of good service from the perspective of the consumer. Service might be associated with:

1 *speed:* the faster the transaction the better;

2 *ease:* the less effort required on behalf of the recipient of the service the better;
3 *advice:* the more accurate and useful the information and judgement imparted prior to the act of exchange the better;
4 *trust in the product:* the more the process of exchange reassures the consumer that the product is sound the better;
5 *value for money:* the lower the price at which the desired item can be obtained the better;
6 *social participation:* the more acceptable and sustained the interpersonal interaction in the process of exchange the better;
7 *social honour:* the more the consumer is made to feel socially comfortable the better.

There are, no doubt, other possible elements of good service, but what this list suggests is that it would be hard for any provider to maximise all at once, that there is plenty of space for misunderstanding or failure in the management of personal service delivery, and that there are likely to be differences in satisfaction with any arrangement depending upon the types of customer involved and the types of service offered.

If we apply this catalogue of the functions of service to the commercial meals sector then we have some basis both for classifying types of outlet and the dimensions along which diners evaluate food and service. Some customers, on some occasions, value speed, which the fast food corporations capitalise on by their concern with instant delivery, but which other outlets must take some account of since service is often criticised for being too 'slow'. The degree of effort that the customer is prepared to invest also varies, with some restaurant regimes eliminating all staff labour through 'self-service', while other establishments absolve clients from even the energy required to remove their overcoats. The extent to which the diner might want advice is more potentially problematic, with the minimalist version being a picture of the dishes on sale on the wall, the maximum level a personal verbal description of different dishes or wines and a recommendation regarding what would be most pleasing. Trust in the quality of the food is partly fostered by the service staff, their appearance often standing as proxy for the hygiene standards, as well as the care involved in food preparation in the kitchen. It is comparatively unusual for any negotiation to occur in a British restaurant about the price of a meal, but the system of tipping has some impact on notions of value for money. The growth of the theme restaurant, and the use of staff as entertainers (see Crang, 1994) is one means by which customers are induced to participate. But equally any restaurant is a site where the overall atmosphere is created by both staff and customers together, such that everyone present is to some extent participating in a social ritual and the satisfaction of each person present is partly dependent on the behaviour of all others.

Finally, the appropriate status relationship between server and client varies from the servile to the cavalier, is one which seems to vary between national cultures, and which is sometimes scripted and regimented by the restaurateur, sometimes imposed by the waiting staff and sometimes negotiated between staff and customer. Traditionally, in the UK, the character of this relationship has been a strategic one, and levels of formality have been key criteria for evaluation. Terms like subservient, surly, supercilious, courteous, overbearing, intrusive, distant, etc. are used by restaurant critics to describe 'service' and while these are sometimes a function of the personal character of staff members more usually they reflect a decision on the part of proprietors about the nature of the establishment. The earlier literature on waiters suggested that they operated a series of strategies which were intended to intimidate and control the customers. Hostility, or at least, mutual suspicion, was typical of the relationship. On the other hand, some recent literature (Sosteric, 1996 and Marshall, 1986) notes that customers and waiting (particularly bar) staff become friends, or at least acknowledged acquaintances, among whom mutual company is valued regardless of the original primary commercial purpose of the relationship. However, this may be comparatively rare in the restaurant trade because people eat out too infrequently for lasting relationships to be struck; and also because a good many staff are casual and temporary.

The restaurant as a site is further complicated because there is not just customer and provider but also different sets of companions. Presumably staff treat large parties, courting couples, family groups and business meetings in rather different ways. Some interactions with staff are noted as potentially problematic: dealing with the wine waiter; complaining on behalf of a member of the party; having somebody else speak for you to the staff; being put down in front of companions by a waiter; being embarrassed by ignorance or lack of knowledge of conventions; etc. It is worthy of note that contemporary books on etiquette feel it necessary to devote extended attention to proper conduct in the restaurant, with ordering, choosing, tipping and paying being the practices (over and above dinner table manners) which command attention and therefore, presumably, are potential sources of anxiety or embarrassment (e.g. Beyfus, 1992: 213–22).

The restaurant being primarily a commercial operation, the staff are functionaries in the pursuit of a sufficient profit, although the commercial nexus may be concealed. As with many other service industries, hiding the commercial thrust behind attention to the individual, whether wishing people a good day, enquiring about their children or discussing the weather, is a means of humanising the exchange. This may be necessary because trade is deemed an activity of dubious worth, so the more it can be concealed the better. It may also be a conscious strategy for maintaining customer loyalty or even persuading customers to buy more than otherwise would be appropriate. It could equally be that social interaction is valued by many people, including the bored salesperson, and that the intrinsically entertaining element of conversation, even (or perhaps especially) in transient situations, is enjoyable.

Some of the particularities of the social relations involved can be identified by asking people about their experiences in restaurants and by contrasting them with eating out in situations governed by reciprocity, which is the purpose of this chapter.

## Service and formality in the restaurant

How people feel about the process of delivery, the nature of their judgements and concerns, is best recovered from qualitative interviews. Our interviewees gave us many reasons why they went where they did, why they enjoyed meals and why they liked particular venues. In the course of this we discovered a good deal about how people evaluated service and that it was in an important degree related to an overriding notion of formality.

In our interviews, discussion of service occurred mostly in the context of asking people about particular meals eaten recently, though sometimes this led to reminiscences about other occasions and gave an opportunity for people to talk about what they liked and disliked about service more generally. Interviewees were mostly satisfied with service and probably took limited notice of details. For instance, many people found it hard to recall what waiting staff were wearing. There is probably a concern for appropriate technique, but only one person described the service at their last meal as 'pretty poor actually' (Janice) in the light of semi-insolent indifference on the part of the staff. The main recurrent complaint arose from courses not arriving at the same time for all guests, which sometimes happened in partly self-service regimes.

The language describing the encounter between customer and serving staff suggests the existence of three dimensions, time, the establishment regime and style of personal interaction.

The majority of interviewees made reference to time when asked about the quality of service. Concern with time was sometimes expressed in minutes, with the length of delays between arrival, having an order taken and the appearance of the first part of the meal on the table. This was very important for some interviewees who were always anxious that service should be quick. However, most recognised, and accepted, that these intervals would depend on the type of eating place and how busy it might be. But besides the absolute times involved, there was also a more subjective sense of acceptable tempo.

Evaluative judgements of service suggest the existence of several polarities, satisfaction being expressed when the event falls acceptably in the middle of the continuum. The temporal dimension entailed avoiding either feeling rushed or being kept waiting too long. Quite a number of people said that they did not mind even quite long intervals before ordering or between courses and they were susceptible to feeling unduly hurried. But it was even more widely observed that staff might hover around waiting to take your plate away and hoping that you will vacate your table soon so that other customers can be accommodated. People did not expect to spend a very long time over a meal in a restaurant. One couple argued about whether a meal they described had lasted as long as three hours, quite clearly in the context of being surprised that it might have done. On the other hand, to feel *slightly* rushed was sometimes seen as evidence of efficiency.

Interviewees clearly recognised the differences between restaurant regimes.[1] Description tended to be in terms of procedures and process: whether ordering preceded being allocated a table, where and with whom an order was placed, etc., identifying different forms of service. Some, like Anne (see below), expressed a very strong preference for bar meals in terms of the character of regime because she seemed ill at ease with the conventions of dress, payment and tipping in restaurants. People who were most comfortable with semi-self service regimes – ordering and paying at a counter and then having food delivered to a nominated table – seemed intentionally to avoid places with more formal arrangements.

An important part of the process of selecting a venue, preference for type of regime can be subsumed in terms of a notion of levels of formality. The way that this is conceptualised in the relationship between customer and staff is on a continuum between intrusive and inattentive service. The word 'intrusive' was used by several interviewees and this was clearly something reprehensible. The character of the dilemma was succinctly expressed by Rose: 'you want your waiting staff to be attentive, you know, make sure everything's all right, but you don't particularly want to be pestered every two minutes'.

A distinct, though related dimension concerns the mood of interaction with staff. Our interviewees used two different contrasts, between enthu-

---

[1] By restaurant regime we mean the comparatively clear, rule-governed system for managing the situational and interpersonal aspects of the meal experience.

siastic and indifferent, and between friendly and impersonal. There was a certain ambivalence about over-enthusiasm, an occasion in an Italian restaurant where the waiters 'were crazy rather than anything else', 'they were all crazy', was enjoyed as a performance but tinged with ambivalence because 'I think one of them liked my little sister'. A couple, Jean and David, while discussing service, recommended a place because they 'always have a good laugh'. On the other hand, Sheila expressed sorrow for the situation of the staff in an up-market place: 'I felt they were a bit down-trodden, you know', whereas 'I think it's nice if the waiting-on staff are enjoying themselves'. She also explicitly condemned staff who, it appeared, 'couldn't care less'. There is an expectation that staff will appear to care.

If staff might be over-enthusiastic, it seemed that they could hardly be too friendly. Forms of recommendation included: being 'welcoming'; 'smiling and you know very courteous'; and 'I like people to be friendly and smile when they bring your food, and ask if everything is alright.' The opposite attitude was condemned: 'if the waitresses are not pleasant . . . that's not good' (Chris). This view found its extension in a comment from Sheila: 'it was efficient but cool and detached, nothing personal about it' (see also Box 7.1). She continued to describe a meal at The Golf Club in the following way:

you know I probably wouldn't go again. Not because the food wasn't nice but I don't know, it's not a place I would choose to go, it's not a homely place. I like to go to homely places like the pub down the road, they have a log fire and you know, you know the landlord and landlady. Yeah, that's more impersonal, you never saw the same waitress twice, they had a lot of staff on.

It is perhaps interesting that reference to friendliness was always considered a feature of the individual staff member and there was no concern that it might be insincere. So whereas the restaurant regime, its organisation and timing, for example, were seen as strategies for increasing profits, the courteousness, politeness and friendliness of waiting staff were taken entirely at face value. In the light of the fears inspired by waiters in the past this may be one of the most important signs of a shift to more informal and acceptable types of service delivery.

The terminology used to commend good service included not just friendliness but also occasionally homeliness. As Smina said of a place she liked:

Yeah, it's quite homely, quite friendly. Because some places you feel oh you know when you go, should I be there or not. It's quite nice, it's nice and welcoming and like all the staff are very friendly too, always coming to ask you is your meal all right, is everything fine, for whatever they bring to you, is everything all right. So it's quite good.

One theme that came up repeatedly in the interviews was the issue of formality, which was a criterion for evaluating different places. One of the strongest expressions of aversion to formal places came from Anne (a housewife, in her twenties with husband and two children) who dwelt upon the topic at length. She expressed a strong dislike of restaurants, and was very favourably inclined towards pubs instead. She explained her preference largely in terms of formality, expressing a great dislike for anything that was formal. 'I don't like going anywhere that's formal. I can't stand anything formal. I had to go to a wedding on Friday, it's just an absolute nightmare for me.' Anne expressed the view that in order for her to enjoy eating out, the experience had to be free from stress, and pressure to 'dress up' for eating out was a source of displeasure. Other elements of Anne's dislike of restaurants included the timing of the meal, not knowing in advance how much the bill would be and tipping. Overall, she preferred the self-service associated with bar meals, partly because of discomfort with conventions regarding tipping and payment, and partly to avoid surveillance.

Other (though not all) respondents thought about different venue types as residing somewhere on a scale of formality, some being more formal than others. The significance of formality for respondents was evident in commentaries about various public eating places. Both John and Sheila were very explicit about different types of commercial venues and their different levels of formality.

obviously if you go to somewhere like a Wotsit's or Pizza Chain it will be obviously far less regimented than if you go to a Classic's or a Gourmet's or somewhere like that, equally the people in there will tend to be different types of people and the dress would tend to be different. If we went to Wotsit's in the evening I could probably feel I could get away with a pair of jeans, where if we went in an evening to one of the other places I mentioned I would go in a suit or a jacket and trousers, invariably a suit. So that in itself tends to put things on a different level of formality in any event. (John)

References to formality often related to particular institutional aspects of the meal experience, like dress codes, bodily posture rules, the timing of the meal, etc. Formality indicates an awareness, on the side of the customer, of a variety of structural aspects which accompany the activity and serves as a means of evaluation of these structural aspects. References to formal aspects of the eating out experience were always accompanied by an evaluation as to whether these were considered 'good' or 'bad', liked or disliked.

The overwhelming impression from the interviews was that people were aware that they might be made to feel uncomfortable if they went to certain types of restaurant, particularly to ones whose regimes were considered excessively formal. The threshold of formality, however, varied between interviewees, with younger working-class people most likely to have low tolerance. Different levels of tolerance for formality might be indicated by responses to three attitude questions on the survey which enquired whether people agreed (strongly or slightly), neither agreed nor disagreed, or disagreed (slightly or strongly) with a number of propositions. Confronted with the statement 'I dislike eating out in places that are formal and stuffy', 62 per cent agreed, but 22 per cent disagreed. And to the statement 'I like to go to places where the other diners are smartly dressed', 33 per cent agreed and 49 per cent disagreed. And to the claim 'I feel comfortable in any type of restaurant', 68 per cent agreed, 21 per cent disagreed.

However, it seemed that most people simply avoided those places which they considered overly formal. This was made possible partly because people tended to go to the same venues more than once and because if picking a new place they would often do so on the recommendation of other like-minded people. Feeling comfortable, avoiding embarrassment, acting appropriately were all important, but there was little sense that our interviewees felt they were being pushed around by the waiting staff, as might have been the case in the establishments described by Whyte or Mars and Nicod. If there were inequalities of power between staff and customers they were not of that type. Power is probably more diffused than before, being mediated rather than directly exercised by waiting staff. If anything it was management that customers primarily held responsible for any defects in the timing, organisation or atmosphere.

If we return to some of the criteria of good service identified in the first section of this chapter, we find some evidence that several are actively and consciously employed by customers. The ones that are most readily identified to discuss the character of service are speed, advice and social participation. This is revealed by the most common complaints. Interviewees complain about slowness, though defined relatively in the context of the particular type of place and occasion; that staff may be too intrusive, or too inattentive, was a second major source of discontent; a friendly and sufficiently enthusiastic manner on behalf of serving staff, again defined by context, was a third dimension of critical judgement.

Other elements of the list of potential evaluative criteria were invoked less frequently. Ease and trust in the product were consciously considered but more often when interviewees gave general reasons why they liked or disliked eating out. The pleasure of being served was a significant reason, especially for women, for wanting to eat out, and worries about hygiene were voiced on several occasions by those who were not fond of restaurants. Value for money tended to be invoked in discussions about selecting between restaurants, not a matter immediately associated with considerations of staffing, though of course that is certainly a consequence of the commercial decisions of proprietors. The matter of social honour was not much raised, and when reference was made to expressive aspects of social hierarchy it was usually in reference either to the regime and its organisation, or to other diners, rather than to waiting staff. So several interviewees referred to places as 'posh', as 'lah-di-dah', and one described a group at another table as 'toffee-nosed' and used them to sum up the character of the restaurant. But it seemed that generally the structural relationships with waiting staff were not particularly problematic.

One additional measure of appropriate service emerged from another source of complaint mentioned on several occasions. Technical incompetence of waiting staff was sometimes commented upon, but usually condoned in terms of inexperience. But interviewees did tend to complain if food for each person at their table did not arrive simultaneously. This appeared to be the most disconcerting of potential technical errors and probably underlines the persistence of rituals associated with the injunction that no-one should start eating before all are provided for. This might be interpreted as evidence of the persistence of a code of manners capable of arousing discontent if some major elements of the ritual process are transgressed. It is probably a more grave mistake than selling unappetising food, suggesting thereby that the satisfactions derived from the social rituals of companionship – eating *together* – outweigh those of the food itself.

As we will show, there is not a great deal of difference in taste between men and women, either as regards which restaurants to use or what types of dishes to eat. Nonetheless some of the rituals surrounding service have, at least traditionally, clearly gendered aspects. An automatic assumption that men in mixed company in restaurants should order, taste the wine, complain and pay are all aspects of etiquette capable of causing irritation. Such practices are perpetuated by some staff and some customers, with the former tending to assume that if a man is part of the company, he, by default, should be addressed. In certain respects these behaviours parallel the shaping and reproduction of relations of dominance and subordination during meal times within households and confer plausibility on the claim that the restaurant is a masculine domain where both the food options and the organisational regimes are primarily addressed to the requirements and desires of men. Thus Wood, extrapolating from Mazurkiewicz's (1983) argument that women are marginalized in hotels due to conventions regarding use of public space, contends that 'Women still tend to be regarded [by the catering establishment] as important only as ancillaries to male partners or children, and women customers without men tend to be regarded as problematic' (Wood, 1990:4), and that 'women in restaurants are carefully controlled, frequently marginalised and sometimes excluded' (1990: 4). Mazurkiewicz said that women may experience marginalisation as a result of remnants of historically constructed understandings of gender 'appropriate' conduct in the public sphere. Wood suggests, in addition, that suppliers of hospitality assume – rightly or wrongly – that the 'man' in the customer group has control over the economic resources of the group, and consequently treats 'him' with more deference than 'her'. The corollary is that women get 'poorer' treatment than men (Wood, 1990, 1992a, 1995). However, such occurrences may be in decline.

We have information about decision taking and rituals which offer scope for gender practices to occur, both within company groups, and between customers and serving staff. Decision-taking informs us about the nature of power and control within the various groups in which women participate. The survey indicated some gender differences in decision-taking, though much depended on the company with whom women ate.

Considering the 134 respondents whose last meal out was in a commercial venue solely in the company of their partner, male respondents were just as likely to say that they or their partner had suggested going out (36 per cent and 34 per cent respectively) and somewhat less likely to say that the suggestion had been a joint decision (at 25 per cent). Female respondents, on the other hand, were more likely to say that their male partner had proposed eating out (45 per cent) and equally likely otherwise to say that they had suggested it or that it had been a joint decision. Where respondents ate out with partner and other family members, there was an equal likelihood of the suggestion coming from either partner.

As regards determining where to eat, women were marginally less likely to have had an input when going out as a couple or with family. Among those who ate out with friends only, more females claimed not to have had a say, but this difference was solely due to group size; in company groups of five and over, 67 per cent of women said that they had no input in where to eat, compared to 25 per cent of men. No such pattern was found in smaller friendship groups.

There was a pronounced difference over paying the bill. In the case of respondents eating solely with their partner, where one partner paid for the meal, ninety-five of those who paid were male and thirteen were female. A similar pattern was evident amongst respondents who ate out with partner and other family members. When eating solely in the company of friends, there was a much higher degree of sharing (73 per cent).

The qualitative interviews revealed more complexities (see Martens, 1997 and 1998). Nevertheless, overall, decision-taking and gendered rituals symbolising relations of dominance and control varied according to the composition of the company group. Couple-only occasions exhibited greater gender differentiated conduct than those involving other groups.

If women had resented being treated as ancillaries to their male partners or had noticed being treated in an inferior manner to other customers, female respondents might have liked less the service they received than their male counterparts. The evidence, if anything, suggested the reverse, with a slight tendency for women to appreciate service more than men. The qualitative interviews also contained observations about the quality of service which interviewees had received and no women complained explicitly about the marginalisation of women in general nor of they themselves feeling marginalised by service staff (see further Martens, 1998). Indeed, compared with many other leisure pursuits, restaurants offer customers a 'comparatively safe, quasi-public environment in which to enjoy many of the genuine pleasures of the modern experience' (Martens and Warde, 1997:149). To the extent that unmannered and indecent behaviour within such establishments is discouraged, women eating out in groups are relatively protected against unwelcome intrusion by men – whether customers or serving staff. Overall, eating out was a relatively popular way of spending time with other women, with 8 per cent of last occasions reported being of women-only groups.

## Comparing commercial service and private hospitality

All interviewees agreed that there was a difference between eating in 'private homes' compared with 'public establishments', though they differed as to which they preferred. Formality was mentioned by almost every respondent in comparing commercial with private hospitality, and dislike of formality was clearly communicated. A preference to eat at the home of friends and family was related to the pleasure of relaxation, and its antithesis, the restriction entailed in observing formal rules of appropriate public conduct. Expressions of preference for 'home entertainment' were also related to an awareness and appreciation of the work this entailed for the host(s).

Relaxation was mentioned only once (negatively) in discussions of restaurant service, but was a much vaunted reason for liking private hospitality. Two specific themes, presentation of self and time pressure, were isolated in making comparison between public and private sites and both were referred to in terms of the greater opportunity for relaxation in a friend's home.

The first theme, presentation of the self, reflected awareness of the 'demands' that restaurant regimes make on 'the self', but also included commentaries on the implications for personal behaviour when strangers are present. The general feeling this generated was expressed by Sheila, who preferred eating at the home of friends to eating in a public venue because it is 'more relaxed, you're not on show'. Pressures to 'dress up', something which may relate to establishment regime as well as the presence of strangers, were felt not to be as pressing when eating at the home of friends. For Debby, this was one aspect which contributed to her greater enjoyment of eating at friends'.

DEBBY: Well it's just relaxed, you just sit round or have a chat and . . .
INTERVIEWER: You find that more relaxing than going to a restaurant?
DEBBY:  Well it's not so formal, no. You don't get really dressed for going round to a friend's house than when you go to a restaurant . . . .

Eating in public stipulates control of bodily demeanour. Yet, certain bodily postures, like 'slobbing out', putting your feet up, and taking your shoes off, were seen as enhancing efforts to relax and were all considered permissible when eating at the home of friends. Trisha was able to relax more at a friend's house by lounging in front of the television: 'Sometimes it's nice to go to a friend's because you don't have to make as much of an effort as if you were going to a restaurant so, and erm you can lounge around in front of the telly and erm you know chat and really just relax and sit and chat about things.' This indicates that eating in public places entailed some level of undesirable self constraint.

A second aspect of comparison associated with judgements about formality was the experience of the passage of time. In Sheila's case, eating at a friend's home was more relaxed because 'you can take as long as you like, sit at the table for as long as you like. I like that.' Other interviewees also said they enjoyed eating out best when they did not feel rushed in any sense, and for them, this was more likely to be found in the home of friends or family. Indeed, for guests in a private house, the longer the event lasted the more enjoyable it was proclaimed. 37 per cent of respondents spent more than three hours on their last occasion. It seems that people eat at a more leisurely rate when in someone else's home and there is plenty of time on such social occasions to take off one's shoes!

Other comments reflected the different degrees of freedom respondents felt they had in different sets of company. Eating in commercial venues inevitably meant eating in the company of strangers as well as people one knew better, whereas this was not the case in someone's home. John felt more on guard in a restaurant:

at the end of the day you are going out to you know this is your leisure time and you are endeavouring to relax, and I think a little bit when you are out you do tend to be on show a little bit. I am a person who is in general what you see is what you get. So I have a very high embarrassment threshold and that it just doesn't bother me, and I will say things in public that possibly you shouldn't say, that would embarrass other people. Well I'll say . . . I'm not never offensive, but they will say you can't say that somebody might have heard you, you know, and that possibly is a little bit, makes one guarded a little bit, can't relax in the way that you would be able to do with friends.

Equally, Smina agreed that when in the company of family members only, she could joke around, whilst in a restaurant she would generally be on her best behaviour. Finally, Mary could not relax properly in restaurants because she felt that the presence of others imposed certain rules of conduct on her and those who ate with her. The behaviour of her grandchildren, who invariably went with them when they ate out, was emphasised in her explanation:

I think when you tend to go to restaurants and er like I say, especially if you're with children, I think people tend to stare at you if your children knock something over or mek a noise. I prefer to be in my son's house like that than go in a restaurant and have people er, giving you sort of a, like children should be perfect.

A key aspect of the experience of eating out is the relationship among diners. There are two sorts of relationship, that among those at the same table who are the companions in a party, and in a commercial establishment also that between different parties. Attitudes towards other parties, strangers in effect, are mixed. There is generally little inter-party interaction, suggesting that the restaurant is a form of 'quasi-public space' (see Martens and Warde, 1997). The restaurant appears as a space containing a number of private reservations (tables), from which mutual inspection of the tenants of other reservations is permitted, and where your own behaviour is restrained by the gaze of others. So, eating out is not necessarily commendable for its encouragement of public conviviality and co-existence. Rather, it is more like private behaviour in a public place. However, the pleasures that derive from being in a public space where one can watch and be observed should not be underrated. Sheila commented that among her main reasons for eating out was: 'To go and sit there and have a look round and you know, have a look at other people and what they're doing, and things. They're probably wondering what I'm doing but that's all right.' She added that she liked to talk to 'complete strangers yeah, the stranger the better'. The restaurant permits enjoyment of some aspects of urban living: it satisfies desires for new experience, for seeing and being seen by others, for observing fashion and for succumbing to the seductive-ness of variety, while protecting its customers from the more dangerous, uncontrollable and unpredictable consequences of sharing public space.

But these aspects of the urban experience may also be irksome or onerous:

INTERVIEWER: Are there any things you dislike about eating out?
JOHN: I can't think of any. I mean obviously if you get somebody who is sitting on a table next to you who is either, you know, a raving idiot or just ridiculously over-friendly, though that can be irritating but it's not something I would think, oh I don't want to go out because that could happen.

Concern was quite strong among some interviewees that they were under public surveillance in a restaurant and that this was, if not distressing, at least unpleasant. Anne captured the ambivalence of being comfortable in public places when she explained her strong dislike of restaurants: 'you can do a lot of people-watching in pubs, more so than in like cafés – unno-ticed people-watching. [But] when you go to a formal restaurant you feel like everybody else is watching you as well.'

## Power and informality

The concepts used to evaluate service in commercial establishments are time (potentially wasted, lost or incapable of being filled, or the sense of being rushed), attitude of staff (friendly or over-friendly, personal or detached, intrusive and casual), efficiency (lack of skill or knowledge), and aspects of regime (dress codes, rituals of ordering and payment). This vocabulary and its application support several conclusions. People recognise differences between types of place and associate them with different regimes, often ranking according to degree of formality and often talking about them in class-discriminating fashion. Many have a particular preference for some types of regime, there being systematic variation in thresholds of formality, as well as in other dimensions of quality. Preferences are also to some degree situational. For instance, some interviewees said that they liked getting dressed up and going to a smart restaurant sometimes on a special occasion, while at other times preferring something less demanding.

There is little evidence that customers are intimidated by waiting staff. When reference was made to aspects of social hierarchy, for instance, it was usually concerning either the regime and its organisation, or other diners, rather than waiting staff. But it seemed that generally the structural relationships with waiting staff were not particularly problematic. This might be in part because eating out has become a much more informal activity than it once was. Not only is there a wide variety of establishments with different levels of formality, but the staff themselves are increasingly less likely to be full-time professionals with sufficient social *gravitas* to manipulate their clients. In fact, the overall evidence shows little consciousness of the exercise of power in commercial eating out situations. Not only did we fail to find staff exercising power over customers, but we found little evidence of the reverse either. The type of scenario where diners are said to be beginning to rile the staff (Fattorini, 1994) was not one that emerged from our interviews. Nor did we find much evidence of the restaurant having a masculine ambience or having a strongly patriarchal form. Conscious appreciation of inequalities of power in the contemporary restaurant was uncommon.

Even so, the existence of appropriate codes of conduct in restaurants was acknowledged. There is potential for embarrassment, as some of our interviewees observed, and there may therefore be some support for Wouters's (1986) claim that informalisation simultaneously requires, as part of the civilising process, greater self-discipline. Certainly, with one exception, people seemed concerned that they should always behave appropriately, including being suitably quiet, fittingly dressed, physically restrained and so forth. There are codes of conduct which constrain people, but these seem to be largely self-imposed and self-policed. Perhaps this supports Beck's (1992) observation that traditionally mediating agents, in this instance waiters, are becoming increasingly irrelevant as individuals negotiate and regulate their behaviour directly in view of larger and shared cultural understandings about appropriate behaviour. In any case, one important mechanism for avoiding social embarrassment is, as we have shown, that people simply avoid places that they consider too formal. There is a process of self-selection in operation governed by people's wish not to feel 'uncomfortable'.

Wood (1994b) argues that during the twentieth century hotels have become increasingly like homes, evidenced by the provision of tea and coffee-making 'facilities', a television for private use, a drinks cabinet, a private bathroom, etc. It is debatable whether there is a general trend, from the point of view of consumers, to want more private and quasi-domestic provision. In hotels, room service was once the principal means by which residents, particularly women, obtained commercial meals. It survives as a luxury service, one which enhances privatism. We have seen that standards of service in restaurants are quite often measured against the criterion of friendliness and homeliness. Clients in restaurants, in explaining their discontent with formality, tend to look for domestic virtues. Chris's ideas about good service in restaurants rested on a direct comparison between eating out and home entertaining, through which she expressed her view that hospitality in restaurants should approximate the hospitality she gave her guests when she entertained.

I have to say that the things that I don't like about eating out, is if you're treated, if the waitresses are not pleasant, or . . . You like to get the service as well as the food. You like to be treated nicely, don't you? And you know also you like to treat them nicely. Some people are bit off-hand with waitresses too, I don't like that either. But I do like if I go out I like people to be friendly and smile when they bring your food, and ask if everything is all right, and ask if you need relishes and things like that. Without you having to ask them. I think that's quite important. 'Cos if you were at home you would go round is everything all right for you, is there anything else you want. You do that don't you, make sure your guests are all happy. I think it's important for them to do that to you as well.

This raises the question of the extent to which commercial establishments (whether hotels or restaurants) are setting the pace as regards defining the appropriate standards of service or, instead, whether they are being propelled by changing household arrangements to offer new and different forms and levels of service. Mennell (1985) claims that restaurant and domestic kitchens are tending to converge, both in their equipment and the kind of food they might deliver. He does not identify the direction from which the impetus for convergence arises, though there is no reason why it should not be from both. Does the emergence of the celebrity chef mean that the dinner party is now cooked from a special cookery book? It seems not if we look at what gets served domestically. Dinner party menus are varied, with some hosts and hostesses consciously experimenting, some seeking least effort, some prioritising time spent with guests over food content, some always using tried-and-trusted dishes. As chapter 7 will show, domestic hospitality does not mimic or imitate restaurant meals in specific content.

The two contrasting sites for eating out permit reflection on whether these are separate spheres, whether the public event is governed by the same, or by a different set of rules. Sennett (1976) thought there was considerable virtue to there being different codes of conduct for private as opposed to public behaviour. He was concerned that every activity would get absorbed into the private sphere and that the skills associated with dealing with strangers, and with public discussion of the common good, would atrophy. This might transpire if the restaurant regime sought to emulate the private event. If customers like Chris were to get their way and waiting staff came to behave like hostesses, would this reduce the repertoires available for human interaction and signify a process of domestication and privatisation? Culturally, it may involve the flattening of experience, the reduction of differentiation between different spheres of activity and the reduction of the manners of public interaction to the familiarities of home. Alternatively, though, we might suggest that if stiff formality is the mode, mood or tone of interaction in the public sphere, then it is hard to weep over its demise. Part of the more general process of informalisation, the shift of restaurant service towards the more familiar, friendly, entertaining and casual might be welcomed. Indeed, homogenisation of experience has the merit of reducing the likelihood of social exclusion.

# 7  Last suppers

This chapter presents a detailed description of some of the minutiae of the experience of dining out: what exactly did people eat?; how did this come to be decided?; where, when and with whom did they eat?; and to what extent did they prepare for the occasion in advance? The purpose is to survey the diversity of the experience. The evidence comes from questions asked of both respondents and interviewees about the very last occasion on which they had eaten a main meal away from home.

The chapter focuses on the ways in which the promise of variety is experienced and used. Some would maintain that increased variety of choice is the greatest benefit of consumer culture and would therefore welcome the fact that in the field of food there is now more choice than ever. Such a claim might reasonably be advanced on the basis of the contents of supermarkets and on the number of commercial outlets selling cooked dishes of many sorts. Indeed, according to Mennell's (1985) influential diagnosis, 'increased variety' is one of the two dominant trends of food provisioning in the twentieth century and the spread of restaurant-going is a significant element of the shift.

Wood (1995) is sceptical, arguing that some of this variety is illusory, a pretence wherein commercial organisations, for reasons of profitability, tend to offer increasingly standardised and uniform food and service. In *The Sociology of the Meal* (1995: 83–4), he claims that: 'at the heart of the menu system of hotels is the "cooked dinner". Indeed, cooked dinners occupy the same central position as a model of culinary provision in the hospitality industry as they do in the domestic food system.' By 'cooked dinner' he means that the central dish of a meal comprises meat and two vegetables, a format widely recognised in the UK (see Murcott, 1982; Charles and Kerr, 1988). He notes that 'the "cooked dinner" dietary system is primarily a male system that many women would not adhere to if they had a unilateral and unencumbered choice' and maintains that the class and gender relations of the commercial meal experience 'parallel (and occasionally diverge from) patterns of domestic eating' (Wood, 1995: 87).

The similarities are a cause of standardisation across the field of food. He argues that the mass appeal of the cooked dinner poses a problem for caterers. Innovation is relatively risky, but nevertheless necessary to induce people to spend their money on eating out. Consequently producers provide people with the same foods which they eat at home, which encourages 'stable and predictable markets' (1995: 98), yet creates

an illusion of variety, of choice ... achieved in part by the tendency of the food and hospitality industries to emphasise the value of the situational qualities of food rather than food itself. Variety and choice are believed to exist because relatively similar food products are perceived as possessing a range of secondary characteristics that, over time, consumers have been socialised into valuing more than any intrinsic qualities of foods ... What standardisation entails is a levelling of consumer expectations of food in both the public and the private domain, a levelling of 'taste' ... (1995: 99)

This argument posits that most British consumers are conservative in taste, experience limited variety of foods and dishes and have similar culinary experiences in both domestic and commercial spheres. Our data allow us to evaluate these propositions.

Based on an analysis of what was eaten during last main meals eaten out, we consider to what extent British food preferences betray conservative and uniform tastes. We also discuss the consumers' expectations. Although we have no data on what people cook and eat at home in their everyday household situations, we do have information on what they are served and how they are treated as guests in other people's homes. Comparison between commercial and communal modes of eating out permits inference about whether the same dishes are expected from the domestic and the professional cook and whether the associated rituals are similar. We examine systematically the relationship between commercial and domestic events by focusing on three of the four key elements of contemporary Western meals (see chapter 5) – the structured menu, mannered rituals and companionship. We also adopt a terminology to distinguish between three modes of meal provision; the domestic (involving only household self-provisioning), the communal (where visitors are present) and the commercial. The communal mode, in which food is provided in a private non-commercial setting for guests, has two modalities, delivery to friends and to non-resident kin. In our survey sample, 585 meals were eaten in a commercial venue, 180 in the homes of non-resident family and 146 in the homes of friends.

Menu structure refers to the content and combination of foods served to, or selected by, a diner. A structured menu contains several elements, the main dish, of which the 'cooked dinner' is an example, is one; while others include supplementary food items, the number of courses, their food contents, the order of courses and type of cuisine.

All respondents were asked to list the foods eaten on the last occasion they took a main meal away from home (although the survey is a useful tool for identifying what people actually ate, some care in interpretation is necessary when considering the recording).[1] That eating out might satisfy a considerable range of food tastes is suggested by table 7.1 which lists thirty of the menus reported, chosen to illustrate diversity. Menus varied with respect to the number of courses eaten, the type of main course, starter, or dessert and the drinks consumed. As well as giving menu details, table 7.1 also lists some of the characteristics of the recipient and the context within which the meal was consumed. As well as indicating a certain order to the practice, the list gives some evidence of considerable variety in tastes.

Steak, a variety of roast meats, Yorkshire pudding, chips, roast potatoes, peas, carrots and tomatoes all featured as part of the main course, as did lamb biryani, squid, moussaka, burritos, carpaccio, lemon chicken, shabu shabu, and braised sea cabbage (see table 7.2 on various food items eaten). In the whole sample, meat was recorded six times more often than fish. Beef was the most popular meat, constituting 37 per cent of all meats recorded, followed by chicken. Scares about beef have clearly not meant its avoidance when eating out or when entertaining guests. Beef was equally likely to have been eaten by those visiting commercial venues, homes of family or the home of friends. However, it was eaten more in 'British' and 'fast food' than 'ethnic' venues.[2] Beef consumption at last meal out was relatively greater among men than women, among those whose father's occupational class was working class, among 'white'

---

[1] Information about everything respondents had eaten during their last main meal eaten out was requested, including information on starter(s), the main course, other courses and dessert(s). Interviewers were asked to 'probe fully for exact details, don't accept general answers e.g. if soup/ice cream what kind, if meat what kind/how cooked etc. What vegetables are served with main course, what type of potato. Are sauces/custard served with dessert.' However, the detail of recording varied to some extent between interviewers. In addition, variations are likely in the detail with which respondents remembered items. It is likely that meat and fish items were recorded more systematically than, for instance, vegetables, carbohydrates or gravy.

[2] Venues were grouped together, in a rough-and-ready manner, into 'British', 'fast food', 'ethnic' and 'other'. 'British' style venue include traditional steakhouse, bar food area of a public house, a restaurant attached to a public house, hotel restaurants and so-described 'other British style restaurants'. Under 'ethnic' venue types we included specialist pizza house, Indian restaurant, Chinese/Thai restaurant, Italian restaurant, American style restaurant and 'other ethnic restaurant'. A further category, 'fast food' included fast food restaurant, fish and chip eat-in, motorway service station, in-store shop/restaurant, and café or teashop.

Table 7.1 *Last menus and their diners*

---

Ten one-course menus

(1) *Pizza, Hawaii kind, served with a salad including lettuce, tomato, cucumber, etc. Drinks: soft drinks.*
*Socio-demographic details*: Woman; 40s; married; couple and children; junior non-manual and personal services; partner is service class; father is working class; household annual income £10,000–£20,000; 'white'; Bristol.
*Other meal features*: Commercial; 'ethnic' style venue; just a social occasion; 2 in company; Saturday evening; costs: £5–10 per person.

(2) *Beef burgers (fried), chips and beans. Drinks: beer/lager.*
*Socio-demographic details*: Man; 10s; single; living with parents; junior non-manual and personal services; father is working class; household income not known; 'white'; Bristol.
*Other meal features*: Commercial; 'British' style venue; convenience/quick meal; 3–4 in company; Saturday lunch time; costs not known.

(3) *Three spiced sausages cooked in mushroom sauce with fresh herbs, including bay leaf and juniper berries, served with a mixture of swede and mashed pots. Drinks: wine.*
*Socio-demographic details*: Man; 40s; married; couple and children; no job recorded; partner is service class; father is intermediate class; household income > £50,000; 'white'; London.
*Other meal features*: Commercial; 'other' unspecified venue; convenience/quick meal; eaten alone; Wednesday lunch time: costs £5–10.

(4) *Paella (with fish) and mixed salad. Drinks: tap water, wine.*
*Socio-demographic details*: Woman; 40s; widowed/divorced/separated; lone parent; intermediate non-manual; father is intermediate class; household income £10,000–£20,000; 'white'; London.
*Other meal features*: Commercial; 'ethnic' style venue; just a social occasion; 2 in company; Friday evening; costs: £5–10 per person.

(5) *Haddock (fried in batter) and chips. Drinks: spirits.*
*Socio-demographic details*: Woman; 20s; married; couple and children; intermediate non-manual; partner is service class; father is intermediate class; household income £20,000–£30,000; 'white'; Bristol.
*Other meal features*: Commercial; 'fast food' style; convenience/quick meal; 3–4 in company; Sunday afternoon; costs: £5–10 per person.

(6) *Beef curry and rice. Drinks: beer/lager.*
*Socio-demographic details*: Man; 30s; married; couple only; junior non-manual and personal services; partner is working class; father is service class; household income £40,000–£50,000; 'white'; Bristol.
*Other meal features*: Commercial; 'British' style venue; just a social occasion; 2 in company; Tuesday evening; costs: £5–10 per person.

(7) *Steak (medium-rare), served with chips, salad and mushrooms. Drinks: wine.*
*Socio-demographic details*: Man; 20s; single; living with parents; professional; father is intermediate class; household income not known; 'white'; Bristol.
*Other meal features*: Commercial; 'British' style venue; purpose 'other' unspecified; 2 in company; Saturday evening; costs not known.

Table 7.1 (*cont.*)

| Ten one-course menus |
| --- |

(8) *Rice, chicken, yam, banana and salad. Drinks: soft drinks.*
*Socio-demographic details*: Woman; single; lone parent; semi/unskilled manual;
father's occupational class not known; household income not known; 'black
Caribbean'; London.
*Other meal features*: Commercial; 'ethnic' style venue; convenience/quick meal; 3–4 in
company; Thursday afernoon; costs not known.

(9) *Chicken salad and chips. Drinks: soft drinks.*
*Socio-demographic details*: Woman; 10s; single; living with parents; junior non-manual
and personal services; father is working class; household income not known; 'white';
London.
*Other meal features*: At the home of friends; just a social occasion; 3–4 in company;
Friday evening.

(10) *Bacon, sausage, egg, beans, fried bread and chips. Drinks: tea/coffee.*
*Socio-demographic details*: Woman; 20s; single; lone parent; supervisor/skilled manual;
father is working class; household income < £5,000; 'white'; Bristol.
*Other meal features*: Commercial; 'fast food' style venue; convenience/quick; 2 in
company; Monday lunch time; costs: £5 per person.

| Ten two-course menus |
| --- |

(1) *Nut cutlets, sweet corn, runner beans, garden peas, and cheese potatoes, followed by cherry
pie and cream, followed by cheese and biscuits. Drinks: tea/coffee.*
*Socio-demographic details*: Man; 30s; married; couple and children; professional;
partner is working class; father is service class; household income
£10,000–£20,000; 'white'; Preston.
*Other meal features*: At the home of family; just a social occasion; 5–9 in company;
Friday evening.

(2) *Sausages, beefburgers, chips and baked beans, served with branston pickles, tomato sauce
and mayonnaise, followed by tinned peaches and pears. Drinks: tea/coffee.*
*Socio-demographic details*: Woman; 30s; widowed/divorced/separated; lone parent;
semi/unskilled manual; father is working class; household income £5,000–£10,000;
'white'; Preston.
*Other meal features*: At the home of friends; just a social occasion; 5–9 in company;
Saturday early evening start.

(3) *Prawn cocktail, followed by chicken moussaka, rice, vegetables and cheese. Drinks: beer/lager.*
*Socio-demographic details*: Woman; 20s; single; living with parents; supervisory/skilled
manual; father is intermediate class; household income not known; 'white'; Preston.
*Other meal features*: Commercial; 'British' style venue; just a social occasion; 5–9 in
company; Saturday evening; costs not known.

(4) *Garlic mushrooms, followed by gammon, pineapple, peas, chips. Drinks: beer/lager.*
*Socio-demographic details*: Man; 30s; single; living with parents; semi/unskilled
manual (working class); father is working class; household income not known;
'white'; Preston.

Table 7.1 (*cont.*)

---

Ten two-course menus

---

*Other meal features*: Commercial; 'British' style venue; just a social occasion; 3–4 in company; Sunday afternoon; costs not known.

(5) *Mexican enchiladas, followed by burritos, chicken sauce and fried beans. Drinks: wine.*
*Socio-demographic details*: Woman; 30s; (living as) married; couple and children; junior non-manual and personal services (working class); partner is intermediate class; father is working class; household income £30,000–£40,000; 'white'; Bristol.
*Other meal features*: Commercial; 'ethnic' style venue; just a social occasion; 5–9 in company; Thursday evening; costs £10–15 per person.

(6) *Lasagne, chips, salad (including tomato, lettuce and cucumber), followed by trifle and cream. Drinks: wine, tea/coffee.*
*Socio-demographic details*: Man; 60s; married; couple only; semi/unskilled manual; partner is working class; father's occupational class not known; household income £5,000–£10,000; 'white'; Bristol.
*Other meal features*: At the home of family; just a social occasion; 3–4 in company; Thursday evening.

(7) *Spinach and cream cheese pancakes, followed by lamb in honey and ginger sauce, potatoes (dauphinoise) and mangetouts. Drinks: pre-meal apéritif, tap water.*
*Socio-demographic details*: Woman; 30s; (living as) married; couple and children; junior non-manual and personal services (working class); partner is working class; father's occupational class not known; household income £30,000–£40,000; 'white'; Bristol.
*Other meal features*: Commercial; 'ethnic' style venue; special occasion; 10–19 in company; Saturday evening; costs: £10–15 per person.

(8) *Corn and mushroom soup, followed by rice noodles. Drinks: soft drinks.*
*Socio-demogaphic details*: Man; 20s; single; living with parents; employer/manager; father's occupational class not known; household income >£50,000; 'Chinese'; London.
*Other meal features*: Commercial; 'ethnic' style venue; convenience/quick meal; 3–4 in company; Saturday early evening; costs: £5–10 per person.

(9) *Shish kebab, followed by chicken vindaloo and fried rice. Drinks: mineral water, spirits.*
*Socio-demographic details*: Man; 50s; married; couple and children; semi/unskilled manual; partner not in employment; father is working class; household income £10,000–£20,000; 'white'; Preston.
*Other meal features*: Commercial, 'ethnic' style venue; just a social occasion; Friday very late evening; costs: £10–15 per person.

(10) *Hummus, followed by salad, donar kebab and chips. Drinks: soft drinks.*
*Socio-demographic details*: Man; 20s; single; living in student type household; no job recorded; father's occupational class not known; household income <£5,000; 'other' not further specified; London.
*Other meal features*: Commercial; 'ethnic' style venue; convenience/quick meal; 2 in company; Tuesday evening; costs: £5–10 per person.

---

Table 7.1 (*cont.*)

---

Ten multi-course menus

---

(1) *Prawn cocktail with green salad, followed by grilled sirloin steak, french fries, vegetables (cannot remember which), mushrooms and onions (no gravy), followed by black forest gâteau (no cream), cheese and biscuits, and After Eight mints. Drinks: wine.*
Socio-demographic details: Woman; 50s; married; couple only; intermediate non-manual; partner is working class; father is working class; household income £5,000–£10,000; 'white'; Preston.
Other meal features: at the home of family; just a social occasion; 5–9 in company; Saturday early evening start.

(2) *Dim sum (small hors-d'oeuvres, with various meats, Chinese green leaves and bean sprouts), followed by noodles, mixed meat (chicken, beef and pork), fish balls and squid, followed by oranges. Drinks: tea/coffee.*
Socio-demographic details: Man; 20s; single; living in shared accommodation; intermediate non-manual; father's occupational class not known; household income not known; 'other' not further specified; London.
Other meal features: Commercial; 'ethnic' style venue; just a social occasion; 2 in company; Friday evening; costs: £5–10 per person.

(3) *Lebanese mezze (small dishes), followed by Lebanese mixed grill, shish kebab, chicken kebab, pitta bread and Lebanese rice, followed by 'stringy cream thing' and coffee; Drinks: wine.*
Socio-demographic details: Man; 10s; single; living with parents; no job recorded; father in service class; household income unknown; 'white'; London.
Other meal features: Commercial; 'ethnic' style venue; just a social occasion; 5–9 in company; Sunday afternoon; costs: £15–20 per person.

(4) *Melon, followed by chicken, herbs, buttered mushrooms and sautéd potatoes, followed by home-made Swiss roll, lemon fromage frais and mascarpone cheese. Drinks: wine.*
Socio-demographic details: Woman; 50s; (living as) married; couple only; junior non-manual and personal services; partner not in employment; father's occupational class not known; househod income < £5,000; 'white'; Bristol.
Other meal features: At the home of family; just a social occasion; 5–9 in company; Sunday lunch time.

(5) *Lentils and chopped crudités (chopped vegetables), followed by pasta with bacon, mushrooms and cream sauce, followed by Viennetta and fresh strawberries, followed by cheese (cheddar and cream cheese) and oatcakes. Drinks: mineral water, wine, beer/lager/spirits, tea/coffee.*
Socio-demographic details: Man; 30s; married; couple only; employer/manager; partner is service class; father is intermediate class; household income £40,000–£50,000; 'white'; London.
Other meal features: At the home of friends; just a social occasion; 3–4 in company; Saturday evening.

(6) *Avocado with parma ham, followed by roast beef, Yorkshire pudding, roast potatoes, parsnips, leeks and carrots, followed by cheese (brie, stilton and cheddar) and biscuits. Drink: pre-meal apéritif, wine.*
Socio-demographic details: Man; 20s; single and living alone; no job recorded; father's occupational class unknown; household income £10,000–£20,000; 'white'; Bristol.

Table 7.1 (*cont.*)

---

Ten multi-course menus

*Other meal features*: Commercial; 'British' style venue; special occasion; 3–4 in company; Sunday lunch time; costs: > £20 per person.

(7) *Fish soup, followed by barbecued duck, jacket pots, peas and mixed salad, followed by lemon water ice. Drinks: mineral water, beer/lager.*
    *Socio-demographic details*: Male; 30s; married; couple and children; employer/manager (service class); partner is intermediate class; father is service class; household income £40,000–£50,000; 'white'; London.
    *Other meal features*: Commercial; 'British' style venue; special occasion; 3–4 in company; Sunday afternoon; costs: £10–15 per person.

(8) *Chicken satay, followed by roast leg of lamb, carrots, creamed cauliflower, broccoli and sautéd potatoes, followed by chocolate gâteau, followed by cheese and biscuits. Drinks: tea/coffee.*
    *Socio-demographic details*: Woman; 50s; married; couple only; self-employed; partner is intermediate class; father is intermediate class; household income £10,000–£20,000; 'white'; Preston.
    *Other meal features*: Commercial; 'British' style venue; special occasion; 5–9 in company; Friday evening; costs: £15–20 per person.

(9) *Garlic bread, followed by chicken tikka masala with nan bread, followed by banana roulade. Drinks: soft drinks.*
    *Socio-demographic details*: Woman; 30s; (living as) married; couple and children; self-employed; partner is working class; father is service class; household income £30,000–£40,000; 'white'; Preston.
    *Other meal features*: Commercial; 'British' style venue; just a social occasion; 5–9 in company; Sunday lunch time; costs: £5–10 per person.

(10) *Raw vegetables: carrots, cauliflower, peppers, baby sweetcorn and radishes, served with garlic mayonnaise, followed by vegetarian smorgasbord (6–7 different dishes, including samosas, moussaka, green salad, mixed salad, potato salad, rolls and butter) followed by date sliced pastry. Drinks: mineral water, beer/lager.*
    *Socio-demographical details*: Woman; 50s; married; couple and children; professional; partner is service class; father is service class; household income £40,000–£50,000; 'white'; London.
    *Other meal features*: Commercial; 'other' style venue; special occasion; >50 in company; Tuesday early evening; costs not known.

---

*Notes:*
Under *socio-demographic details* we have supplied information about: sex, age, marital status and household type. This is followed by the respondent's occupational class, the occupational class of partner (where applicable) and of the respondent's father. Where known, household annual income, followed by the ethnic category the respondent chose as most adequate, and city of residence.

Under *other meal features* we have listed: whether the meal happened in a commercial venue or a domestic home, and if the latter, whether the hosts were friends or family. If the meal was commercial the venue type has been added (our crude four-fold distinction between 'ethnic', 'British', 'fast food' and 'other' venue type is used). This is followed by the purpose of the meal; how many people were present, what day of the week and time of day the meal began and, for commercial meals, the cost.

Table 7.2 *Number of food items recorded as part of main course during the last main meal out*

|  | Total | Commercial | All communal | of which family | of which friends |
|---|---|---|---|---|---|
| *Meats* | | | | | |
| Beef | 259 | 172 | 86 | 47 | 32 |
| Pork | 45 | 27 | 18 | 11 | 6 |
| Lamb | 49 | 29 | 20 | 9 | 9 |
| Bacon/gammon/ham | 47 | 33 | 14 | 9 | 4 |
| Sausage | 33 | 21 | 12 | 6 | 6 |
| Chicken | 237 | 123 | 114 | 72 | 37 |
| Turkey | 28 | 14 | 14 | 8 | 4 |
| Total | 692 | 415 | 276 | 158 | 98 |
| *Fish* | | | | | |
| Total | 112 | 89 | 23 | 11 | 12 |
| *Carbohydrates* | | | | | |
| Potatoes | 528 | 321 | 205 | 129 | 60 |
| Rice | 118 | 69 | 49 | 21 | 27 |
| Pasta | 61 | 32 | 29 | 7 | 21 |
| Bread | 82 | 63 | 19 | 9 | 9 |
| Pizza | 46 | 38 | 8 | 2 | 5 |
| Pastry | 72 | 36 | 36 | 24 | 11 |
| Total | 783 | 483 | 299 | 163 | 116 |
| *Vegetables* | | | | | |
| Cooked vegetables | 447 | 236 | 211 | 127 | 66 |
| Salad | 148 | 110 | 38 | 21 | 16 |
| Salad and cooked vegetables | 37 | 29 | 8 | 2 | 6 |
| Total | 632 | 375 | 257 | 150 | 88 |

*Note:*
Total meat, fish and carbohydrate recordings are not necessarily equal to the sum of individual food items because respondents who recorded more than one meat, fish or carbohydrate item were only counted once. 783 respondents recorded one or more carbohydrates.

respondents and among those living in Bristol and Preston. Age, household type, respondent social class and household income did not make a difference.

With the exception of chicken, which families frequently presented to kin, no significant differences were found in the recording of other meats. Families were much more likely to serve each other meat, less meat being consumed when eating out commercially or being entertained by friends. Significantly more fish was recorded in commercial than communal settings. Carbohydrate accompaniments were most commonly recorded for meals at the home of family and least often at the home of friends. Potatoes and pastries were more likely to have been recorded by those eating at the home of kin, bread and pizza featured more on the menus of those eating out commercially, whilst friends served each other more pasta. Cooked vegetables featured more commonly on communal plates, salads and a mix of salad and cooked vegetables at commercial tables.

As we noted before, the 'proper meal' and the 'cooked dinner' have a high profile in the British sociology of food. Brought to light by Murcott in South Wales in the 1980s 'the cooked dinner' is one where meat and two vegetables, of which one is potatoes, not chipped, becomes a 'plateful' because linked on the plate by gravy. Charles and Kerr (1988) saw it as the template for the food content of the 'proper meal' and Wood isolates it as a key indicator of the conservatism of the British diner and the bridge between the domestic and the commercial sphere. We therefore examined the reported menus to see how often, and where, the 'meat and two veg' format appeared. According to the survey, 342 main courses consisted of meat served with at least two vegetables. In terms of their ostensible content these were therefore 'proper meals' or 'cooked dinners' (though 'gravy' was explicitly recorded in only 60 of these meals).

Near equal numbers of 'meat and two vegetables' meals were eaten in private homes and commercial venues (175 and 166 respectively), which means they were proportionately much more prominent in domestic entertainment (where half of all meals were of this type). This difference was due solely to entertaining between extended family members; 63 per cent of the 180 family meals were of this type. Given that 'meat and two veg' dominated the dinner plates of meals hosted by parents or sons and daughters, it appears that families keep the habit of eating 'proper meals' together.

'Proper meals' were more likely to be served on 'special occasions' (111 out of 238 such meals were 'meat and two veg'), whilst 'convenience/quick' meals were unlikely to be 'proper meals' (only 26 out of 137). It seems, as suggested by Wood (1995: 92), that special occasions require 'richer variants of domestic cuisine'. Compared with other dishes, meat and two vegetables were more likely part of a two- or three-course meal and particularly likely to be accompanied by a dessert (of 470 desserts served, 225 accompanied 'meat and two veg' meals). Those served in commercial venues were more often part of three- or four-course meals. Overall, 'meat and two veg' meals were more likely to be served on Sundays, and in the middle of the day or early evening for communal meals.

Compared with other meal types, 'meat and two veg' was preferred by respondents over forty, those in Preston and Bristol and married couples

Table 7.3 *Last main meal eaten out: main course*

|                          |       | Frequency | Per cent |
|--------------------------|-------|-----------|----------|
| No main meal eaten       |       | 65        | 6.5      |
| Insufficient information |       | 27        | 2.7      |
| Roast beef               |       | 73        | 7.3      |
| Other roast              |       | 151       | 15.1     |
| Meat in sauce            |       | 70        | 7.0      |
| Steak                    |       | 94        | 9.4      |
| Pies + puds              |       | 29        | 2.9      |
| Pizza                    |       | 46        | 4.6      |
| Pasta                    |       | 65        | 6.5      |
| Sausages                 |       | 21        | 2.1      |
| Casserole                |       | 19        | 1.9      |
| Fish and chips           |       | 17        | 1.7      |
| Burgers                  |       | 29        | 2.9      |
| Salad                    |       | 13        | 1.3      |
| Curries                  |       | 79        | 7.9      |
| Vegetarian               |       | 30        | 3.0      |
| Flans + quiches          |       | 3         | 0.3      |
| Fish in sauce            |       | 14        | 1.4      |
| Other                    |       | 156       | 15.6     |
|                          | Total | 1001      | 100.0    |

with children. Working-class respondents were more likely to be served such a meal when eating at the home of extended family, while those assigning themselves to an ethnic category other than 'white' were less likely to partake. While Wood (1995: 87) claimed the 'cooked dinner' symbolises a dietary system which is primarily male, sex did not make any appreciable difference to consumption.

We also sought to compare the incidence of the cooked dinner with other recognisable meal formats. So, although acknowledging that classifying dishes is inevitably tinged with arbitrariness, we produced a rough-and-ready taxonomy of forms of main courses. The dishes we identified and the frequency with which these were consumed are presented in table 7.3 which shows that just over half of main meals (532) could be allocated to six frequently occurring categories: roast beef, other roast meats, meat in a sauce, steak, pasta and curry dishes. Roast meats of all kinds were particularly common in family entertaining. Meat in a sauce and steak, on the other hand, featured more frequently on commercial plates. Pastas and curries were equally likely to be served commercially and communally, although friends were much more likely than extended family to serve curries.

Table 7.4 *Last meal: courses eaten and their composition*

|  | All meals reported | Commercial | All communal | of which family | of which friends |
|---|---|---|---|---|---|
| *Number eaten* | | | | | |
| Starter | 402 | 300 | 102 | 42 | 50 |
| Dessert | 470 | 233 | 237 | 134 | 85 |
| *Percentage eaten* | | | | | |
| One-course | 29 | 33 | 23 | 19 | 27 |
| Two-course | 41 | 36 | 49 | 57 | 43 |
| Three-course | 28 | 29 | 26 | 22 | 29 |
| Four-course | 3 | 3 | 2 | 2 | 1 |
| Total (N) | 936 | 585 | 351 | 180 | 146 |

Our classificatory scheme identified exactly the same number of main dishes (342) as having non-British 'ethnic' inspiration as were denoted 'meat and two veg'. Such dishes were more likely to be eaten in commercial venues and in homes of friends, to be consumed in smaller company groups (two to four), to be shunned on special occasions, to be part of one- or two- course meals, and to be taken most frequently on Thursday, Friday and Saturday evening. The socio-demographic characteristics of those eating 'ethnic' dishes were much like those of respondents who made frequent use of ethnic restaurants (see chapter 4).

67 per cent of commercial meals and 77 per cent of meals in communal settings involved more than one course (see table 7.4). Starters were more popular in commercial venues, desserts in domestic settings. The proportion of respondents eating more than one course during their last meal out increased when the last meal had been a 'special occasion' or 'just a social occasion'.

Starters eaten during the last main meal are listed in table 7.5. Soup was the most popular starter, recorded eighty-one times. Soup and fruit were popular dishes served during home entertainment. Prawn cocktail, meat and vegetable starters were equally likely to appear at home or in a commercial venue. Bread was eaten on forty-six occasions and, with four exceptions, this occurred in commercial venues.[3]

Desserts were eaten by 470 respondents, 237 of these in a domestic venue. The most popular type of dessert was ice cream; 67 people had eaten this in a commercial venue whilst 55 had eaten it when being enter-

---

[3] On thirty-one last main meal occasions, another course was eaten prior to the main meal, making these four-course meals.

Table 7.5 *Last meal: type of starter eaten*

| Type of starter eaten (in numbers) | All | Commercial venue | Domestic venue |
|---|---|---|---|
| Soup | 81 | 53 | 28 |
| Prawn cocktail | 37 | 27 | 10 |
| Fruit | 32 | 14 | 18 |
| Bread | 46 | 42 | 4 |
| Fish starter | 34 | 27 | 7 |
| Meat starter | 24 | 18 | 6 |
| Vegetable starter | 86 | 67 | 19 |
| Indian starter | 30 | 24 | 6 |
| Other[a] | 37 | 33 | 4 |
| Total | 407 | 305 | 102 |

*Note:*
[a] Other includes Chinese, Mexican, cheese, egg, pasta and other unspecified starters.

tained at the home of friends or family. Pies, tarts and crumbles were especially popular for home entertaining; of 82 portions served, 54 were in a domestic context. Cakes and gateaux were also popular, with 42 chocolate and 79 non-chocolate varieties being served. Other desserts mentioned by name included fruit (47 instances), pudding (40), pavlova/meringue (21), profiteroles (7), pancakes (7) and cheese (5). The desserts were served with a variety of accompaniments, 79 with fresh cream, 32 with custard and 18 with syrup or sauce.

The evidence of the food content of meals eaten out suggests considerable diversity. The number of different food items, the range of dishes and their cuisines of origin, and the patterning of meals indicates that in aggregate variety is abundant. On this evidence it would be perverse to claim that the population of England has uniform and exceptionally restricted tastes. However, the prominence of main course dishes in the 'meat and two vegetable' format, and of roast meats generally, indicates the persistence of traditional habits. One question that arises is whether the pursuit of variety is a general one, or whether only a minority of people are adventurously developing new tastes.

### Mapping food tastes

One antinomy of contemporary food tastes contrasts neophilia, the love of the new, and neophobia, fear of novelty. Our interviewees provided examples of both tendencies. Debby, a woman in her twenties, apropos of having tasted a companion's swordfish, which she pronounced 'quite nice', said, 'I won't order anything I don't know. If I don't know what it tastes like I won't order. I'm very, you know, stick to what I know.' Her conservatism meant that she would only eat that with which she was already familiar. Smina, also in her twenties, indicated a similar reluctance to try new foods:

INTERVIEWER: Would you say that you like to try out new things when you go out for something to eat?

SMINA: No, not a lot. We normally get the same things that we like. But no we never try new things unless we take somebody along with us, and then we order different dishes and try different ones. If it is just me and my husband we normally get the same thing.

Such positions contrast with Trisha, the most explicit neophiliac, who practised totally open-ended experimentalism, which meant she tried something different on every occasion:

Yeah, well, I mean I hadn't tried Indian food 'til about two years ago and I didn't think that I would like it and I've never been offered it at home but when I tried it I thought it was really nice and you know there's so many varieties that you can eat so you should just try different things, even if you don't like them at least you know for the future. So we do tend to, especially when we go out, we don't choose the same thing on the menu. You know, every time we go out we tend to like go somewhere different and try a different meal and things like that. We get a bit [of] variety.

Another indicator of the distribution of neophilia derived from attitudes reported in the survey. Distinctive and mutually exclusive clusters of attitudes emerged from factor analysis, 'I like what I know', 'home-is-best', and 'interested learners' being identifiable groups, suggesting that conservative and neophiliac tendencies co-exist in the population.

Some of the main courses described in the previous section may serve as proxies for conservative and neophiliac tendencies. *Pace* Wood, the 'cooked dinner' implies continuity between domestic and public cooking, and is an aspect of conservative British food tastes. By contrast, dishes with an 'ethnic' inspiration, including pasta and curries, might be read as evidence of neophiliac tendencies, at least when eaten by 'white' respondents. The attitude that 'home is best' was stronger amongst those who had eaten a 'meat and two vegetables' main course the last time they ate out. Those tending to say 'I like what I know' were less likely to have eaten a meal with 'ethnic' connotations. There were also significant differences in this tendency between those who had eaten steak, and those who had eaten other roasts and pasta, with those who ate steak being most highly predisposed to the opinion 'I like what I know' and those eating pasta the least. 'Interested learner' tendencies were stronger amongst those who had eaten a main course with ethnic connotations.

Given that 74 per cent of survey respondents agreed with the statement 'When I eat out, I like to choose things which I don't eat at home', it seems strange that a substantial majority of our respondents had eaten their chosen main course on a previous occasion. Survey respondents were asked 'have you ever eaten this dish out before?' and 'have you ever eaten this main course at home in the last 12 months?' Of the valid responses, 17 per cent were trying their main course for the first time while eating out, and 38 per cent of people had not eaten the same dish at home in the last year.

The second question is of particular importance. Where respondents had eaten made a difference. Nearly 46 per cent of those who had eaten out commercially, compared with only 25 per cent of those who had eaten out communally, claimed not to have eaten that dish at home in the previous 12 months.[4] In other words, almost half of those who had eaten out commercially said the food was different from what they eat at home. Those who had eaten in one of the 'ethnic' venues for their last meal were even more likely to say that they had not eaten their main course at home in the year prior to interview; 53 per cent claimed this compared with 43 per cent of those eating in a 'British' style venue and 37 per cent of those eating in a 'fast food' venue. This is strong evidence that customers do eat different food in the commercial than in the domestic sphere. Nevertheless, in the majority of cases people dining out have eaten the same main course at home, presumptive evidence of convergence.[5]

Many were familiar with their main course choices, reporting having eaten them away from home on a previous occasion. This eventuality, however, reflects more than simply conservative food tastes of the kind displayed by Debby when she claimed to have eaten 'steak, every night, for two weeks' on her recent holiday. Repetition may also reflect mood or the availability of a favourite dish, as was clear from John's response to the question what influenced his choice:

How you feel at the time I suppose. I suppose sometimes you want something light, sometimes you are ready to dive in, sometimes you are feeling adventurous, other times you are feeling you want to be safe with your choices. Erm ... just depends on the menu. I mean if there is something that really takes my eye on the menu, then I'll go for it. If it is a menu that's been tried and tested and I've been there before, then I'll more often than not go for an old favourite that I know I'll be reasonably happy with.

For John and others, one influence was perception of risk of disappointment, significant when opportunities to eat out were limited. Even people

---

[4] No significant difference was found in this answer between those who had eaten at the home of family and friends.

[5] The likelihood was less for those eating ethnic main dishes.

who consider themselves 'adventurous' return to familiar dishes some-times. Moreover, diners do not have unrestricted choice. Whereas cus-tomers in commercial venues usually choose from a given menu, guests of domestic hospitality mostly have to eat what is placed in front of them, though hosts may consider the food preferences of guests to some degree.[6]

Another explicit reason repeatedly given for choosing the same dish was that particular commercial venues offered little variety in their menus. Katrine, for instance, ate out with a large group of friends, and they tended to choose particular venues for those nights out. These were typically not 'ethnic' style restaurants, because not all her friends enjoyed 'foreign' foods, and they were places where they 'could stop for the night'. Katrine expressed the view that such places did not offer much choice, hence she ate steak more often than she cared for: 'It's usually a steak when I eat out and that's it. Not very adventurous I don't think, but I don't think they have like a lot of choices at these places. You know, like you have steaks and you have gammon or you have a chop, it's mostly basic things anyway, but with different sauces on.' Katrine's experience arises from her limited control in choosing where to eat. Because of the particular company, her personal preferences are subjected to those of her group of friends, and the venues selected do not cater for Katrine's desire for something different. Disappointment in the food that is generally on offer may in part be the reason why Katrine places so much emphasis on 'different sauces', which makes the steak she eats out different from those she eats at home. The potential importance of this type of 'situational entailment' (see Warde and Martens, 1998) is clear when we consider which meal types prevailed in what commercial venue types. A significant 75 per cent of commercially provided 'meat and two vegetables' meals were in 'British' style venues, as were 82 per cent of roast beef dishes, 75 per cent of other roast meats and 78 per cent of steaks. By contrast 65 per cent of 'ethnically' inspired meals were eaten in an 'ethnic' style venue, as were 66 per cent of pasta dishes and 76 per cent of curries.[7] Where one eats to a significant degree determines what one eats.

We found both neophobic and neophiliac views and behaviour amongst our 1,001 survey respondents. We doubt the claim that British diners are predominantly conservative, though a proportion of them are.[8]

---

[6] 80 per cent of those who had eaten at the home of friends or family indeed said that there had been no choice in their decision of what to eat.

[7] Incidentally, 18 per cent of 'ethnically inspired' dishes were eaten in a 'British' style venue and 11 per cent in a 'fast food' venue.

[8] See chapter 3 for a discussion of the socio-demographic characteristics of the 'I like what I know', 'home-is-best' and 'interested learner' tendencies amongst the survey sample.

Overall our sample appeared to contain about equal numbers of diners with conservative and neophiliac tastes. Diners can and do try foods they have not eaten before. 17 per cent of our sample had not previously eaten their last main course. This may seem rather small, but since these diners eat out on average eighteen times a year, many must be trying dishes they have never eaten before. Nevertheless, whatever their preferences, in some situations diners may be compelled to eat familiar foods. Situational constraints mean that often a diner has little influence over where and what he or she eats, so repetition of main courses does not necessarily reflect negative attitudes towards new foods.

In advancing his argument for convergence, Wood tends to focus entirely on the food content of main courses. However, there are many other aspects of eating out which might suggest significant symbolic differences from home: witness interviewees' perceptions of what counted as 'offering a change'. One aspect contrasting eating out with eating at home centred on distinctions between 'rich' and 'light' foods, on quantity and on the manner in which restrictions on food consumption are controlled or relaxed. Martens (1997, 1998) showed that notions of appropriate quantities and 'richness' of foods eaten in different situational contexts pervade food practices. 'Novelty' and its opposite 'tradition' are not the only influences contemporary consumers face when making everyday consumption decisions (Lupton, 1996; Warde, 1997). Concurrent pressures to indulge and to constrain exist. Restraint in food intake is induced by contemporary concerns with health and body image, concerns which Mennell has termed the 'civilisation of appetite' and which, according to him, is now an almost universal experience in the West. Wood also acknowledges the relevance of this antinomy, observing that such everyday concerns for 'healthy eating' are neglected by caterers who perceive their market to be one characterised by a 'predominantly hedonistic experience' (1995: 92). Nevertheless, he conveniently overlooks this as an aspect of potential variety.

By way of illustration, let us return to the course structure of meals eaten out, as it offers insight into diversity in food quantity. Diners see eating out as an opportunity for eating more. A high proportion of our respondents desired to eat more than was usual at home; 43 per cent of respondents agreed with the statement 'When I eat out, I like to eat more than I do at home', whilst 40 per cent disagreed. Female interviewees acknowledged that they eat more than normal when eating out, often because such meals involve more courses. [9] As we saw above, 67 per cent

---

[9] Indeed, Wilson has argued that contemporary routine domestic meals are mostly one-course meals (1989:175).

of commercial meals out and 77 per cent of meals out in domestic settings involved more than one course (see table 7.4), a significant difference.

Another way in which our interviewees distinguished between eating out and eating at home centred on the cooking time, expertise and cooking style involved in meal preparation. For instance, when Janice was asked what influenced her choice of what to eat when she ate out, she replied: 'What sort of things? I suppose I go for things in restaurants that do take what I consider quite a lot of cooking, are quite intricate to prepare and things that obviously because of that I wouldn't have time [to make myself]'. In Anne's case, eating out and the ready meal market offered her the opportunity to eat lasagne, something she might not eat otherwise because 'I'm no good at making lasagne, the pasta is never right'. Other interviewees said that they could and did make certain dishes at home, but that professional cooks made different or superior versions. Smina was adamant that the shish kebabs they ate in their favourite restaurant tasted completely different because cooked on charcoal whilst those at home were done in the oven. And Sheila puzzled with the idea what it was that made the pizzas at Don Giovanni's better than her home-made ones.

I can make home-made pizzas but they're not as good as the ones you buy from, you know, Don Giovanni's. They're good them, I don't know what they put in them but they're really good. And they have, and the ovens they use are better for the base, I don't know, and the cheese and what have you.

Yet others appeared to get special gratification out of the different sauces surrounding their food, or the way the food was presented, as Chris suggested:

I suppose it's just like the little additives that you wouldn't bother with at home, that make it look really presentable, beautifully presented and also as I say all sorts of little bits of different kinds of fruit that I don't normally buy to make it look really appetising. And it's not necessarily part of the meal, it's a decoration on the plate to make it look appetising. I like that.

All diners may not experiment wildly with unknown food when they visit restaurants, but they probably satisfy a desire for change in other ways. Interviewees said that they liked to try 'different' things and to 'have a change'. In addition to their food, they were referring to a different activity or a different place from the everyday. The latter was the case for Andy, who enjoyed getting out of the house: 'Just a chance to go out and do something a bit different it's quite nice. Er, you know living in a one-bedroom flat it can get a bit restrictive. Er, so it's nice to get out now and again.' However, change also referred to other aspects of the event. Smina's reasons for eating out were to 'Just enjoy yourself mainly. It gives

you a change though doesn't it mainly. Gives you a change from cooking.'
For others it was the event that was different. So Jenny said 'Because it's
nice, I enjoy, I enjoy getting ready to go out as much as going out, I enjoy
getting dressed up and going out.' The quest for change and variety is not
necessarily sought in novel foods.

So, eating out commercially or communally offers experiences
different from everyday domestic eating. Not only is there potential for
trying unknown foods, but also familiar dishes where methods of cooking
and presentation are different. Meals out also give diners a chance to
indulge every so often and to distance themselves from everyday places
and activities.

There are variations in conduct, in the common practices and modes of
behaviour associated with commercial and communal settings. As Visser
(1991) says, many rituals accompany dinner. We did not collect material
on all possible facets, but we have information on planning and dressing
for meals and their timing. We can also show how these vary depending on
the purpose of the meal and where and with whom people dined.

The survey suggests that meals eaten out are more often pleasure than
necessity. Of the 936 last meals out, 238 were said to be a 'special occasion', 530 were described as 'just a social occasion', 137 were said to be
'quick or convenience' meals, and 27 were work-related. Purpose and
venue were often linked. Amongst the commercially sourced meals, 29 per
cent were said to be for a 'special occasion', 48 per cent were recorded as
being 'just a social occasion', whilst 19 per cent were merely 'convenient'.
'British' style commercial venues served the purpose of 'special occasion'
particularly often, with nearly 60 per cent of such meals being celebrated
in these venues. For special occasions, 'safe' venues get priority. For a
social occasion, although as many meals were taken in an 'ethnic' as a
'British' style venue, proportionately 'ethnic' venues were more popular
for this purpose. Nearly 70 per cent of those eating in a 'fast food' venue
considered their meal 'convenient' or 'quick'. Respondents were more
likely to celebrate a special occasion by eating in a restaurant than in
someone else's home, while communal meals were more likely to be
described as 'just a social occasion'.

In commercial venues eating alone was uncommon: of 585 respondents who ate their last main meal in a commercial venue, a mere 21 said
that they had eaten alone. Eating in the company of a partner was very
popular, with 302 (52 per cent) respondents eating their last meal out in
the presence of their partner and 134 (23 per cent) respondents eating
that meal only with their partner. Eating out with family members was
also common, with 216 respondents eating with one or more family
member. 105 diners had eaten out with partner and kin. Friends were

Table 7.6 *Communal meals: the home in which the last meal was eaten*

|                              | Frequency | Percentage |
|------------------------------|-----------|------------|
| Parents                      | 77        | 21.9       |
| Son/daughter                 | 34        | 9.7        |
| In-laws                      | 38        | 10.8       |
| Brother/sister               | 28        | 8.0        |
| Other family                 | 3         | 0.9        |
| Friends                      | 146       | 41.6       |
| Someone I work with          | 2         | 0.6        |
| Business associate/colleague | 1         | 0.3        |
| Don't know / not answered    | 22        | 6.3        |
| Total                        | 351       | 100.0      |

Valid cases 351     Missing cases 0

also important as company; 228 meals (39 per cent) were reported to have been in the presence of one or more friends and 132 respondents had eaten out solely with friends. Work colleagues, a boss or business associates were uncommon companions: 44 respondents had been in the presence of such company, whilst 27 meals were consumed with work colleagues only.

As regards communal settings, table 7.6 shows that more meals were eaten at the homes of family than friends (180 compared with 146), and more meals were eaten at the home of parents than other specific family members. Only three meals were eaten at the home of a work-related host, which, like eating out commercially, stresses the comparative insignificance of this kind of socialising. Table 7.7 shows how often the respondent ate at the home of the friend or family that he or she had visited last. Variation reflects the relationship between host and guest. For instance, where respondents ate at the same home every week, this was likely to be the home of close family (particularly parents), whilst less frequent visits were made to the homes of more distant relations. Monthly and six-monthly visits were more likely to be to the homes of friends.

Eating at the home of friends was predominantly done by younger respondents (under forty), although respondents in their twenties and thirties were also particularly likely to eat at the home of their parents. Those living alone were more likely to eat at the home of friends, as were lone parents, whilst older single householders were quite likely to eat at the home of a son or daughter.

The degree of organisation prior to the meal was related to its purpose. For instance, most respondents knew where they would eat out for a

Table 7.7 *Last meal: how often do you eat a main meal there?*

| Value Label | Frequency | Per cent |
|---|---|---|
| This is first time | 20 | 5.7 |
| At least once every week | 57 | 16.2 |
| At least once every month | 99 | 28.2 |
| At least once every 3 months | 86 | 24.5 |
| At least once every 6 months | 50 | 14.2 |
| Once a year | 23 | 6.6 |
| No answer / don't know | 16 | |
| Total | 351 | 100.0 |

Valid cases 335   Missing cases 16

special occasion a few days or longer in advance. Since special occasions are often meant to gather together a particular group of people to celebrate, prior organisation is necessary. In contrast, mere 'social occasions' were much less premeditated; 17 per cent of respondents had decided a week or more in advance where they would eat out, but 40 per cent made up their minds less than an hour before, many at the instant of passing the venue. Instant decision-making was even more evident for those taking a 'convenience' meal.

To the question 'did you dress specially for the occasion?' 68 per cent of respondents answered 'no'. That these figures should not be taken at face value is clear from our in-depth discussions. What to wear was a concern of almost all our interviewees – there was a consciousness about the presentation of self when eating in the company of others and interviewees held a distinct sense of what clothes befitted specific activities and occasions, but this did not mean that all dressed up in their 'best' or smart clothes for every occasion. Steve, Lisa and Andy had 'dressed up' the last time they ate out commercially. Steve, for instance, had visited a fashionable restaurant in the middle of Manchester with his girlfriend, and had dressed up in his 'best togs', his 'most fashionable things' (also see Sheila in Box 7.1 below). But not all commercial eating venues or occasions were thought to require 'dressing up', and in some instances casual clothes were considered more appropriate.

Expectations concerning dress were more relaxed when eating at the home of family or friends compared with eating out in restaurants and similar establishments. Only 22 per cent of respondents who had eaten their last meal in a 'private home' claimed to have dressed up specially, compared with nearly 40 per cent eating last in a commercial venue (see also chapter 6). Respondents were much more likely to dress for a 'special

**Box 7.1 Sheila's Christmas lunch with colleagues**

Sheila and her colleagues had a Christmas lunch at The Golf Club restaurant before Christmas. It is situated about ten miles outside Preston, and is a place where Sheila had never been to before, and where she would probably not go again. Every year, Sheila explained, they enquired about the Christmas menus of various venues, these would be circulated and a decision would be made. That year, the choice had fallen on The Golf Club restaurant.

Being a fraud investigator, Sheila had a good memory for detail, and she was able to describe the proceedings of the lunch in some detail. On the morning before the lunch, all her colleagues, including herself, had come into work all dressed up. 'We all went to work in our going out gear . . . Everybody looked really funny you know. Looked around the office, who's that, got make-up on and lipstick and you know fancy earrings and everything. Chiffon scarves draped round the place.' As the venue was ten miles away, many (including Sheila) drove to it in their cars. She remembered parking next to a Rolls-Royce or was it a Bentley? Before being seated, their boss offered them all a drink, which they had in the bar. Sheila had a whisky.

Sheila explained in some detail what she had eaten: 'for a starter I had chicken livers. They were whole chicken livers and they were quite well, they were well browned and they had walnuts in them, and it was served on a very well-presented salad . . . it was all very fresh. And then there was a soup or sorbet course and I had the sorbet. I thought I'd better have that 'cos I thought there's going to be a lot of food here, and I'd enjoyed the chicken livers so much I ate them all. And then for a main course I had salmon, and that was with broccoli and carrots and little potatoes with the skins on and a blob of flavoured butter with the salmon, but I love that. And what else was there. Oh there was cauliflower cheese with it as well and sliced curried potatoes but I didn't have those, 'cos they didn't seem to go with the salmon. And it was really nice. And for pudding I had Paris breast, which I've never had before. It was two circles of choux pastry with some fresh fruit inside and just to the side of it was what I think was custard cream type of stuff, and there was cream in with the fresh fruit, in between the choux pastry. And it was very nice, yeah. And then there was mince pies. And a nice touch I thought was, they brought on the whole nuts in their shells and nutcrackers. Then there was coffee and it was nice, it really was an excellent lunch. And everything was cooked just right, you know the vegetables were firm.' Sheila herself drank spring water during the meal, which came from blue bottles of Welsh spring water which decorated the table when they sat down. Little alcohol was consumed at their table, because many were driving, but some drank white or red wine.

Their table, Sheila remembered, was a long one, whilst other guests were seated around round tables. It was decorated with Christmas crackers 'and bits and pieces', but it did not have the 'very nice Christmas decoration' that featured on the tables of the other guests. Sheila also noticed that the glasses on their table were plain, whilst those on the other tables were cut glass. The restaurant itself was 'really plush, very tasteful pastel colours'. Sheila believed that they were in a new annex to the older Georgian building, and the annex had been built to copy that style. The restaurant itself looked out over the green expanse of the golf course. The waiting staff were 'smartly dressed in black and white uniforms'; they were mostly young women and 'they all looked about sixteen or seventeen', with

Box 7.1 (*cont.*)

an older male waiter, whom Sheila believed to be in charge. During the meal, they were served by different waiting staff, and the service, according to Sheila was 'efficient but cool and detached, nothing personal about it'. The timing of the service agreed with Sheila. She called herself a slow eater, and wondered whether, in fact, the timing was related to when she finished.

Sheila certainly appeared to have taken her time to look around, for in addition to all these features, Sheila remembered and described some of the other customers in the venue. In one corner was seated an older man with a smartly dressed young woman, who appeared not to talk much. There were other couples, too, who looked like golf club members. Around one large round table, which had a Christmas decoration and a crystal vase in the middle, was seated a group of young men, who wore 'very expensive clothes . . . one chap had a yellow and black dickie bow'. And there was another 'works do' in a room to the side. Sheila and her colleagues speculated that the young men around that table were sales reps. They had come in with their briefcases, and all had small mobile phones. They spoke with 'loud voices, and darling, nice to see you . . . and the main topic of the conversation was what company car they all wanted'.

The meal cost them £15.50 each.

occasion' than for a 'social occasion'. Not surprisingly, those who had eaten for convenience reasons or had visited a 'fast food' venue were the least likely to have dressed specially.[10]

Meal times also matter. In many contexts, both institutional and domestic, meals have been central markers of the routine of social life. Food events of different kinds punctuate and structure daily, weekly and annual cycles. It is widely believed that eating has now become less routinised, that neither the form of meals, nor their timing, are as regular and predictable as in the past. Eating out, because discretionary and comparatively infrequent, is not governed by rigid temporal rules but nevertheless has its own rhythms, with meals for different purposes concentrated disproportionately in particular time slots.

Nearly two thirds of last meals eaten in commercial venues took place at the 'weekend' (including Friday). Fridays and Saturdays are by far the most popular days for eating in restaurants. Such concentration is understandable for, as Lisa explained, the social meals with her friends happen on Saturdays because 'nobody's up for work Sunday'. Of the 585 commercial meals eaten out, 30 per cent had happened on a Saturday, and a further 19 per cent on a Friday. Sundays were also popular, with 16 per cent of respondents eating their last meal out then, and they proved particularly important for celebrating 'special occasions'. Monday, with only

[10] No differences were found in dressing conventions when meals were provided by friends as opposed to family.

---

**Box 7.2 Anne's barbecue at the neighbours'**

Anne and her husband Bert, who live in a small two-bedroomed terraced house characteristic of Preston, socialise quite a lot with their neighbours. One couple they are particularly friendly with (they play cards in each other's houses at least once a week) invited them to a barbecue they were organising to celebrate Bill finishing his university degree. This was not the first time Anne had been at a barbecue at their neighbours', and Anne and Bert had organised barbecues themselves that summer, too. The other guests invited were all friends of the neighbours. The barbecue was to start at 6 o'clock in the evening. Anne said that she did not change clothes for it, but that she took with her chicken legs marinated in tikka masala, which were partially cooked. She always did this with chicken for the barbecue because of 'health' reasons; you never knew whether barbecue chicken was properly cooked, and according to Anne, there was a risk of food poisoning.

Anne went over in time to help her neighbour Joyce with the preparation of the 'other stuff'. Her husband was engaged with Bill in getting the barbecue going. The 'other stuff' included salads and garlic bread. In the end, they had to wait quite a while before the first meat was cooked, until 8 o'clock, because there had been delays in getting the barbecue hot enough to cook the meat. Then the party got going, with everyone drinking lager, and eating the salads, the garlic bread, Anne's chicken legs and sausages and burgers. Anne commented that she did not necessarily eat more that she would normally do, but that she certainly ate more meat than she would normally do.

The barbecue was held in the back yard of Bill and Joyce's house. The question 'what were the surroundings like?' was accompanied with laughter, as there is nothing special about a back court where nettles grow out of the walls. The atmosphere had been good, however, with music playing from speakers which were situated in the yard, and lively conversation on topics which were different from Anne's everyday conversation. Anne went home at half past eleven, where she took over from the baby-sitter; another neighbour. Bert, she believed, came back some time during the night.

---

6 per cent of last meals, was the slackest day for commercial meal providers.

Evenings were the most common time for eating out. The most popular hour for starting a main meal out was between 8 and 9 o'clock in the evening; 22 per cent of respondents had started their meal at this time. A further 17 per cent started their meal between 7 and 8 o'clock and 10 per cent between 9 and 10 o'clock in the evening. Almost half (45 per cent) of evening meals lasted between one and two hours. 20 per cent lasted less than an hour, 27 per cent lasted between two and three hours, whilst 8 per cent of respondents sat for longer than three hours. Meals eaten out on Saturday were more protracted: 41 per cent of these lasting between two and three hours. Also, 40 per cent of meals lasting longer than three hours occurred on Saturday night. The average communal meal appears to move at a more relaxed pace, 37 per cent lasting longer than three hours compared with 8 per cent of commercial counterparts. There were some interesting relationships between timing and venue. Eating out in the middle of the day (between noon and 3 o'clock) and in the early evening (between 5 and 7 o'clock) was frequent on Sundays. Meals in 'ethnic' restaurants tended to occur on Thursdays, Fridays and Saturdays. Meals in the early part of the week occurred more often at lunch time and in the early evening, were shorter in duration and were more likely to be taken in fast food outlets.

Domestic entertainment was more strongly concentrated on particular days and times, being predominantly a weekend activity, with 67 per cent of such meals taking place on a Saturday or Sunday. Sunday is the day *par excellence* for family entertainment. Of the 132 communal meals on a Sunday, 92 were hosted by respondents' families, and just over half of these meals were eaten in the middle of the day, a vestige of the traditional family Sunday lunch. Friends are more likely than family to entertain each other on a Saturday, the temporal sequencing of such events replicating those in the commercial sector. Friday was less popular for domestic entertainment than for eating out commercially; only 40 out of 148 Friday meals were communal. Reflecting weekly rhythms, Friday, as the end of the normal working week for domestic as well as paid workers, may be inappropriate for the time and effort consuming nature of entertaining.

### Diversity, convergence or anomie?

This chapter has identified several reasons why consumers see eating out as different from everyday domestic eating. Meaningful aspects of the consumer's quest for variety include not only the chance to eat different foods (and this may well not be the most pressing reason), but also the opportunity to get out of the house, to get a change from everyday routine and to escape the controlled food intake increasingly evident in everyday food practices. Wood's (1995) emphasis on the idea that the variety offered in the eating out process is an illusion obscures and belittles those meaningful practices.

We agree with Wood that the illusion of novelty is actively created by food producers, but the quest for variety by consumers is in part independent of this (Warde, 1997). The search for small differences which confer a touch of individuality without taking a person too far from the group norm is a most important consumer strategy. Wood perhaps overemphasises the operation of illusion in the food field. Pizza or lasagne, whether made from scratch at home, bought ready made from the supermarket, bought as a take-away, eaten whilst sitting down in one of the multitude of venues that have them on the menu, or even at the dinner table of a friend, are in one sense the same basic foodstuffs. Equally, it might be argued that the steaks eaten by Katrine and Jenny differ only in their sauces and presentation. Yet, in the survey steaks were described in many ways. They were, for instance, identified by type (T-bone steak, rib steak, sirloin steak, rump steak, beef steak and (double) fillet steak were all mentioned), by accompanying sauces and ingredients (steak with mushrooms and mushroom sauce, onions, barbecue sauce, as well as peppered steak, Chateaubriand steak, steak Diane, steak with baluchi dressing and tampaquina steak with chilli were all eaten), as well as by cooking technique (respondents commented on eating rare rump steak, medium rare steak, well-done steak, grilled steak, plain steak, and steak burger). It is not obvious that consumers capable of recognising and discriminating among so many ways of preparing steak are deluded about variety.

While the catering industry invents some spurious impressions of variety there is a sense in which the complexity and range of all cuisine is based on recombinations of a relatively small number of ingredients and meal formats. The creation of many different versions of dishes is an inherent aspect of culinary cultures. Soups have always been made with different kinds of ingredients and served in different ways, ice cream has always had different flavours, pizzas different toppings. Diversity also arises from regional culinary cultures (e.g. wines and cheeses) and from their hybridisation (Mennell remarks on smoked reindeer pizza (1985: 329)). 'Variations on a theme' are hence not peculiar to the commercial market.

Concentrating on producers, and with limited appreciation of consumer motives, Wood exaggerates convergence between public and private eating. Our findings suggest systematic differences of experience between communal and commercial meals. Depending on where our respondents ate the last time, they were likely to have eaten different food items, different main dishes and a different numbers of courses. They also tended to have dressed differently, eaten at a different time of day and over a different length of time. There was some sense, in addition, that communal eating required less overall adherence to self-presentation rules like those about dressing up.

Without an analysis of what diners eat when they eat out commercially and communally, it is impossible to appreciate the ways in which meal patterns diverge. For instance, 'meat and two veg' were eaten both commercially and communally, but proportionally more were eaten communally. The prominence of 'meat and two veg' in communal provision is due to families providing such meals to other extended family members, particularly on Sundays. Method of cooking also differed. Roast meat was served in both modes of provision, but in communal provision almost all the meat was roasted, while commercial venues served almost all the steaks and 'meat in a sauce' meals.

Neophilia is a major mechanism driving contemporary consumption. The general climate of opinion advocates exposure to new products, new experiences, new pleasures. Industry constantly seeks to innovate, to design commodities which generate 'innovation rents'; advertisements, popular magazines and media programmes celebrate novelty; and consumers may feel inspired to follow fashions and buy the most up-to-date products or inventions. Innovations in the preservation, transportation, biotechnological invention and retailing of foodstuffs allow late twentieth-century society to offer unprecedented opportunities for individuals to indulge any interest in new culinary experience. The extent to which people explore such opportunities and the extent to which these are gratifying rather than anxiety-provoking is a matter of some importance as regards eating out.

Pursuit of the new has been associated with deregulation and the experience of anomie in the food field (Fischler, 1980). The loss or lack of rules guiding meal consumption may affect all aspects of meals, including the meal content and sequence, mannered rituals and company. Rampant pursuit of new items may be interpreted to mean that rules guiding what is appropriate to eat have disappeared. Equally, rules guiding the sequence of meals may be deemed lost as Western diners no longer accept a course structure, or throw the existing pattern of starter–main course–dessert into disarray. In addition, Gofton (1990, 1995) and Falk (1994) have argued that the temporal structuring of food consumption is becoming increasingly irrelevant, while the prominence of eating alone may be seen as an indication of the breakdown of rules that make eating a social activity. Eating out might be used in support of such arguments. For instance, it confronts diners with untried foods, cooked by a stranger, that may be eaten alone or away from the immediate family. However, we dispute this conclusion. Eating out, whether commercially or communally, is by no means a deregulated activity. How, otherwise, would one explain the quite distinct patterns found, not just in terms of what was eaten, but also in terms of who eats out with whom and associated codes of conduct? It is precisely regularities – in timing, course structure, preparation, etc. – that make meals eaten out distinctive.

# Part IV

# Enjoyment: the attractions of eating out

Western, capitalist and especially Protestant cultures have a long history of ambivalence towards consumption (Hirschman, 1982; Schama 1987; Sombart, 1967). Consumption smacks of luxury, waste, unnecessary expenditure, self-indulgence, excess. Antithetical to the puritan virtues of work and thrift, consumption is morally suspect. Campbell (1987) detected a paradox. Capitalist development required that some people, even if not the early Protestant entrepreneurs, purchased and used the increasing number of items produced. To generate the expansive material culture of modernity required an urge to consume as well as an urge to accumulate, a Romantic as well as a Protestant ethic. The urge to consume is now well established, as observations about wants being unlimited imply.

In Campbell's view it was the replacement of a traditional with a modern hedonism which explained the continual transformation and extension of consumption norms. No longer was the search for fulfilment simply a matter of seeking maximum repeated exposure to known pleasures, but had become a matter of imagining and anticipating novel and ever more stimulating gratifications. Modern hedonism thus instilled the inevitability of disappointment, for this is an attitude which depends upon the endlessly renewed quest for more rewarding, more exquisite, more self-enhancing experiences.

Hedonism is increasingly identified with consumer culture. Spending money, rather than wasting time or indulging sensual desires, characterises its contemporary form (Cross, 1993; Schor, 1992). However, consumerism is not simply an expression of hedonism. Much consumption is simply routine. After all, survival depends upon the many commodities necessary for physical, emotional and social reproduction; most people must purchase food, pay for housing, travel to meet friends and kin, and so forth. Some level of consumption is absolutely necessary and in an advanced capitalist society there is no realistic option but to go to market to obtain the wherewithal to subsist. Even the most ascetic, frugal and self-sufficient people cannot avoid being drawn into the culture of modern consumption.

People reasonably expect some degree of gratification from consumption. Consumption should be pleasurable and, given its scale in the contemporary world, it would be remarkable if it were not. True, there are some people for whom food appears a major enemy, and others for whom it seems a constant dull threat, yet few would wish to retire from eating. The attitude of indifference is, however, much more widespread (e.g. Lupton, 1996), a phenomenon of some general importance in the understanding of consumer culture. Nevertheless, a universal drive like the relief of hunger is insufficient to explain particular desires, like wanting to eat out. Surely many people are not sufficiently interested in food to want to bother to invest the additional money required to eat out? General accounts of modern hedonism require elaboration in terms of the specifics of particular practices, their rationales and rewards.

The final phase of a chain of consumption is that of enjoyment, where one experiences some sense of gratification, whether positive or negative. Enjoyment relates both to the intrinsic experience of the act of consuming a product or service and to the short- or long-term benefit that the consumer thereby derives. Arguably, in the past too much attention has been devoted to utilitarian aspects of benefit, like whether the item consumed was good value for money or functionally fit for a practical purpose. While these are important considerations, they typically neglect sensations, emotions and sentiments associated with consumption, and tend to reduce the values obtained to a form of economic calculation. Items which are not susceptible to evaluation in terms of price tend to be eliminated from consideration. To have shared in lively conversation, to have passed time in congenial company, to have presented oneself attractively to others are possible benefits derived from dining out, but they are hard to subsume under the accounting procedures of economics. Nor are they likely to be in the forefront of people's consciousness when deciding whether, or where, to eat out. These gains, part of the substratum of eating out, cannot be guaranteed on any particular occasion and require some collective effort to achieve. Such intangible benefits are contingent; they do not follow necessarily or predictably from the channels of earlier phases in the production – consumption cycle; provision, access and delivery are not sufficient determinants of outcomes in terms of enjoyment. In this section we seek to develop a set of categories of types of gratification which give some analytic grip on the complex processes involved in the derivation of enjoyment in acts of consumption.

In our view, far too little attention has been paid by sociologists of consumption to this last phase 'enjoyment', or what is otherwise called 'final consumption' or 'final use'. Very few studies attempt to explore what it feels like, what good and bad sensations are aroused, what are the sources of gratification and dissatisfaction associated with actual experiences of consuming – sitting in a concert, using a computer, playing a piano, watching a television programme, or eating a meal. By comparison we know in vast detail the processes and experiences associated with producing goods and services; studies of work satisfaction and the nature of labour processes are legion. One might expect that equal attention would be given to the differential appreciations of recipients of such services. Do people like the dinners they are given?; what sort of satisfactions do audiences obtain from watching television?; are they similar to those derived from listening to live music?

There are many plausible causes for sociological neglect of such questions among which three seem especially important: a tendency to operate with utilitarian assumptions; a tendency to view consumption as instrumental to other social ends rather than as having intrinsic value; and a tendency to refuse to accept that people are the best judges of the meaning and value of their feelings of satisfaction.

The principal reason for neglect has been the hegemony of neo-classical economics among the social sciences. By presuming that consumers are not constrained to buy particular goods or services, and that purchase reflects a reasoned schedule of preferences directed to affording each their greatest pleasure, it seems reasonable to deem that consumers derive satisfaction from their activities. This assumption has been widely incorporated into sociological accounts. Sociologists, inexplicably and partly by default, have tended to adopt the utilitarian assumption that people must, if they have chosen to consume one item rather than another, anticipate, and in all probability achieve, satisfaction. It is comparatively rare to enquire about the subjective senses of gratification that are derived from consumption activities. It is psychologists (for reviews see Csikszentmihalyi, 1992; Lane, 1991) who have made the greatest contribution to the empirical understanding of the sources and experiences of happiness, though these come primarily as understandings of the individual psyche, and ignore the social components of pleasure. One effective demolition of the inadequacies of a utilitarian account of pleasure is advanced by Lane (1991) who argues, *inter alia*, that it deflects attention from the experience of pleasure by reducing all to a spurious addition of satisfactions.

Second, much of sociology has viewed consumption solely as an activity instrumental in social struggles for power. Such accounts have little interest in the experience of final consumption precisely because they are presumed directed to ulterior benefits – wealth, status, position, etc. This view is deeply etched into the analyses of major sociological contributors like Weber and Veblen. It also runs through the work of Bourdieu, in his understanding of the role of cultural and symbolic capital in the process of establishing and displaying distinction. Among recent elaborations, Hirsch's (1978) notion of positional goods and Featherstone's (1991) speculation about the social project of the cultural intermediaries draw on the same mechanism. Consumption is about strategic individual or collective action. There is no doubt that consumption has been, and still is, used to mark social position, a function even more central to status-oriented societies. But from that point of view, how, and indeed whether, people get intrinsic enjoyment from those activities, is largely irrelevant. Concentration on the competitive instrumental aspect of consumption tends to see the primary satisfaction as the enhancement of social power, and any expressed or felt gratifications as, if not mere rationalisation, subsidiary. Such a focus cares little for the experience of enjoyment.

While most instrumentalist accounts concern invidious comparison between social groups, recently fashionable accounts of the construction of self, or self-identity through consumption also posit instrumentalist reasoning. To the extent that one's purchases are oriented to the presentation of self then it is their effect – making a performance credible and persuasive – rather than their intrinsic features, which is of primary interest. Though such accounts leave more scope for appreciating consumption behaviour as expressive, it is that which is expressed or alluded to, rather than the activity itself, which is paramount.

The third longstanding tendency in sociological analysis casts doubt on how accurately people appreciate the level, quality and sources of their satisfactions. If people's subjective senses of satisfaction are somehow worthless or deserving of contempt, or if people are generally misled about what makes them happy, then concentration on the experience of such activities may seem unrewarding. Such a presumption has often led to attribution of false consciousness (temporary or permanent) to consumer behaviour and thereby to imply some objective hierarchy of pleasures. The most eminent version was advanced by the Frankfurt School, although it has suffered a recent eclipse in the face of some robust defences of popular culture. Adorno (e.g. 1991) is notorious for his argument that mass culture induced a state of distraction which prohibited serious cultural appreciation. Marcuse (1964) also claimed to identify false needs created by modern industry which deluded citizens into believing that the pleasures of consumption might render alienated workers happy. A contemporary, relevant contribution in this vein is Finkelstein's (1989) account of dining out. She denies the value of asking people whether they like eating out because they always say yes and can cite a train of commonsensical, though mistaken, reasons why. She argues that restaurants are particularly inauthentic contexts for human interaction because they are organised to determine mood and behaviour to such a degree that customers are prevented from recognising that they are being manipulated.

If the dominant and traditional approaches in sociology have failed to pay much attention to the experience of consumption there are others, mostly of recent vintage, which have made some attempt to approach the question. Most are preliminary and somewhat partial. These fall into a number of different types. One draws on evidence of pre-industrial recreation to give some impression of expressive, even bacchanalian, ways of obtaining pleasure, thereby seeking to reintroduce the passions and the emotions to current ludic events (e.g. Bakhtin, 1968; Bataille et al., 1991). A second perspective has involved ethnographic work, in mainstream cultural studies, particularly in relation to youth cultures and subcultures, which concentrates on what people do, and why, in natural contexts of consumption. Studies of media audiences, of the pleasures of watching favourite television programmes (Morley, 1992) or reading popular magazines (Ballaster et al., 1991; Hermes, 1995), convey such information. Some of the best work, avoiding any form of instrumentalism, has concerned enthusiasms which convey some understanding of the commitment, involvement and creativity of non-work, commodity-deploying recreational activities (Hoggett and Bishop, 1986; Finnegan, 1989; Moorhouse, 1991). A third approach draws on psychoanalysis for concepts of desire and applies them to practices of buying and selling to explain the persistent demand for additional items (see Bowlby, 1985; Radner, 1995). Fourth, there have been studies of shopping behaviour, which show that this is a differentiated activity and that the satisfactions are complex and uneven; indeed some shoppers are calculative and rational, others impulsive, addicted, entranced or seduced (Lunt and Livingstone, 1992; Falk and Campbell, 1997). Fifth, quality-of-life studies have asked people in some detail about their level of subjective well-being, permitting some empirical assessment of the role of consumption in this process (e.g. for a résumé, Lane, 1991). Sixth, there have been some excellent studies of material culture, of what objects mean to their owners, landscapes to tourists, pictures to the visitor to the art gallery, all of which give some insight into the pleasures of consumption in different forms (e.g. Miller, 1987; Appadurai, 1986; Csikszentmihalyi and Rochberg-Halton, 1981). Several of these have in common the well-founded observation that consumption is not simply an outcome of rational and calculating determination of the order in which to meet needs, an insight which is encapsulated in the widespread denial that consumption is any longer a process primarily led by calculations of the use-value of goods and services (e.g. Baudrillard, 1981).

So there are exceptions to dominant sociological approaches. However, they have yet to deliver systematic, coherent, detailed under-standings of enjoyment. Further conceptual and empirical work needs to be undertaken, which is the objective of Part IV. In chapter 8 we review evidence about the degree of satisfaction and pleasure derived by our respondents and interviewees from episodes of eating out. We question whether high levels of expressed satisfaction can be accepted at face value and consider the preparedness of people to complain and the topics of complaint. However, satisfaction seems genuine, so we go on to try to explain the responses, partly by suggesting that eating out delivers a number of different sorts of gratification which we collate systematically by reference to scholarly analyses of pleasure and happiness. In chapter 9 we attempt to apply the taxonomy of enjoyment in the analysis of our interviews. This provides grounds for a more systematic elaboration of the nature of the phase of enjoyment involved in eating out.

# 8    Eating out as a source of gratification

Much of the sparse analytic literature has tended to be highly critical of the nature and standards of eating out in Britain. Restaurants are condemned variously for the quality of the food from a gastronomic point of view (e.g. Driver, 1983), for standardisation accompanying the introduction of mass production techniques (e.g. Wood, 1994a) and for offering oppressively inauthentic contexts for social interaction (Finkelstein, 1989). Indeed, there are many reasons for anticipating negative reactions towards eating out experiences. There is evidence of appreciable ambivalence about food in general. Thus Lupton (1996:143) reports that 'some interviewees demonstrated an overwhelming interest and enjoyment of food; others seemed to have very little interest in food, viewing it simply as a way to survive rather than a source of pleasure'. Similarly, Purcell (1992) found a significant proportion of her Oxford sample considered food nothing more than a biological necessity: food is merely fuel. In addition, there is widespread current concern not to be overweight which, *in extremis*, manifests itself in serious food disorders, suggesting that occasions which require more eating may be unattractive (see Bordo, 1993). Furthermore, much concern is expressed that many British foodstuffs are potentially damaging to health; there is considerable suspicion of the food production system which might make eating in restaurants, where one is ignorant of the sources and qualities of the raw ingredients, seem particularly risky. Finally, English food has not traditionally had a reputation for excellence, rather the contrary.

Mistrust or indifference towards food is not the only reason for having reservations about dining out. Studies of kitchens and restaurants document the way that waiting staff develop strategies for controlling, and sometimes embarrassing or shaming customers, which would suggest that some experiences of eating out must be personally distressing. Even in places which are normally pleasant, there must be some occasions when the food is poorly prepared, the dish selected uncongenial, the people at the neighbouring tables irritating, or the waiter or waitress in a bad mood. Finally, as the frequency of eating out increases and people

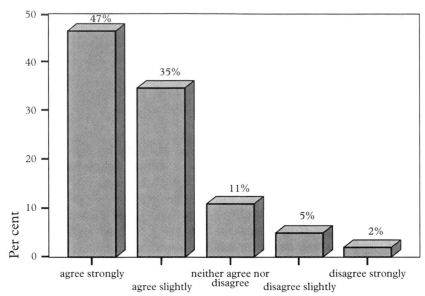

Responses to the statement 'I always enjoy myself when eating out'

8.1 Satisfaction derived from eating out

become more experienced, diners will have greater opportunities for comparison between different restaurants and different dishes, such that it might be predicted that their aspirations and expectations would rise and they would thus become more critical of individual meals.

In the light of all these potential drawbacks, one remarkable feature of the survey of English urban populations was the great sense of pleasure and satisfaction that people claim to derive from eating out. Respondents registered overwhelmingly high levels of satisfaction. As Figure 8.1 shows, 47 per cent of people agreed strongly with the proposition 'I *always* enjoy myself when I eat out', and a further 35 per cent registered agreement. Only 7 per cent disagreed. Moreover when asked 'How much did you enjoy the overall occasion when you *last* ate out?', 82 per cent said they liked it a lot and a further 14 per cent said they liked it a little (see Figure 8.2). We also asked about the extent to which people liked the various different elements of that meal experience. Again an overwhelming majority of respondents were very pleased with almost every aspect of the occasion. Aspects of sociability were the most likely to be pleasing, with over 95 per cent of people saying they liked the company and the conversation. But 94 per cent said they liked the food, 87 per cent the service, and the same proportion thought they had

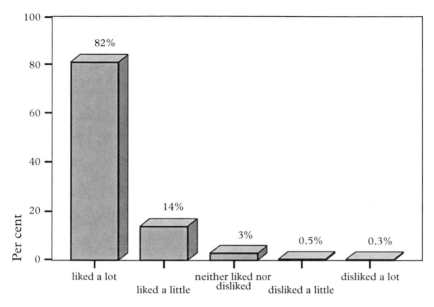

8.2  Overall rating of last eating out occasion

received value for money. The least appreciated feature was decor, but even then more than four out of five people said that they liked it (see Figure 8.3).

One of the outstanding findings of our study was the very high degree of satisfaction with eating out recorded by interviewees and respondents. Table 8.1 indicates answers to questions about how much various aspects of the last main meal eaten away from home were liked by respondents to the survey, distinguishing between those meals eaten on commercial premises and those in somebody else's home. People get maximum enjoyment from eating in someone else's home, though clearly the pleasures of restaurants are not far behind in terms of their capacity to deliver satisfactions. No-one at all disliked the company when eating in a domestic setting, and only two respondents in a public venue said that they disliked the company 'a little'. Similarly dissatisfaction with the conversation was minuscule. In every instance a larger proportion of people were likely to prefer the various elements of the experience in the domestic than in the restaurant setting. That this also stretches to the food is a point worth noting. There are slightly more failures to obtain a response from people eating in the houses of their friends and family. This may be sign of some reluctance to criticise aspects of meals which are gifts, though in some

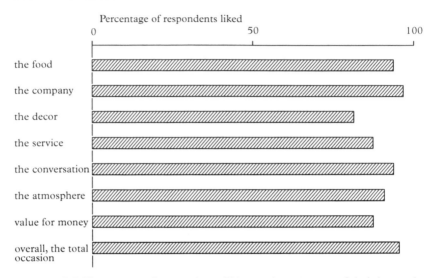

Percentage of respondents liked

8.3 Percentage of respondents liking various aspects of their last eating out experience

instances it may simply have seemed inappropriate to answer questions about, for instance, the quality of the service in a domestic setting.

It is possible that respondents operate with different standards of evaluation when judging a meal in a private as opposed to a commercial setting. But the evidence from the qualitative interviews suggests that this was probably not so; people commented in such a way as to note the differences between the two situations while still applying the same evaluative criteria. The difference in satisfaction with the atmosphere between commercial and domestic modes might perhaps indicate a continued preference for privacy, and some ambivalence about eating in public. The atmosphere in the home is created and supplied entirely by the host(ess) and selected guests, who will normally be expected to value each other's company. There can be no intrusion, or effect upon the proceedings by pure strangers. Of course all the guests need not know one another, but they may be assumed to have some basis for common conviviality such that there are strong social guarantees of their compatibility. At the same time, the lack of much registered distaste for commercial atmospheres suggests that diners are not much distressed by fellow customers nor by the trappings of the aura created by restaurant owners.

The commercial features of eating out receive least acclamation: there is less than overwhelming praise for the decor, the service and value for money. The difference in the proportion of superlative judgements is greatest between commercial and domestic locations with respect to

Table 8.1 *Satisfaction expressed with various aspects of the last meal eaten on commercial premises or in the home of another person (percentages by row)*

| | liked a lot | liked a little | neither liked nor disliked | disliked a little | disliked a lot | didn't know or no answer |
|---|---|---|---|---|---|---|
| | | | How much did you enjoy the food? | | | |
| commerical | 80 | 13 | 3 | 2 | 1 | – |
| domestic | 85 | 10 | 2 | – | 0 | 3 |
| | | | How much did you enjoy the company? | | | |
| commercial | 89 | 6 | 3 | – | 0 | 2 |
| domestic | 92 | 5 | 1 | 0 | 0 | 3 |
| | | | How much did you enjoy the decor? | | | |
| commercial | 56 | 24 | 15 | 2 | 1 | 1 |
| domestic | 68 | 16 | 10 | 1 | 1 | 4 |
| | | | How much did you enjoy the service? | | | |
| commercial | 65 | 22 | 6 | 4 | 2 | 1 |
| domestic | 78 | 8 | 7 | 0 | 0 | 7 |
| | | | How much did you enjoy the conversation? | | | |
| commercial | 80 | 14 | 4 | – | – | 2 |
| domestic | 86 | 9 | 2 | – | 0 | 3 |
| | | | How much did you enjoy the atmosphere? | | | |
| commercial | 72 | 18 | 6 | 2 | 1 | 1 |
| domestic | 89 | 6 | 2 | 1 | – | 3 |
| | | | How did the place rate as value for money? | | | |
| commercial | 67 | 17 | 6 | 5 | 2 | 4 |
| | | | How much did you enjoy, overall, the total occasion? | | | |
| commercial | 81 | 14 | 3 | 2 | – | 1 |
| domestic | 90 | 6 | 1 | 1 | 0 | 3 |

*Notes:*
– indicates less than 0.5 per cent, 0 means no response in the category.
Total number of meals (n) in commercial venue = 585, in domestic venue = 351.

decor, service and atmosphere. These are also the dimensions on which we get the largest number of absence of reply with respect to the domestic situation. This might seem to imply a liking of familiar domestic surroundings and continued ambivalence about the formality of being served, there presumably being limited ritual about service in many of the cases of domestic delivery.

Ultimately, it is unclear whether it is the domestic setting, or the fact of being a guest, which is the primary basis for these levels of satisfaction. When someone else paid in a restaurant (on 184 of the 585 reported last occasions), 85 per cent said that overall they liked the meal a lot, and a further 10 per cent said they liked it a little, so that 95 per cent recorded liking the occasion. When the respondent had paid (150 instances), 77 per cent reported having liked the meal a lot, and 94 per cent reported liking it either a lot or a little. When payment was shared, 83 per cent of respondents professed to liking the occasion a lot, and 96 per cent liked it to some degree. This suggests that being in receipt of a gift is best even in a restaurant, though without achieving the same level of enjoyment as in a private home. Sharing payment is almost the same. However, paying for oneself is likely to reduce the rapture, though even then this does not spoil the occasion much. However, it is obviously better to receive than to give!

The interviews give us a somewhat different, more nuanced under-standing of the nature of the satisfactions derived from eating out. People have differing orientations. Some people are very concerned about the quality of the food and decisions about where to eat out, and indeed whether to eat out, are determined on culinary criteria. Thus one interviewee said:

But it was very nice, you know it was lovely. It was like pillared, it was lovely. And always felt very nice, you now, they always have decorations on the food and they do all that business and it feels special, you feel that you are being pampered. The food is excellent. It's almost like your own excellent food at home and your dinner party, but without the work yourself. (Chris)

Others were more concerned that they experience variety, of types of food and environment, through eating out. It was less the quality of the food, more novelty or doing something for a change that was important. However, like our survey respondents, interviewees in Preston placed the joys of sociability at the head of their list of reasons for liking eating out. Convivial conversation was a primary source of enjoyment. Thus Meg, when asked what she liked about eating out, said: 'I mean there's twelve of us went once, and if you let them know how many's coming, we all sat round a big table and it was really good you know, talking and everything. It was really smashing, yeah.' Jane, while also commending the attractions of escaping domestic work, unsurprisingly another principal factor among female respondents, suggested that variety and company were principal reasons for liking to eat out:

Being waited on and being treated nicely, not having to keep going into the kitchen to, you know, prepare. The atmosphere, and company, and being able to choose from a varied menu. What else is there I enjoy in restaurants? That's it. The company, atmosphere, different kinds of food that you wouldn't make at home, having the choice, being waited on, all those things.

Although there was general enjoyment of eating out there were some perceptible differences between responses to eating in commercial and domestic circumstances.

### Are customers really satisfied?: a methodological interlude

There are three potentially serious objections to using the data advanced in the previous section as a basis for exploring issues of pleasure and enjoyment. The first, explicit in Finkelstein's (1989) account, is that expressions of enjoyment about eating out should never be taken at face value. The second is that the findings are an artefact of the measurement device, of ambiguous questions or of the use of inappropriate or unreliable quantitative techniques to determine people's attitudes. The third objection is that since people are not forced or obliged to eat in restaurants they would automatically say that they enjoyed doing so.

Counter-intuitively, Finkelstein, in *Dining Out*, claims that 'the practice of dining out is . . . a rich source of incivility' (1989:5). Her central thesis is that restaurants are organised in such a way that dining out does not require the 'engagement' of customers in the creation of their own environment of sociality. Thus the decor, service and atmosphere are designed in such a way as to relieve us of the 'responsibility to shape sociality', and this 'weakens our participation in the social arena' (5). Finkelstein challenges the authenticity of the feelings of pleasure reported by people as arising from eating out. She discredits lay perceptions of the experience:

Although over the years, from conversations and interviews with dozens of regular diners . . . I have collected data on why people dine out, and the pleasures they derive, this data has always had a limited use. In answer to my question of why dine out, the answers were repeatedly that it was fun, a convenience, a habit, an entertainment, a pleasure. In answer to any suggestion to the contrary, with reminders of meals when the food was of poor quality or overpriced, when the waiter was instrusive or the restaurant too noisy, my respondents most often excused these as being rare, circumstantial, and unfortunate. It was not admitted that such discomforts may indeed be integral to dining out and so should always be expected . . . a consideration of why individuals displayed such limited analytic insight into their own conduct suggested, in hindsight, that the process somehow thwarted scrutiny. (19–20)

So, Finkelstein maintains that people go to the place with the ambience appropriate to their purpose, behave in accordance with its associated conventions and hence derive guaranteed, if superficial, satisfaction. There is some truth to this; as we will suggest, dining out requires a form of social arrangement whereby diners must behave in ways which will not detract from each other's enjoyment, which entails that people will, wherever possible, seek an atmosphere which is mutually pleasing. The restaurant plays a part in providing an appropriate background. But this is not a sufficient explanation of high levels of satisfaction. Finkelstein's explanation overlooks the fact that places have different meanings for different people; what promises to achieve a particular effect varies between people. Her position also leads to a dismissive, or certainly a non-inquisitive, attitude towards pleasure. Thus she lists some of the reasons why people say they eat out and proceeds to dismiss them as imaginary or illusory, rather than to interrogate the responses (see further Martens and Warde, 1997). By better understanding the remarkable level of satisfaction achieved from eating out we might both identify and categorise different types or sources of pleasure and further elucidate the social and cultural significance of the expansion of the practice of eating out.

It is always possible that any statistical finding is misleading or meaningless because it is an artefact of the measurement device employed. Many sociologists have contested the appropriateness and reliability of the use of quantitative survey techniques to establish attitudes. It might be objected that 'I always enjoy myself when I eat out' is an ambiguous proposition about which to ask for a response. One basis for ambiguity might be the term 'enjoy'. Perhaps our respondents are unable to estimate accurately the gratification derived. However, psychological investigations suggest that people probably have quite sound grounds for estimating what makes them happy and that they can answer sensibly and meaningfully on such topics (Lane, 1991: 435–6). They are therefore likely to know whether or not they usually derive gratification from eating out, etc. Alternatively, perhaps our respondents are prepared to use the term to describe low levels of gratification. Since it is one of our contentions that the vocabulary of pleasure is imprecise it would be foolish to dismiss this possibility out of hand. Nevertheless, to say that one enjoyed something is usually to confer moderately strong praise, implying more than that it was found adequate or merely routinely satisfactory. We can be reasonably confident that any positive answer to the question would imply at least a moderate degree of gratification. Whether respondents took full account of the presence of the term 'always' is intuitively less likely. Since the available responses, part of the battery of opinion questions, were in terms of strength of agreement or disagreement with a statement ('agree strongly', 'agree slightly', etc.), ambiguity could arise regarding what was meant by the 35 per cent of respondents who agreed 'slightly' with a proposition including the term 'always'. Perhaps it would mean that they usually, or more often than not, enjoyed themselves. That would indeed diminish the apparently dramatic level of enjoyment, but would still leave eating out as a very strongly recommended activity.

We cannot hope to convince those who deny that quantitative techniques are ever valid. Indeed, their objections might be partially sustained by the evidence from the qualitative interviews where, when pressed, many indicated some reservations and qualifications about eating out. However, analysis of discussion of complaint does not give sufficient grounds for rejecting the claim that people do overwhelmingly enjoy themselves when eating out.

The dominant legitimating ideology about consumer markets probably predisposes people to vouch that they like what they have selected. People will tend to affirm the wisdom and appropriateness of their purchases, to say that they like what they receive because they chose it. Disliking what has been freely chosen may imply foolishness, carelessness, lack of foresight, culpable ignorance or profligacy. Poor choices often require an excuse. There are reasons why people might express commitment to their decisions about how they have spent their income and passed their time. People may feel a responsibility for their decisions. However, this does not prevent them from critically evaluating the experience of eating out. The ideological effect is not a blanket one. Our qualitative interviews demonstrated that having chosen a restaurant or a dish does not preclude conscious dissatisfaction. Contrary to Finkelstein's view, customers do complain and, apparently more often, contemplate complaint.

Hirschman (1970) summarised three generalised responses for dealing with the experience of belonging to a declining organisation – exit, voice and loyalty. This typology has been adapted to apply to many situations of dissatisfaction, including that of the disgruntled consumer. One of the virtues of the market is said to be that it offers painless exit from situations which are unsatisfactory; deciding never to return to a restaurant is one response to an unsatisfactory meal. Alternatively, the customer might complain in the hope of having a grievance remedied, sometimes anticipating a future visit, at other times merely to secure a sense of adequate restitution. Finally, for a variety of reasons, diners might feel dissatisfied but suffer in silence even while expecting to return on a future occasion. The alternatives are indicated Table 8.2. Evidence of each was reported, demonstrating the complexity of the reasoning surrounding these abstract alternatives.

People claim overwhelmingly to be prepared to complain if an unsatisfactory meal is delivered (see Table 8.3), implying that lack of satisfaction would be disclosed explicitly. If that were so, absence of complaint might confirm high levels of contentment.

People do complain. Our interviewees had complained about

Table 8.2 *Alternative strategies for diners in the face of dissatisfaction*

|                 | Complain       | Feel discontented |
| --------------- | -------------- | ----------------- |
| Probable return | Voice          | Loyalty           |
| Never return    | Voice and exit | Exit              |

Table 8.3 *Percentage of respondents who would complain if served an unsatisfactory meal in a restaurant*[a]

| Agree strongly | Agree slightly | Neither agree nor disagree | Disagree slightly | Disagree strongly | Don't know/ not answered |
| -------------- | -------------- | -------------------------- | ----------------- | ----------------- | ------------------------ |
| 60             | 24             | 6                          | 5                 | 3                 | 2                        |

*Notes:*
N = 1001
[a] Responses to the statement, 'If I was served an unsatisfactory meal I would complain.'

unhygienic behaviour by staff, contaminated food, the temperature of the room, staff clearing up and preparing to close before they, the customers, were ready to leave, poor quality of foodstuffs, undercooked food (particularly bloody steaks), food served at the wrong temperature and failure to deliver dishes simultaneously to all diners at the table. In addition, some instances were reported where interviewees explicitly regretted not having complained. So, for example, Sheila told us, 'I really should have said, "don't sweep while I am eating my pizza, if you don't mind" ' and Liz said of a visit to a very prestigious regional restaurant 'the melon was musty and I said something to my brother, and sort of as head of the party he should really have said [some]thing, but I let that go'. Customers are aware that they have rights, even obligations, as consumers to complain that failure to receive anticipated standards of service is grounds for dissatisfaction. Complaint is a necessary part of a consumer culture and there is evidence of a sense of both the right and the obligation to complain.

Very few interviewees suggested that they would never complain, though some (also a few) asserted that they had never had cause. When asked to recall defective aspects that Finkelstein would consider significant, they may decline to, as was the case with Jane.

INTERVIEWER: Do you remember an occasion when you were served bad food?
JANE: No not really. I think we've been quite lucky really. I can't remember.

Yet, even though Jane could not remember negative experiences herself, the mention of 'lucky' by her might suggest that she was aware that others, friends or family with whom she discussed these matters, did have negative experiences.

On a number of occasions interviewees gave reasons for refraining from complaining, for suffering in silence when they might have, or even felt that they ought to have, protested. Some feared that it might be painful or costly to complain. One reason, which might be described as the kitchen's revenge, was anticipation of retaliation. There was an awareness that if food were sent back the kitchen staff had an opportunity for defiling the food. Thus John said, 'I have sent things back, but I'm very wary of sending things back . . . something would have to be fairly offensive for me to send it back on the basis that you do hear horror stories, and things do happen where they say right fine so "let's put a little bit of cigarette ash in it".' Spittle and insects were the other examples offered.

Most were clear that foreign matter in the dish required complaint. Scepticism about whether, even in such circumstances, complaint would result in redress was, however, another reason for silence. Thus, Rose reported an incident: 'There was a very large screw in the middle [of a plate of garlic mushrooms], and [we] brought the waiter over and said "There's a screw in here" and he said "Oh, that will be off the pan in the kitchen, thanks", picked up this thing and that was that.'

In some instances there can be no effective practical form of redress; for instance when meals fail to arrive at the same time, the most unacceptable form of service mistake, the error cannot be rectified. However, there would be a possibility of financial compensation. Significantly no-one reported having refused to pay for a meal or dish, and no-one reported having been excused payment for something that they considered unacceptable.

Some occasions entailed that one person, by virtue of their role within a particular party, had the right of complaint but if they did not exercise that prerogative it would be impertinent for anyone else to. This seemed to be the case when Liz (above) attributed this responsibility to the head of the party. The role was also attributed to the person who had chosen the venue; only if they complained, or commented adversely, was it acceptable for other companions to offer a negative judgement. The converse of this was a sense of responsibility felt by the person for recommending or choosing a place to go with friends or family: it was probably because she had recommended the pizza house that Sheila was prompted to make a written complaint.

Sometimes people might be disturbed but consider that the offence was one to be anticipated when eating out. Thus Sheila, who dislikes people smoking at adjacent tables, said, when asked about general dislikes, 'You know there's a good chance of it going to happen, it's no good making a big fuss about it, you just end up with indigestion.' Interviewees also made reference to mitigating circumstances, as with a hotel proprietor who was suffering from a terminal illness which meant that the establishment was struggling: Liz said about 'The worst food I've ever eaten in the whole of my life, I think', 'Had he not been ill I would probably have complained more strongly about it.' A further form of reasoning that precluded vociferous complaint concerned who was actually responsible for, say, an unacceptable dish. 'I wouldn't make a fuss but I just say well I'm not eating that . . . It's the poor waiters that you've to complain to isn't it . . . Not their fault is it?' (Jean).

Finally, it was calculated whether, in total context, complaint was justified. So one interviewee (Sheila) said that she went regularly to a place where the vegetables were poor but since everything else was very good there was no ground for dissatisfaction. There were many borderline cases between justified and unjustified complaint. These tended to be apparent where people declared themselves dissatisfied or discontented with some aspects of the occasion but did not think that overall overt complaint to the management was merited. This tended to lead to retrospective grumbling about a meal. So people grumbled about the price, a poor version of a tandoori dish, a presentation 'where there's no finesse', but without regarding these as grounds for formal complaint. Such criticisms were frequently accompanied by an observation that the meal had been enjoyed for other reasons. One instance was generalised upon by Katrine: [1]

just sometimes if the meat is not cooked enough or the steak or something. We found one . . . we had peppered steak, all of us complained that the steak was tough. But that was, you only talk about it afterwards, you know, like on the way home, so that's it, we talk about it. Nobody complained to the management or anything. I think it's 'cos we enjoyed ourselves.

Many respondents were willing to excuse the failings of establishments. Most striking was Janice's report of a 'bar-type' lunch where the food 'was

---

[1] Katrine was a woman who did report two occasions when she had made complaints, though the memories seemed difficult to recall – an undercooked steak and the staff forgetting to bring food for two people in the party.

so salty I couldn't eat it', 'some had finished their meal before the others were served' and where they had had to listen to a faulty jukebox for fifteen minutes.

INTERVIEWER: Altogether a few hiccups?

JANICE: Yeah, yeah, but I mean because of there being a group of us we weren't that concerned really, I mean we quite enjoyed the meal on the whole.

INTERVIEWER: What? Mainly because of your companionship, your friends being there?

JANICE: Yeah, yeah.

Christine, an interviewee in Preston interested in food, recounted an occasion when the food at a restaurant was disappointing. Having said that she would never go back, she was asked whether her dissatisfaction was discussed at the time. She replied, 'Well not at the time because we were, you know, having a nice family outing and so we were talking about various other things . . . But afterwards I said to Norman "That wasn't really good was it?" So that was a discussion between him and me afterwards.' Reluctance to complain was not a result of failing to observe a deficiency, nor indeed because she would never complain, but because it might spoil things for other people and make the event seem less congenial than it otherwise might. Although many people were concerned with the quality of the food, they were prepared to overlook it because maintaining an atmosphere of companionship and mutual enjoyment was even more important.

Forms of complaining behaviour included sending a dish back, writing a letter afterwards, bringing an unsatisfactory situation to the attention of the staff and declaring never to return. The tone of complaint was clearly a matter which interviewees gave thought to. So, one interestingly apologetic style of complaint related to a dirty glass table-top in a café:

'the glass was really smeary, and you know I couldn't [eat off it], I had to ask him to wipe it down, you know, to polish it because it just, I couldn't face eating off it, you know. So I said 'I'm not being funny but I'll do it myself. Give us your cloth' . . . and when he'd shined it up he says 'is that alright now?' And I said 'yes, that's alright'. (Sheila)

Others considered just how much 'fuss' should be made about a defective meal or performance. There is some reluctance to 'make a fuss'. Jean presented herself, somewhat ambiguously, as a vigilant consumer. Asked about a hypothetical situation where a table was not available she said, 'I'd tell them I would. I'd go mad. I wouldn't sit there and suffer in silence like some people do. Not me, no', and 'if I'd had something that's horrible I would complain'. As she explained, 'you are paying for something you expect it to be right, don't you'. But nevertheless she also maintained that she 'wouldn't make a fuss but I would ask them, say this is not right you know. I mean it's very rare that you ever get that . . . most places it's all right. I tend to go out, we go for a meal where we know it's all right.'

However, the principal form of complaint is a declaration like 'so I don't think we'll go back there again'. A statement of this kind was made by the majority of the interviewees with whom the theme of dissatisfaction was discussed.[2]

People might expect to find themselves in an uncongenial restaurant sometimes, although it would appear from our survey data that people do insulate themselves from this possibility by revisiting the same restaurants. In response to questions about the last eating out experience, 62 per cent said that they had been to that same venue before. Among these over 99 per cent said they enjoyed themselves overall. 84 per cent of respondents said they would be likely to return again to the venue they had last visited. Again, this is likely to be a very substantial proportion of those for whom it will be practically possible to return, given that some meals will be taken of necessity miles away from home. One of the strongest guarantees of satisfaction is, indeed, returning to a place which is familiar, and most of the accounts of poor meals were in unfamiliar places, especially on holiday, but also on occasions when the planned destination of an outing was for some reason closed or full.

From our qualitative evidence we conclude that although interviewees were prepared to, and sometimes did, complain, the number of complaints were few. The overall impression was that the benefits greatly outweighed the costs, that people's initial and predominant reaction was one of pleasure, that the expressed reservations were few and varied from person to person. Our interviewees were basically very content with eating out. Asked what they disliked about eating out some would say nothing despite quite extensive probing. An example of a generally satisfied customer was Jenny, who said 'we've never really had a bad meal', and after much probing declared, 'we haven't been anywhere where we've had to send anything back or we've been disappointed'. It took some people quite a long time to recall occasions when they had complained. On reflection they sometimes dredged up stories about situations where complaint had occurred or would have been justified.[3] At least as often as they lodged complaints, interviewees could remember grumbling, either at the table, or more often afterwards. The image of Britons as reluctant to complain may thus be justified, though those most familiar with restaurants were more likely to complain (see chapter 3 on

---

[2] Katrine, Chris, Sheila, Liz, Rose, Jenny, Trisha, Janice; eight out of thirteen.

[3] Thus, Jenny did recall both being given a cramped table on one anniversary and poor service on another occasion which decided her not to go back.

'experienced consumers'). This suggests that it is relatively easy for restaurateurs to keep customers satisfied, but also that many dissatisfactions
go unreported. We might also note that when asked what they disliked
about eating out, events involving private hospitality were never cited,
even though such occasions were prominent in the interviews.

The qualitative interviews revealed evidence of critical reflection on
dining out (see Martens and Warde, 1997). The adequacy of meal experiences were the subject of conversation and judgement. Nevertheless there
was an interesting discrepancy between the evidence from the survey,
which suggested a willingness to complain, and that of the interviews,
where there were many situational reasons for forbearing to do so. The
number of formal complaints to the establishment were few. However,
rarely were the criticisms, even in situations where something went
grossly wrong, sufficient to lead interviewees to deny that they enjoyed
the occasion. So, even though the qualitative interviews provided evidence of more dissatisfaction, particularly under prompting, several
interviewees categorically answered 'No' to the question 'are there any
things you dislike about eating out'.
  Hence, we are inclined to dismiss the potential objection that the
findings to be explained are spurious and we assume instead that people
really do enjoy eating out. If there are firm grounds for enjoyment in this
particular domain of consumption it is worth trying to account for its
attractiveness in terms of different dimensions of modern capacities for
gratification. So, in conclusion, we agree with Finkelstein that people are
extraordinarily satisfied with their experiences in restaurants. However,
we disagree with her interpretation of the condition. Enjoyment has its
roots in processes other than misperception or manipulation. People are
discerning, can be critical and do complain on occasion. Reluctance to
complain, of which there is evidence, is a consequence of a number of
considerations. One is the ease of exit; the simplest and least taxing means
of criticising any establishment is the avowal never to return. That many
people go back to places where they have previously had good experiences is one sound reason for high and genuine levels of satisfaction.
What remains remarkable is that even in situations which were recognised
as being unsatisfactory in key respects, people mostly recorded a positive
judgement on the event as a whole. A second important consideration is
that the maintenance of an agreeable atmosphere among companions is a
more important consideration than enforcing exacting standards of
service within the establishment. This suggests that dining out does
involve mutual engagement and a commitment to sociability. No doubt
restaurant regimes have an impact and an influence; there are different

sorts of regime and the more experienced and enthusiastic diners use them for their own purposes, relying upon a tacit understanding that most customers will comport themselves in a manner appropriate to the context. The conventional behaviour of the restaurant is as much enabling for the customer as it is convenient for the restaurateur.

### Gratification and the definition of eating out

The reliability of the gratification derived from eating out is in part a result of the shared understanding of the term. Whereas Finkelstein took the meaning of the term for granted, we asked people what they meant by eating out. Given their understanding of the activity (see chapter 3), it would be surprising if the expectation was not one of potential pleasure. If someone makes a special journey, invests discretionary income in order to eat a substantial meal, on a special occasion, without requiring personal toil and in company, then he or she might anticipate physical and emotional gratification. The lay definition may colour our respondents' reactions to questions about the gratifications derived from meals eaten on commercial premises.

They expect to enjoy themselves; that is what eating out is and unless something very disturbing occurs they will declare themselves content. Nevertheless it would be unwise simply to assume that this is evidence of some verbal trick. We should not assume that people are so inured by the equation of eating out with enjoyment that they will always feel gratified by such an event. Our data suggest justifiable anticipation. Regarding eating out on commercial premises, there is a strong correlation between people saying that they always enjoy themselves and their liking the last occasion. It is, therefore, worth exploring whether there are substantial foundations to their overwhelming tendency to be pleased. The positively valued elements in the definition of 'eating out' throw considerable light on different dimensions of gratification that can arise from final consumption. The reasons why these component elements of eating out combine to a definition of a pleasurable event give grounds for understanding some of the principal dimensions upon which other consumption activities may be deemed enjoyable.

### Towards a systematic vocabulary of gratification: a theoretical interlude

Philosophical debate about the origins of happiness, and whether some gratifications can be deemed more valuable than others, runs back into classical antiquity. We cannot hope to resolve it here. Nevertheless, consideration of the various types and sources of gratification involved in eating out suggests that a systematic framework of concepts might be developed for sociological purposes. This would be useful because the gratifications associated with consumption can only be evaluated intelligently in the light of others arising from different sources.

There are many terms in use to describe gratifying experiences, and the key sociological point is that there is, always has been and probably always will be a struggle over the definition of what should count as satisfaction, pleasure and happiness, and how best to achieve them. The establishment of a conceptual hierarchy often serves as an instrument of power and preferment for particular, usually elite, groups. Consequently, an appropriate sociological response is to examine the history of such terms, and to investigate who values contemplation over sensuality, immediate over deferred gratification or sight over touch.

Sketchily, it seems that notions of satisfaction and happiness develop differently in different academic disciplines. Many disciplines, from biology to theology, recognise bodily pleasures, though the merits of indulging them are often disputed. Philosophers have concentrated on the gratifications arising from contemplation, on mental activity, on aesthetic appreciation, on ethical bases of happiness and on the sense in which to be happy involves deserving to be happy. Economists have been concerned with how to be happy most efficiently, examining the application of instrumental and calculative reasoning to the practical objective of gaining a degree of satisfaction. Psychologists, having actually asked people what gives them satisfaction and what makes them feel good, have identified the realms of activity which people report to have given them the greatest happiness. It transpires that work – because it develops people's skills, gives them a sense of self-control and gives a sense of achievement – is one principal source; the other is personal relationships. What remains for sociology to add is a better understanding of the gratification that arises from especially those social relationships that involve active participation and mutuality.

In such a light, consider the various positive appeals of the activity of eating out in terms of the categories of pleasure and happiness. There are many different sorts of pleasures or satisfactions that may arise. Traditional sensual pleasures might be derived from aspects of the experience. The expectation that eating out delivers a substantial meal is a basis for undergoing the physical transformation from discomfort to comfort that Hirschman (1982) identifies as a reliable and regular source of pleasure. The absence of toil is another, universal, feature of eating out which is also a predictable basis for gratification. This is not to say that work is never gratifying; far from it. But release from routine practical activity and the social responsibility for preparing food, when welcome, is another likely source of gratification. On this topic, a multiple linear regression analysis of responses to the question 'would you like to eat out more often?' found significantly more affirmative replies among women. The economic exchange component, whereby the customer buys service, is a source of satisfaction as is the potential opportunity to try new food. Most restaurants will offer some opportunity for experimentation in food consumption, whether this amounts to offering ingredients or dishes previously unknown to the customer, elaborate presentation that would be absent from daily domestic meals, or merely the variety of flavour and texture that arises from the techniques of a different cook. Reflection on such matters may give rise to complex cognitive comparison and evaluation of the merits of particular foods or venues. Relaxed interaction and conversation with friendly companions is an opportunity furnished by eating out. That this occurs as a special occasion, especially when there is cause for celebration, is likely to heighten the degree of pleasure obtained. The range of gratifications is thus considerable and it is perhaps unsurprising that on balance most meals are at least satisfactory. If the food is considered expensive and the service poor, one may be compensated by the company and by no longer being hungry. The worst-case scenario, where the food is inedible and the company unbearable, is likely to occur very infrequently.

We seek therefore to develop a formalised schema distinguishing types of gratification. Probably none of the disciplines are mistaken in believing that people are pleased by the activities and reflections described. More likely, disciplines may be inclined to exaggerate the importance of those activities which are most central to their concerns. Schematically we might say that there are four realms of gratification, the sensual, the instrumental, the contemplative and the social. The first includes those bodily pleasures which Campbell (1987) associates with traditional hedonism, and which Hirschman (1982) finds superior to the satisfactions provided by consumer durables on the grounds that they regularly and reliably transport people from a feeling of discomfort to one of comfort. The second is the world of achievement, of putting means to valued ends, of securing survival, of honing skills, or securing material advancement and occupational promotion and of making successful presentations of self. The craze for self-improvement that has been said to be a key part of contemporary consumer culture is, in part, instrumental, though it uses expressive means for the successful presentation of self and communication of self-identity. Contemplative gratifications subsume experiences like simple distraction, dreaming and fantasy, aesthetic appreciation, intellectual reflection, religious ecstasy, all of which offer

Table 8.4 *Gratification: a typology*

|  | Types of gratification | | | |
|---|---|---|---|---|
|  | Sensual | Instrumental | Contemplative | Social |
| Low intensity | Pleasure | Satisfaction | Entertainment | Participation |
| High intensity | Joy | Achievement | Appreciation | Mutuality |

some rewards. Finally, there are social pleasures, of which the paradigm case is probably conversation, but which encompass participation, sympathy and trust, and of which companionship is, for the present purpose, a very important instance. These four categories of abstract forms of gratification subsume respectively a number of typical differentiated and recognisable sources of experiences of subjective well-being (see Table 8.4).

This categorisation should be read as one which is sociologically useful rather than in some sense absolutely valid or mandatory. There could no doubt be other formulations which might fit better other purposes. The claim here is that these distinguish between different types of gratification which might result from engagement in particular practices. The different levels of intensity are ones which correspond to everyday sensations and reflections upon experience. The same activity sometimes delivers higher, sometimes a lower degree of gratification. For any individual, some activities reliably deliver the more intense gratifications, which others never will. In respect of which appeal most, we might expect differences between individuals, though we might also expect these to be socially sorted and historically transformable. Attempts have often been made by different social classes, groups, institutions and agencies to establish some form of hierarchy among these gratifications, often in a self-serving way. Those involved in the culture industry – artists, television producers, critics, arbiters of taste, et al. – have an interest in persuading us that the values of the imagination are more rewarding than those of the accumulation of capital, say, since this would confer greater esteem and practical influence upon them. If there is a trend towards the aestheticisation of everyday life, then that is a process which will serve their interests particularly well. As Bourdieu would have observed, this is part of the strategy of one social group to legitimise the culture that is distinctively theirs. The role of the cultural intermediaries is also one of determining which practices or items within any particular kind of activity are likely to give the most intense gratification. When a writer of a restaurant column evaluates a meal at a particular establishment he or she is precisely trying to transmit a sense of the degree of enjoyment which a reader might obtain from eating there. Some restaurants do offer food worthy of contemplation, many probably do not.

It might be observed that to suggest the existence of different levels of intensity does not intrude on the much more highly contested question of whether there is some objective hierarchy of activities which will for all people, or should for all people of sound mind, good taste and social competence, deliver more rarefied joys. While we consider that the defenders of popular culture against apparently elitist positions like that of Adorno have probably overstated their case, we are not here proposing that poetry is in any way better than pushpin in its capacity to extend human happiness. Rather we would want to observe that: there are different types of gratification; that these arrive with differing degrees of intensity; that people are currently at liberty to pursue them in different combinations; that anyone might try to maximise one of them and express little concern for the others; that it is likely that different groups of people will exhibit different priorities in this regard; that different societal value-systems, particularly at different stages of historical development, are likely to rank some above others; that there is some scholarly value in identifying such changes; and that even within an individual's lifetime there may be a process of abandoning some in favour of others. This is a notion which is explicit, but unformalised in the work of Hirschman, whose argument in *Shifting Involvements* (1982) is particularly thought-provoking in this regard.

Hirschman developed an intriguing argument about the limits of mass consumption. He maintained that some forms of consumption were inexhaustibly pleasing: these were mostly the same items that Campbell (1987: 69) identified as traditional pleasures. These pleasures were contrasted primarily with the pleasure derived from such manufactured objects as white goods (e.g. refrigerators) and automobiles, which gave only a temporary sense of 'satisfaction'; a refrigerator, even if proving pleasing when first delivered, soon becomes taken for granted and thereafter, while useful and convenient, is neither stimulating nor humanly rewarding. He surmised that therefore the appeal of consumer durables had an inherent tendency to diminish. Those disillusioned by their accumulated purchases would, he argued, turn again to political mobilisation, because the associated social involvements provided some intrinsic sources of gratification. Bored with possessions, the affluent consumer would rediscover the positive attractions of company and personal interaction associated with participation in a collective endeavour. However, recognising that political movements and organisations also had tendencies which alienated members, he admitted the possibility of return to the private pursuit of possessions offering, finally, a cyclical model.

Hirschman's conjecture has its limitations. In the face of a seemingly inexhaustible demand for new consumer durables the basic projection is empirically suspect. There is no evidence to suggest that even the more affluent members of the richest societies conclude that they would be better devoting their attention to public participation or 'obituary-enhancing' activities rather than accumulating possessions. The poorer and younger members of such societies are less likely to favour such a refocusing of their motivations. Second, the argument revolves around attitudes towards the most inert of objects, white goods. However, other items which convey a certain level of glamour, like cars and fashionable clothes, and those which may be used for purposes of self-development, like musical instruments, sports equipment or books, have much greater potential for attracting extended concentration. Yet increasingly it is services, often in the form of events, which consumers covet. These are characterised not by a passivity in relation to an inert object, but themselves involve active participation. Arguably it is the event-like character of eating out that makes it especially appealing. Thus, Hirschman engages in a comparison most favourable to his argument, between durables, pleasure and participation. His concentration on only three potential types of gratifications – satisfaction, pleasure and (only one particular form of) participation makes for a very partial case.

Nevertheless, Hirschman gives a striking formulation of the fundamental insight that there are different spheres of gratification, that individuals and groups might shift their involvements over time, that the opportunity for meaningful social interaction is a basic good in limited supply which is mostly only acquired through ventures into the public arena.

### Elements of enjoyment

It is readily apparent that eating out, in its ideal and its actual form, has much potential for being enjoyable. It is always likely to be a source of pleasure and of social involvement, since all get fed and very few people eat out alone. It will usually be a source of entertainment, always one of satisfaction in the sense that the diner will be the recipient of the fruits of someone else's labour, and it will often in addition be considered fair exchange, as reasonable value for money. Moreover, it may provide a source for contemplative gratifications of aesthetic appreciation, and also in some instances be a source of esteem in social circles where familiarity with excellent restaurants, varied culinary knowledge and experience, or novel gastronomic events are valued. To a much lesser extent eating out might symbolise personal accomplishment either because it signifies having sufficient discretionary income or because social esteem bestows personal esteem.

The attractions of eating out are perhaps best emphasised through comparison with other fields of consumer activity. Compared with eating alone at home, or buying groceries, eating out offers a more varied range of gratifications. It compares well with passive collective entertainments and with the acquisition of a new washing machine. However, and intriguingly, eating out on commercial premises compares less favourably, though only marginally, with eating at someone else's home.

In chapter 9 we apply the schema in more detail.

# 9 The enjoyment of meal events

In the qualitative interviews several opportunities were offered for people to evaluate the experience of eating out, affording some illustration of the applicability of this schematic classification of pleasures to the language of our interviewees. The invitation to describe the last three occasions of eating a meal out was supplemented by direct questioning, sometimes insistent, about what they liked and disliked about eating out in general – what kinds of places and foods they preferred or would always avoid. Thus much opportunity was afforded for people to discuss their tastes, their reservations and the nature of the gratifications derived. The terms that were used most frequently to describe experiences were substantively without content: people would tend to say of the various elements of the meal event that it was 'nice', 'really nice', 'very nice', 'good', 'enjoyable', 'lovely', 'fabulous' or 'I loved it', 'I liked it'. The vocabulary deployed to describe pleasures was restricted. It was, however, clear that interviewees had a practical sense that there were different types of gratification, some of which appealed more than others to different individuals. We have already indicated (in chapter 3) some of the reasons people gave for eating out and from further analysis of their talk about those reasons, we can infer the nature and relative importance to them of the different types of gratification which combine to make eating out a generally positive experience.

## Sensuality: pleasure and joy

### Pleasure

Sensual pleasures might be obtained from eating out in a number of different fashions. Interviewees made reference to bodily pleasures derived from sitting in comfort, relaxing after a hard day's work and the mild intoxication of alcohol taken before or during eating. However, most specific references to aspects of sensuality and embodiment related to food and eating.

The sensual aspects of eating proved resistant to verbal articulation. A couple of interviewees responded to the question of why they liked to eat out in terms of appetite: 'Cos we're hungry' (Sheila); 'because we enjoy eating' (Peter). Occasionally people mentioned the constraints of travelling which entailed responding to a bodily need for food: 'If you can't get home you have something out. That's if hunger calls or something like that' (David). However, in most cases this was not a principal reason; eating out was not usually necessary. Some people said that they ensured that they were hungry when they went out to eat by consuming less food than normal at meals earlier in the day or intended to eat less subsequently.

Most were explicitly concerned that they should consume an appropriate amount of food when eating out. What was appropriate varied, of course, between individuals. There was general condemnation of the circumstances in which customers were given too little to eat. Sheila used *nouvelle cuisine*, 'where there's one little thing in a little bit of sauce over here on a big plate', to symbolise inadequate portion size and asserted that 'I'd be a bit disappointed with that.' Men in particular were likely to assert that it was important that a meal offer plentiful food, whereas women, and particularly middle-class women, were likely to disagree. Nevertheless, to be left hungry after having paid for dinner was considered highly unacceptable. This was often expressed in terms of value for money, a criterion which mostly referred to quantity rather than quality of food. A typical comment, from Rose, was:

I don't want to leave the restaurant when I've paid for a meal I feel like I need to go to the fish and chip shop. But it wouldn't be one of my priorities. I like value for money, not necessarily a plate full piled high with chips. But if I ordered a meal I'd expect to have value for money. There'd be enough there so that I would feel like I have eaten something like a meal.

Even more poignant was Trisha's, for whom insufficient food was the only thing she disliked about eating out:

I mean I'm not a greedy person but sometimes they don't give you enough for you know, you're like sat there and it comes over and there's not very much on your plate and at the end of it you're not full and you think, oh I've just spent that money on that and I'm not full and I'm quite disappointed really.

Most reflection on sufficiency came embroidered with the normal ambivalences of a society wherein people are highly conscious of diet and body shape. Interviewees as a group made as many statements expressing reservations about indulgence as about pleasure in satiation. Inhibiting notions of greed and gluttony were never far from the surface. Sheila said 'I must admit I am greedy'; Meg said she tended to 'make a pig of meself when I go out'. As in the survey responses, a significant number of people said they tended to eat more than usual and more than was desirable when eating out. However, since eating out was a special event for almost everyone, it was felt to be acceptable. Concerns with weight reduction, and indeed with eating healthily, were often suspended on such occasions. Coping with the potential guilt involved compensation on other occasions. So Trisha, who had joined Weight Watchers a few months earlier, said:

you spend the week like dieting or cutting back on savoury and sweet things and you know at the weekend you just like have one night where you think, oh yes I'll have [what I want and] cut back the rest of the week sort of thing. I'd rather have one really nice meal and diet for the rest of the week.

What in one light might be the failure of the restaurant to serve enough food easily turns into lightly veiled criticism of excessive appetite. Thus Peter's behaviour after his last meal out with a group of friends in the [Merchants] Shopkeepers had been a bit of a joke. Peter had eaten a three-course meal (like the others), but afterwards, when they were back at home, had eaten a bag of crisps. This, according to Sally, had 'horrified' their friends. Peter had to explain apologetically,

it's not that you were overfaced with the food, but I can manage a bit more. Well perhaps that's not strictly true. I think, I do mean plentiful, but in the case of the Shopkeepers I tend to come away feeling quite full and satisWed, but often it's early on, but later on the same evening I can feel hungry again. Maybe the food doesn't contain enough Wbre or something.

Others expressed dislike for being given too much food. Attributing an unwillingness to leave food on the plate to early childhood training, several people claimed often to eat too much almost against their will or better judgement, and did not like being 'overfaced'. Thus discussion was at least as much about delimiting, constraining and controlling appetite.

The most expressive, and almost the only, description of food consumption as intrinsically pleasurable came, both as a joke and an afterthought, from Steve, who explained why he had visited a Manchester restaurant: 'a very fashionable place to hang out, and she likes going to fashionable places my girlfriend, so pleasing her . . . and pleasing my stomach as well'. Nevertheless delicatessen specialities and cream cakes were the reason why Sally ate regularly in one café and anticipation of a three-course meal was an explicit reason why Smina preferred restaurants to other venues.

We do not think that this comparative inarticulacy implies that the sensations associated with the eating of food are unimportant. Comments on feelings of (in)sufficiency do refer to the feeling of comfort that arises from appetite having been satisfied. People presume that any adequate meal event would entail receiving sufficient food to deliver the sense of comfort that Hirschman identified as giving endlessly repeatable episodes of gratification through consumption. Moreover, there were many judgements made in inspecific terms which implied an appreciation of sensual pleasure. For instance, Andy said of a Christmas meal 'I just remember it being very well prepared, very well laid out, very nicely presented and very very tasty food.' And Steve, describing a meal in the Lake District, talked explicitly in terms of hedonism:

I had a pasta dish, it was like a sort of carbonara thing with ham and mushroom and pasta. It was quite good really, a decent plate full and a pint as well because we had a bit of a hedonistic weekend so we were eating and drinking and spending money lavishly, it was very good, champagne and [so forth].

### Joy

Many of the experiences of the senses of taste and smell are comparatively hard to describe (Synott, 1993:183ff.). As Fine (1995b) points out, even professional cooks, who are constantly tasting food to adjust flavours for presentation to customers, have only the most imprecise vocabulary for defining how an item tastes or smells. Perhaps only food writers have an extensive active vocabulary for dealing with such matters, and it is rare that even they effectively communicate what something tastes like. Vocabularies are primarily ones of flavours – as when wine writers talk of specimens tasting of peaches or plums, pepper or gooseberries – but they are often not aspects of a meal which people recall. When interviewees described meals to us they primarily reported the menu, a list of the dishes, rather than the smell or taste. Specific aspects of the sensual characteristics of the food were rarely mentioned. People sometimes listed the ingredients of a dish and gave names to complex items like sauces, but rarely made any attempt to say anything more than whether they had liked them or not. This may be because these sensations are ones that are immediate and because people forget whether the shellfish tasted freshly of the sea, whether the sauce was light or the rice aromatic. If anything, they were likely to recall technical deficiencies, the meat being tough or the vegetables overcooked.

Hence, scarcely anyone actually used complex descriptive language of sensual joy to describe their reactions to their last meal out. It is interesting to speculate why not. Possibly the food fails to inspire such responses. Maybe people fail to register sensations of delight at the time of eating. Perhaps they do, but rapidly forget. Or perhaps most people simply lack the vocabulary with which to express sensual delight: Sheila, one of the few interviewees who attempted to capture sensations, used abstract rather than concrete terms when she said, 'I think you go out because your senses can enjoy the food, and the smell, the taste and the pleasure from eating.' This last alternative may also be consistent with an hypothesis of Fischler's (1995) that Protestant cultures retain a deep resistance to celebrating pleasures, a consequence of there being no earthly means for the absolution of over-indulgence. Certainly the conversations in the interviews contained as much apologetic discussion of greed and discussion of strategies for self-discipline and self-control as reference to the physical pleasures of consumption.

## Instrumentalism: satisfaction and achievement

### Satisfaction

We take 'satisfaction' to be a term describing the acceptability of a particular exchange of money for an item or service. Monetary value was part of the reasoning of most interviewees, with issues of whether particular meals were expensive, good value for money, better or worse than an alternative, and so forth, being commonplace in discussion. As we saw in the previous section, such calculations played an important part in judgements about the acceptability of any visit to a restaurant.

Other instrumental reasons also surfaced. When asked what exactly it was about a meal that justified expenditure, women very often simply cited relief from the obligation to cook. The most striking expression of this was given by Lorna, who was one of only two interviewees who would have preferred never to eat out. Her case is worth examining in a little detail.

Lorna, a full-time housewife and voluntary worker, lived with her breadwinner husband and her fifteen-year-old son (her third child) in a semi-detached house, their two older children both being students who lived at home during holidays. Lorna herself still saw the household as containing five persons. In the first instance, she had not been keen to be interviewed because, she said, they hardly ever ate out. Unlike some of the other respondents, for whom money was a real constraint on the frequency with which they ate out, this was certainly not the case for Lorna and her husband, who shared one of the larger household incomes. She said 'there's no reason at all why we couldn't eat out more if we wanted to, we just choose not to. We'd rather do something else instead.' So on her last birthday, rather than go out for a meal, they went to the theatre.

That is something I will really enjoy, a night at the theatre. It's luxury and it's the same sort of level as I think people would eat out. As a luxury, as a night now and again, as a treat . . . Having a meal out is to save cooking, that's the reason for going out to save having to make a meal.

Her view might be partly explained by the fact that she only enjoyed what she described as 'plain' foods. These were foods and dishes prepared without the addition of too many other ingredients in the form of sauces or wines. Wine, according to Lorna, ruined a nice piece of chicken. At times she would go to 'fancy' restaurants, or engagements where 'fancy' foods were presented. In the past, this had occurred during special occasions (e.g. weddings) or engagements through her husband's work where she described eating the food as being 'courteous', 'putting up' with it, obviously not descriptions of pleasure. But ultimately the only reason, as far as Lorna was concerned, to consider eating out was to save her having to make a meal herself.

Significantly, however, Lorna accepted that if eating out was the only way to socialise with friends or family 'then it would be a price we'd have to pay would be having a meal'. But that was rarely the case. Anyway, she had established a pattern of visiting with relatives 'restaurants' near home, like Inn Foods or the Brown Cow, where they took a main course dish, at a moderate price, and afterwards returned home for supplementary refreshments and further socialising.

Lorna is exceptional in her aversion to eating out, but normal among our women interviewees in rating the exchange of money for relief from burdensome food preparation as worthwhile. It was the second most commonly mentioned reason for wanting to eat out: 'I like eating out, it saves you cooking . . . and it's nice to be served isn't it, and it's nice to have something made for you' (Meg); 'it's a break from doing something yourself' (Liz); 'It's nice to try some food somebody else has made, somebody else is going to clear up and after you just relax' (Jane). None of our male respondents gave 'getting a break from cooking' or 'enjoying the reception of service' as a reason for eating out, even though most of them did prepare meals themselves.[1] Nothing much more is required than relief from labour, something which the commodified version guarantees absolutely. Other qualities of the experience may be just welcome extras. So, when women described eating out as a treat and a luxury, which several did, this was at least as often because it represented a break from routine domestic food preparation or spending too much time at home as because it afforded them particularly pleasurable food.

---

[1] This did not preclude these men from recognising that such reasons were relevant for others around them.

## Achievement

At first sight, eating out is very unlikely to afford the gratifications which social psychologists attribute to the successful pursuit of self-development, that process of striving towards self-improvement, working towards targets or on projects which enhance skills or create increasing mastery over one's environment. Dining out is not much like learning Esperanto, turning a collecting hobby into a profitable venture or climbing a career ladder. It is a less active and less goal-oriented pastime. However, it is not entirely without attributes associated with achievement. As classical sociology noted, if one-sidedly and at the expense of other aspects, consumption practices tend to reflect social position, indicate extent of command over material and cultural resources and may incite resentment or emulation among excluded social groups. As Bourdieu might put it, consumption reflects aspects of hierarchical and competitive social classification systems which turn entertainments into social markers. It is not inconceivable that to have eaten out a great deal or to be familiar with expensive and highly regarded restaurants might, on reflection, seem to be a mark of personal success and might even result in others according prestige to someone who has breadth of experience. Three aspects of this conjecture deserve consideration.

Eating out frequently is indicative of a relatively high degree of personal autonomy and control, part of which has its origins in financial power. Interviewees with lower incomes were particularly likely to say that they would like to eat out more if only they could afford to. Eating out commercially, and as we have seen equally as a guest of friends, is associated with possession of significant discretionary income.

Second, we detected a social class basis for the preference for dining in restaurants specialising in ethnic cuisines. Bourdieu gives us grounds for imputing instrumental attitudes towards consumption. Cultural appreciation is a tool of social preferment, since it reflects a scarce resource, cultural capital, which may be profitably transformed into economic or social capital. Exhibiting cultural distinction may thus act as a claim to social superiority and privileged treatment. Unsurprisingly, none of our interviewees expressed the view that they expected or sought social preferment or esteem because of their consumption patterns. Dining out was never considered by interviewees as a part of a conscious strategy of theirs for social climbing, social display or material gain. Occasional references to the character of particular restaurants or to the behaviour of other customers betrayed a glimmer of awareness that social distinction might be exhibited through dining out, hence the references to 'posh' places and 'toffee-nosed' fellow customers. In discussing 'fantasy meals' we asked

Smina, 'If you were taken out for a meal and your mother was looking after your children, and you could choose where to go and money was no object, where would you go?' Her initial response was to identify an Indian restaurant in Manchester in which she had had a meal very recently and which she had been to on several occasions previously and described as friendly, relaxed and familiar: 'I like the service over there . . . Atmosphere's very nice, relaxing, it's quite nice.' Then she re-considered and reflected that she might like to go to 'a posh restaurant, when we were in London: is it the Hilton or something?' She continued, 'I could do if I win the lottery. Somewhere really posh, really expensive in London, yeah.' When then asked 'you think you would be able to enjoy yourself there?', Smina replied, 'Oh, no, I don't think you would, you'd have to be really upper class then, wouldn't you. You'd have to be a proper snob.' Then, in the process of interrogating the interviewer about how she would feel about the Hilton, Smina concluded that 'It would be an experience to see how, it's like, how the other people live.' As in Smina's case, however, recognition of such social stratification rarely seemed to prompt resentment or aspirations towards emulation among our interviewees.

Third, there is a sense, though comparatively weak, in which to be able to perform 'dining out' is a social accomplishment, something which has to be learned in order that it can be performed convincingly. If this were not so, there would be no need for extensive discussion of the practice in etiquette books, nor grounds for fearing embarrassment when eating in public. The formality threshold among interviewees was one testament to the existence of social barriers. One mother quite explicitly wanted her sons to learn appropriate manners for such events. Of survey respondents, 32 per cent of respondents were unable to affirm that they 'felt comfortable in any restaurant'. Whether they considered this a matter of regret, whether they envied the self-confidence of the others and, indeed, whether those others considered their facility a source of self-congratulation cannot be known, but all are plausible.

The extent to which differences in taste are, consciously or unconsciously, cultivated with a view to displaying or reproducing social status, remains debatable. Empirically, interviewees who expressed the most aesthetic appreciation of the products of the catering industry were from middle-class households and were among the more highly educated. As we saw in chapter 4, the survey supported the idea that greater familiarity with the variety of eating out venues, and most particularly with the range of ethnic cuisine as delivered through specialist ethnic restaurants, were also characteristics of the professional and managerial classes. Those scoring highest on the curiosity index had a distinctive social location. It cannot be conclusively determined from our data whether this was a

function of a benign cultural omnivorousness, inquisitiveness and tolerance, or whether it was a function of a calculated awareness that culinary
knowledge was an important social token of cultural refinement and
social standing. However, it seems highly likely that there is a considerable element of the latter consideration and that the gratifications deriving from aesthetic appreciation, discussed in the next section, are not
entirely separable from their social functions. Erickson's (1996)
Canadian investigation indicated some positive material advantages of
having a wide culinary repertoire for people in particular economic positions. She also showed that some professional and managerial workers,
even while confessing to having no interest in culinary matters, exhibited
considerable knowledge of, and the capacity to talk in a discriminating
way about, different restaurants, implying that this knowledge is socially
necessary or useful rather than of purely intellectual or aesthetic interest
(Erickson, 1991). We are inclined to argue that the acquisition of knowledge and the capacity to discuss food from an aesthetic point of view does
have instrumental value for the middle classes as evidence of possession
of cultural capital and as a way of cultivating social capital.

### Contemplation: entertainment and appreciation

All action deserving of the name requires some mental concentration and
reflection on its purpose. However, the degree of attention varies considerably. Some pursuits, perhaps routine watching of television is the
stereotypical example, do not necessarily entail much concentration. The
broadcaster's notion of light entertainment is a paradigm case: the audience is expected to be amused rather than educated, inspired or challenged. Entertainment, in this sense, is a relief from consequential
thought or personal responsibility, is largely passive, and involves being
only gently engaged in a pastime which is neither practically nor symbolically significant. Being entertained is one end of a continuum of attentive-
ness which runs, at the other, to a passionate single-minded enthusiasm
which totally absorbs and concentrates the mind. In between lies a realm
where people engage to a greater or lesser extent in cognitive and aesthetic processes of recognition, classification, information-processing,
and judgement. It has been argued that late modernity is characterised by
two tendencies increasing such engagement. One is an increase in
'reflexivity', the process in which people monitor, reflect upon and adapt
their personal conduct in the light of its perceived efficacy (e.g. Giddens,
1991). The second is often referred to as the aestheticisation of everyday
life, a process concomitant with the expansion of the culture industries
which propels consumers towards a more aesthetic approach to images,

mundane objects and the presentation of self (Lash, 1995). It might be anticipated that these two tendencies would increase the scope for imaginative contemplation of food.

Food, its consumption and its appreciation, is a field with much space for these gradations of attitude. The extent to which our interviewees and respondents adopt different approaches to the cognitive and imaginative aspects of food is some measure of both the salience of food as a consumer item and the aestheticisation of everyday life. All entail gratification, though of differing intensities. In the field of food the highest level of such engagement is attributed to gourmets and connoisseurs who, in their own view, have cultivated an exceptional knowledge and capacity for discrimination among foods and who, in the view of others, might be said to be groups of people sharing an enthusiasm for food. An enthusiasm might be described as involving extensive knowledge and appreciation of a specialised practice in which the participant has a considerable investment and heavy engagement.

In the past, at least, Britain has not been known for the intensity of its enthusiasm for food; T.S. Eliot's observation that 'One symptom of the decline of culture in Britain is indifference to the art of preparing food' stands for many others of similar provenance (quoted in Santich, 1996: 84). However, it might be argued that aesthetic judgement is increasingly being applied to food. No longer is mere physical sufficiency a standard of evaluation. Nor is it now decreed, as in polite society in nineteenth-century Britain, indelicate to discuss the food being eaten at table, which must surely have militated against its contemplative appreciation. It is now a common topic of conversation; for example, two thirds of our respondents claimed to talk to others about where and what they ate out. Also, our interviews indicated that people pass judgement about their eating out experiences, often in knowledgeable and interested fashion (see also Martens and Warde, 1997). We proceed by considering the different levels of awareness and discrimination apparent among our interview sample.

### Entertainment

We know from other studies that many people claim to seek nothing more from food than relief from hunger and for them food is neither interesting nor worthy of reflection (Halkier, 1997; Lupton, 1996; Purcell, 1992). For such people, eating is likely to be considered a regrettable necessity requiring time which might be more fruitfully spent in other pursuits. Nevertheless, our data suggest that most of them enjoy eating out and that they even express a liking for the food in such circumstances. Even if they take little interest in the food, they enjoy aspects of the experience. Such people are, presumably, entertained but not engaged.

Lorna and Mary among our interviewees avoided eating out if at all possible, and in both cases liked plain food, the food of their childhoods. Neither of them, however, suggested that they strongly and positively disliked the occasions on which they ate out. Lisa, by contrast, professed to liking eating out, but declared she had no wish to increase the frequency with which she did so because it would interfere with other more absorbing entertainments. Indeed, almost half of our interviewees felt they ate out sufficiently often, including those who did so infrequently. Several of them had comparatively narrow experience of eating out and appeared familiar with only a small proportion of the opportunities available to them in Preston and its surrounding area. Dining out was little more than occasional entertainment for many, but was nevertheless considered a rewarding form of relaxation.

### Appreciation

While there was a general interest in food, indicated by people's preparedness and capacity to talk about it at length, few could be described as food enthusiasts. One of the peculiar features of late modern society is the extent of enthusiasms (Bishop and Hoggett, 1986; Slater, 1997). Almost by definition high levels of engagement in any enthusiasm is that of a minority involved in the particular practice. Studies of the social worlds of recreational associations, clubs, commercial practices like art, collecting, etc. indicate that a few people tend to be deeply involved in the administration and organisation of the practice, to whom some others will turn sometimes because they hold powerful positions, sometimes because of their exceptional expertise. Much greater numbers of individuals are less engaged, some participating occasionally in the organised enthusiasm where they are located on the periphery, others merely having a private interest. Involvement varies, and it is a feature of our world that the practices themselves have comparatively few adherents. There are many football fans, but they comprise a small proportion of the British population. There are many fewer leek growers, pigeon fanciers and polo players. Yet there are a vast number of enthusiasms. As Bishop and Hoggett showed, districts within cities are likely to contain hundreds of organised groups. What this seems to suggest is that there is increasing specialisation in consumption activities which require concentrated attention.

A few interviewees talked in the language of gourmet appreciation, compared restaurants, recalled the way that foods were treated and talked of eating fashionable dishes. Jane was one who appreciated the skills of the more accomplished chefs. She was a full-time housewife and mother of two teenage children. Her husband was the only breadwinner and worked as a marketing manager. Jane's household had known more affluent times, and money was a constraint at the moment of interview. Although the household income was one of the highest among our interviewees, it supported two teenage children, as well as a large detached house, and Jane commented that the frequency with which they ate out at the time of interview was lower than it had been in the past. When answering the question whether she would like to eat out more often, Jane did not lack imagination.

INTERVIEWER: And what sort of places would you like to eat out more?
JANE: Money no object?
INTERVIEWER: Well yes.
JANE: Well actually I would like to go to top-class restaurants with the top class chefs like Pierre Bleu's place or up in the Lake District, what is it called – Windermere View. I'd like to go to those types of places. Oh and also round here I've been to Wuthering Heights, you know . . . I'd like to go there again. And then I would speak to friends who've got plenty of money and find out where they've had a nice meal. So those types of places: really nice, top-class restaurants where they make food, cook food that I wouldn't make at home. The last place I would want to go would be a big chain restaurant. I just wouldn't, even with plenty of money, I would go and eat, I'd rather eat at home, you know.

Certainly Jane, who went on to elaborate the grounds of her dislike of some particular chain restaurants, eliminated 'cheaper-type' eating places from consideration.

Chris was another aware of cooking style and presentation of dishes and who maintained that she would not go to a restaurant whose food was not better than that which she could prepare for herself at home. She described dishes served in some of the restaurants she frequented as:

almost like a painting sometimes when it's presented nicely, and they put different little bits of fruit on, and it's displayed nice. Things that I wouldn't normally buy are on the plate, I know I like them . . . I suppose it's just like the little additives that you wouldn't bother with at home, that make it look really presentable, beautifully presented and also as I say all sorts of little bits of different kinds of fruit that I don't normally buy to make it look really appetising. And it's not necessarily part of the meal, it's a decoration on the plate to make it look appetising. I like that.

There were a number of interviewees, mostly younger and dispropor-tionately men, who positively valued novel, often foreign foods, and who routinely passed judgement on the quality of restaurant meals in their experience. They discriminated between good and bad versions of the same dish, and between better and worse restaurants specialising in the same cuisine. Probably none would have thought of themselves as connoisseurs, but their talk did convey some appreciable enthusiasm for eating out. They made comparisons between food they themselves prepared at home, food which their families prepared and food which they had received in restaurants. They were particularly likely to try to match up venue and menu with occasion, seeing some places as appropriate for celebrations, others for more casual outings. In this group, though by no means uniformly well off, the younger ones had college educations and all had middle-class occupations or lived in middle-class households. For these few people, food was an object worthy of cognitive and aesthetic reflection and they had developed a vocabulary for expressing their tastes and judgements.

Only occasionally did interviewees comment at length on the quality and composition of a meal or a dish. For example, chicken livers 'were well browned and had walnuts with them, and it was served on a very well-presented salad', a meal where 'everything was cooked just right, you know the vegetables were firm' (Sheila). The word 'tasty' occurred occasionally. One described as desirable fruit salad where 'you can pick out the fruit and enjoy each flavour' (Rose). But these were very much the exception in paying any attention to the skilled execution on the part of a chef.

We asked respondents how they obtained recommendations about where and what they might eat out. About two in three people said that they took notice of recommendations about where to eat. Friends and relatives were the most frequently used informants (61 per cent and 43 per cent respectively), with only 13 per cent using a newspaper, 5 per cent specialist food guides or books and 4 per cent television programmes. As regards which dishes to try, less than half of respondents (45 per cent) said they took notice of recommendations, and again people (friends, family and colleagues) were the most widely used as informants, with the press being cited by 5 per cent, specialist food guides by 2 per cent and television programmes by 3 per cent. This suggests first that the numbers of people seeking and obtaining information through publicly accessible sources, to which we might expect enthusiasts to have recourse, are comparatively small. It also implies that there are likely to be a comparatively small number of enthusiasts in the UK and that the direct influence of the journalists of the mass media is likely to be limited. That more people listen to the advice of their acquaintances is significant. When it comes to changing people's diets, as we suspect with most other forms of consumption decisions, it is personal contacts and networks which exert most influence. Of course, acquaintances may themselves have obtained their information from mass media sources; indeed, we know that everyday conversations draw heavily on media messages. But as far as influencing behaviour is concerned it is likely that advice has to be transmitted via trustworthy personal informants (Miller and Reilly, 1995). Hence there is a likelihood that groups of people who are personally acquainted will tend to have similar tastes and dispositions.

Contemplative gratifications are common. Some people discriminated carefully between eating places and read consumer guides. Even among the less enthusiastic of interviewees most obtained some enjoyment from discussing and evaluating the meals that they ate out. This form of enjoyment was not especially intense for many, and not of much significance for any of our working class interviewees, suggesting that the aestheticisation of this aspect of everyday life is as yet restricted.

## Sociality: participation and mutuality

### Participation

Hirschman observed that one of the rewards of involvement in public affairs is the opportunity for sociability. Of course, there is nothing very original in the idea: psychologists' accounts of what makes people happy always include the existence of acceptable and trustworthy personal relationships. However, these are increasingly interpreted by the common sense of highly individualistic cultures, as 'pure relationships' which presumes an intense intimacy attained by highly self-reflexive couples. For instance Giddens (1991; 1992) builds his account of personal relationships in a post-traditional society around the model of the 'pure relationship', in essence the intimacy of highly self-reflexive couples. Yet it is doubtful if that serves as a relevant template for more than a small proportion of meaningful interpersonal interactions. Looser ties, with colleagues, friends, acquaintances, association members and so forth, are rarely much valued. Hirschman reminds us of the attractions of such ties. However, he does not explicate the nature of the particular pleasures associated with sociality and sociability.

When asked why they liked eating out, our interviewees most often gave socialising as the reason. When asked 'what sort of things contribute to your enjoyment?' Sheila's first response was 'The social aspect. If the food was appalling and totally inedible but the people were all right I wouldn't mind too much.' Meg replied 'Because we are with friends, it's fun isn't it, you know we have a talk and a socialise. . . I'm an extrovert and I like to be with other people and talk and talk to anybody. Yeah.' Socialising 'with friends' was mentioned most often. Jane explained the pleasure of a meal thus: 'It's nice to enjoy the food and it's also nice, it loosens your tongue, doesn't it, you sit round the table enjoying a meal together. Or it's nice to go with friends. I suppose the sociable aspects . . .' Rather more people said that the appeal of eating out was 'to enjoy the company of family and friends' (Jean and David) than that of a partner. Only a few younger respondents (women) tended to mention that eating out was a desirable way to socialise with their boyfriend or partner:

I think it's easier, when you're sat over a meal, to talk about things. Probably if you're sat with a take-away you tend to be glued to the telly, whereas rather if you're just sat together over a meal you do tend to have a better conversation really because you haven't as many distractions and things like that, it's quite nice. You know, it's socialising involved especially with your boyfriend. (Trisha)

However, other interviewees, and not necessarily older ones, made a point of saying that they did not eat out as 'couples' any more. By this they must have meant that they ate with others in addition to their partners, since of the fifty-nine meal occasions described in our Preston interviews partners had been present on forty-one occasions. This suggests both that eating out is something of an antidote to privatised, couple-centredness and that the pleasure is one associated with a more generalised sociability.

Lisa's description of her regular, though comparatively infrequent, eating out occasions suggested that entertainment rather than an opportunity to refine her palate was at the root of her enjoyment. Indeed, she was perhaps the paradigm case of the awareness that eating together was a sound basis of collective conviviality:

We eat out as a social gathering. I mean we might not see our friends for six weeks but we'll be going out with them for a meal and that's, we all get together for this meal . . . we always make a point to have a meal, to go out with a gang of us, you know. I mean there can be anything up to eighteen or nineteen of us going out for a meal, and we always try and make a point of having one every six or seven weeks.

Held at places where it was possible to dance afterwards, she implied that it was not the food, but rather the fun to be had from her night out with a large group of friends that was her reason for eating out.

A significant number of the eating out occasions reported to us had very many people present and such large gatherings often generated intense appreciation. Thus Andy reported a meal that he had particularly liked because of 'that social experience you know, twenty or thirty friends together, having a good time, in fact that was just before Christmas, that was really enjoyable'.

Some commented positively on the opportunity that eating out offered for forms of public participation. Sheila said she liked 'to socialise, if somebody invited me out for a meal I'd certainly go. Yes, please.' She was one who appreciated the opportunities of the urban experience more generally – to gaze at others and, indeed, to talk to strangers. Mary too liked the fact that 'you're getting out of your house for a bit, aren't you, and you're meeting people. You always chat to somebody, don't you, at some time or another?' Anne, on the other hand, indicated some ambivalence about exposure in public space. She said 'you can do a lot of people-watching in pubs, more so than in cafés – unnoticed people watching. [But] when you go to a formal restaurant you feel like everybody else is watching you as well. You can't start talking about anything 'cos they are all sat there in their happy little couples and they have nothing to say to each other.'

### Mutuality, reciprocity and sharing

The attraction of company is probably demonstrated by the unacceptability of its opposite. To prefer to eat alone is suspicious: people do not like to eat out alone and few do. 75 per cent of respondents agreed with the statement 'I dislike eating alone'; and only 2 per cent reported that they had eaten their last meal without company. It is not self-evident why this should be the case: to eat alone gives more control over what is eaten, when and where. Yet of the satisfactions deriving from eating, some of the most symbolically and emotionally important arise from being in company and sharing food or the occasion.

The dominant Western commercial trend is to make food choice ever more individualistic. A la carte tends to replace table d'hôte, offering each individual a choice of dishes independent of others at the table. Also as the elaborateness of visual presentation of dishes has grown, fewer items are served from a common bowl; the chef is likely to arrange every component, including vegetables and sauce, on the individual plates. The sharing of food therefore recedes. There are however some counter-tendencies. The spread of Indian and Chinese restaurants offers increasing opportunity to share food, to eat parts of the same dishes as companions, as too does the buffet. Some interviewees achieve this in other types of restaurant too. Katrine explained:

KATRINE: I like it when we all go out at night, you know like the groups of us 'cos there's like twenty of us and we're all shouting is yours nice, and we're all having a taste of everybody else's, 'cos we all try to get different. All the ladies, you know, all passing it down the table, and we're all trying different bits, yeah.

INTERVIEWER: Only between the ladies?

KATRINE: Yeah, fellas just eat their own. It's good 'cos if you haven't tried that before and somebody else has tried it and they like it so they're eating it, and

they let you have a taste . . . . So that's how we do it. Or if someone's left something one of the fellas [will say] can I have that? . . . I enjoy it. You can talk, we
have all of us talking over the table. The only thing I don't like is these long
tables [because it restricts conversation]. . . But we have a good laugh.

Katrine's description of a sense of conviviality was heightened because it
involved sharing food. Notably, only the women at the table made a point
of sharing, and the men did so solely in the capacity of dustbin. It was
equally noteworthy that it was almost exclusively women who said that
their reason for liking eating out was because it was an opportunity 'to
socialise', 'to gossip', 'to chat'. Presumably, and our interviewees hinted
at it, men have other more easily accessible channels through which to
socialise, particularly still the pub.

Arguably, one reason for the marginally greater appreciation of the
food at private dinner parties is that the sense of sharing the same meal
and being served from the same platter is heightened. It is inevitably so in
other ways, since the obligation to reciprocity, to return the invitation to
dinner, means that there is some longer-term obligation to share the
labour of providing attractive meals and occasions. That the conversation
at the domestic dinner party was also liked a little more than that in the
restaurant further reinforces the argument that reciprocity enhances the
feeling of mutuality.

### The social importance of mutual gratification

The example of eating out is scientifically valuable because it directs
attention to specifically *social* gratification. In line with the earlier
identification of 'enjoyment' as dependent upon a social context or environment, we suggest that a key basis of gratification is social participation,
particularly in situations where the enjoyment of each person is dependent upon the enjoyment of all, where affect or mood is irredeemably
a joint creation. It is difficult in individualistic societies – with their
associated dominant disciplines of economics and psychology – to
keep in mind the mutual aspects of human existence, the awareness that
social relationships are more than the sum of the attributes, intentions
and motives of individual actors. Psychologists like Lane and
Csikszentmihalyi put self-development and accomplishment at the top of
a hierarchy of human goals. Featherstone (1991), in his model of the
heroic consumer, reminds us that the goal of self-improvement is central
to the current mode of consumption. The notion that the greatest happiness is to be derived from achievement – whether symbolised by personal
ownership of wealth, by occupational success, by power, by an impressive
self-identity – is endlessly insinuated into contemporary reflection on the

human condition. The predominant image is of an active individual exercising control in situations voluntarily entered. Yet while this captures or reflects a key facet of popular consciousness, it fails to appreciate some other sources of pleasure and happiness.

Some aspects of human activity are irremediably social in the sense that they cannot be brought about by a single individual alone. These include joint activities like conversation, gift-giving and sexual intercourse; social relations like trust, co-operation, secrets, generosity, friendship (and their converse of distrust, competition, etc.); and social institutions like community and association. What is important about these is that they cannot be understood simply as the 'social' contexts and environments of individual action; the other people in these relationships are not just a set of background constraints or parameters of action, but are active co-agents whose presence demands mutual adaptation (as is recognised in game theory and rational action theory), or negotiation (as in situations of symbolic interaction), or recognition (for trust and friendship imply mutual acknowledgement). What is particular about these relations is that the individual actor is not in autonomous and independent control; other people are inevitably required to share in the maintenance and consequences of the relationship. Possibly, what is meant by saying that social relationships are a key element of human happiness is that these kinds of specifically social relations are a major intrinsic source of gratification. Of course people may be calculative or manipulative, try to mislead others about their intentions or lack mutual accommodation to the relationship, but in such instances any intrinsic gratification that might arise from sentiments of mutuality will not be forthcoming. You might obtain material benefit by dissembling friendship to curry favour, but you will not be able to enjoy the emotional satisfactions of friendship. Neither can you, by dint of your own will, be someone's friend unless they acknowledge you to be so. There is a reciprocity, or reciprocal co-operation, involved which surpasses the power of the individual to determine.

If someone accompanying me is pleased, I have a better environment. If a companion is displeased it seriously detracts from my pleasure, even though I might eat the same thing, i.e. my consumption is reduced in value and enjoyment in otherwise identical circumstances. And it is not in my power to alter this. Methodological individualists will talk of feelings of gratification as if they are the properties of detached individuals; and it is true perhaps that only individuals have feelings. But often one person can only have a particular feeling if someone else does too. In enjoying a meal situation, *bonhomie* requires others to share in it; the atmosphere is a collective creation, a joint achievement. Admittedly, someone can work to achieve it personally. It is no accident that some people are valued because of their capacities to get other people to enjoy themselves: the good hostess, the outward-going person. There is an art, sometimes formalised into a role like 'master of ceremonies', to encouraging people to participate. But success depends on the co-operation of all others in the party.

Recall the case of Chris, an interviewee interested in food, recounting an occasion when the food at a restaurant was disappointing. Her reluctance to complain was because it might spoil things for other people. Other people's state of mind, or affect, was a constraint on her behaviour. Although she derived low satisfaction from the commercial service, this was of less concern than the maintenance of a mutually congenial atmosphere. The frequency of such behaviour should not be underestimated. A kind of sacrificial affective action, it involves doing something in order to please others, a form of emotional care which is deeply entrenched in, particularly women's, approaches to eating events. (Another form of this was exhibited in Trisha's view that she preferred restaurants to dinner parties because everyone could relax.)

Many potential pleasures which are highly valued are entirely contingent on other people, over whose behaviour no individual has exclusive control. There are many aspects of life which require mutuality, where co-operation cannot be achieved by formal and imperatively co-ordinated action, but rather is reliant upon mutual sympathy, independently and voluntarily granted, for sustaining the activity. Examples might be teenage gangs, marriage, a good night out, and a successful dinner party. Others have to feel the same, to share the same affective condition, to be in the same mood, to be in sympathy. This constitutes the social context of enjoyment.

### Simple and compound enjoyment

Several types of gratification are involved in eating out and the occasion typically provides all these types of gratification, though at different degrees of intensity. Most people are generally highly pleased by their eating out experiences, so much so that it was impossible to use survey responses to explore statistically variation by gender, class or age. Our interviewees almost always derived some physical pleasure from their meals out, and sometimes ate what they considered luxurious foods as part of an episode considered as a treat. Almost all were entertained and some had a sufficient degree of enthusiasm to be interested in evaluating the meals they consumed. They were mostly determined that they should be satisfied, in the sense of getting value for money, and there were some aspects in which they might be said to be involved in a form of social competitiveness from which they derived a sense of prestige. And above all they enjoyed the social aspects of the occasion, the participation in an event, friendliness and conviviality.

Gratifications are not mutually exclusive and one of the primary reasons why eating out is so well liked is precisely that it offers a wide range. Listening to a concert, watching a sporting event, gardening or watching television typically offer fewer. Perhaps eating out offers more social and sensual than imaginative and instrumental rewards for most people. The most common combination of reasons for having enjoyed a meal among our interviewees was the food and the company. Arguably, conviviality and physical pleasure, traditional pleasures in Campbell's (1987) terms, are more reliable than the others and are appreciated by almost everyone.

These gratifications are cumulative, and probably account for the overall levels of satisfaction recorded. The odds of successful delivery of a service strongly favour the restaurateur. Nevertheless complacency would be unwarranted, since quantitatively there remain many unsatisfactory events. However, most people go to restaurants where they feel comfortable, where they can feel confident that they will be supplied with a service which they will appreciate and which will give them a range of gratifications.

However, much of the enjoyment is provided by the group of companions for themselves. Enjoyment derives from participation: for best affect, traditional pleasures are obtained in company. Eating alone or singing in the bath are generally less gratifying than their socially committed versions. Enjoying eating out is dependent on the good will of others, for it is a mutual situation where one makes oneself dependent on other people to achieve the desired level of gratification. Some occasions are of particularly high value, as the shared affect associated with competent participation in a collectively constructed event gives some of the highest of social rewards. Eating out is a social accomplishment, the achievement through voluntary co-ordination and co-operation from which most people, while taking these for granted, derive considerable and justified enjoyment. One feels duly rewarded for having played one's part competently in an event which requires participation. Intriguingly, one cannot be a free-rider in such circumstances because the participation is itself intrinsically rewarding, as it is only by being generous rather than selfish that the pleasures of company can be obtained. In such scenarios it is unacceptable to refuse to play a part despite even limited competence, because technical excellence is much less important than the expression of sincere participation.

Arguably, companionship holds a superior position in the hierarchy of enjoyments associated with eating out. It holds this position partly because of the mutual obligations imposed on people who eat out together to engage in a collective performance directed towards the promulgation of a shared sense of enjoyment, which is dependent precisely upon sufficient acknowledgement of mutual dependence. Moreover, it would appear that this mutual dependence is heightened in situations of being a guest in someone else's home, probably because of the expectation of reciprocity and the greater degree of sharing of foods. For, as Table 8.1 indicated, it was guests in private households who recorded maximum enjoyment of company, conversation and food.

*Part V*

# Conclusion

## Events

Western attitudes towards consumption have always been ambivalent. On the one hand, enhanced levels of consumption are inextricably bound up with rising economic production and offer the opportunity to meet the basic human needs of the mass of ordinary people which most societies in history have been unable to do. On the other hand, consumption is morally suspect, associated with unnecessary luxury, self-indulgent hedonism and rampant materialism. Many recent contributions to this ancient debate have argued that modern consumer culture is morally harmless, and even something which might properly be welcomed and celebrated. The pleasures of consumption, including those obtained directly in commodified form, are real and make a major contribution to human happiness. Among the benefits of the practices supported by contemporary consumer culture are that they generate dignified forms of (unpaid) labour, promote an aesthetic attitude to everyday life, sustain many socially meaningful practices like caring and hospitality, provide entertainment and mental stimulation, ensure unobjectionable levels of comfort, permit expression of personal and group identities in rebellious as well as conformist mode and, of course, stimulate economic competition and create employment. Given these positive attributes, if they also provide people with a sense of satisfaction and gratification then it would be perverse to condemn modern consumerism.

One remarkable feature of the survey of English urban populations was the great sense of pleasure and satisfaction that people claim to derive from eating out. Whether the expectation is so high that diners become reluctant to admit disappointment is uncertain, but our data suggest justifiable anticipation. This we consider to be associated with a more general attitude towards social occasions and events.

That meal events express belonging and mark boundaries of inclusion and exclusion is a staple idea of anthropology. With whom one might share a meal is an indicator of social distance. Most societies seem to distinguish between four categories of person: co-resident kin, other kin and friends, strangers to whom one has some obligation to hospitality, and the remainder. As Douglas and Nicod (1974) showed, in Britain the food served on a meal occasion is also an indication of affinity. The more significant the meal occasion, the more elaborate the food and the closer the ties between companions.

Eating together is usually expected to be a socially significant event, one which has traditionally offered considerable gratification. The idea that a family meal is a basic source of family cohesion is premised precisely on the assumed capacity for sharing food to generate mutual solidarity and co-operation. Despite the family dinner table also being a locus of domestic conflict on some occasions, the presumption is that in the longer run repeated communion will reproduce sentiments of mutual affection. As we saw in chapter 5, the spread of the habit of eating out does not seem to have seriously jeopardised the likelihood of household members eating together, since they tend to go out together too. Whether a meal taken in a public place affords the same opportunity for family bonding is debatable, but there is no particular reason to think it any less satisfactory a context.

It is interesting to speculate whether the addition of the commercial option to eat out has increased the range of potentially meaningful eating occasions. There is no reason to think that the level of domestic entertaining has declined overall as a result of the greater availability of commercial meals. The addition of new sites for eating together might in fact increase the potential size of the circle with whom any individual might eat. Though we have no means of knowing from our data, it is not unlikely that there are people with whom one might eat in a restaurant whom it would never be appropriate to invite home. In that sense, circles of companions may be getting larger for many people and if, indeed, eating together encourages mutual sympathy, then the spread of restaurant eating may increase the sum of human happiness. That this might be the case does depend upon the equivalence of the experience of sharing food with acquaintances in restaurants and in the home. The evidence is probably that these are not equivalent, and that the invitation that involves private hospitality is indication of greater social affinity than a joint meal in a restaurant. Nevertheless, the differences may not be so great as to eliminate all effect. We would hypothesise therefore that social networks of companionship have expanded in recent decades and that this has positive effects for participants.

One assumption is that meals engender sympathy among the diners. Meals are a potential source of immediate social enjoyments of conversation, communicative action which may lead to a better understanding of one another, and also of conviviality, of having fun together. Lisa's regular large group outings to a restaurant were not ones led by gourmet concern, but by the expectation of an exuberant evening with a well-established group of friends. Many of our interviewees (though by no means all) appreciated their meals out primarily because they provided a good opportunity to laugh, joke and chatter with friends. There is no necessary conflict between commodified provision and conviviality.

One further feature of the social aspects of eating out is the importance of the event itself. Our respondents and interviewees considered eating out special, both 'out of the ordinary' and symbolic. Many of the last eating out occasions were for particular celebrations, birthdays, marriages, etc., and being together on such occasions is a mark of social belonging and intimacy. It may be considered a privilege to be at such occasions, not to have been invited perhaps being seen as a slight. One needs to apologise for not being present if invited, again indicating some sense of social obligation to eat together to mark a significant passage of time or a change of social status. The point is that it is important to be present, if it is possible, because the meal symbolises a socially significant, temporally specific occasion. To have eaten the same meal the day before or the day after would not be a satisfactory substitute, even if many of the same people were present. There are two sociological lessons to be learned.

As the number of meal occasions increases, so does the potential for sharing and co-operating with a wider network of people. An implicit assumption on the part of those who feel that the family meal is under threat is that the less frequent such meals, the less attachment family members will feel for one another. The impression is of a negative-sum game where fewer family meals means weaker family bonds. However, the corollary is rarely entertained, that more meals with non-family members have positive effects on social relationships with alternative companions. Yet this might well be so, as it is possible that the spread of eating out will enhance sociality and solidarity among wider networks of people.

This conjecture offers a fresh angle on Hirschman's (1982) thesis about consumer disappointment. He argued, first, that the satisfactions derived from the ownership of consumer durables are prone to turn to disappointment. Second, by comparison, the gratifications from sensual pleasures like eating are much more reliable, because they involve a transformation from discomfort to comfort on almost every occasion. Third, the disappointment arising from consumer durables may lead affluent people especially to seek instead the personal rewards of political participation. However, Hirschman is unpersuasive because he focuses on goods and neglects services. Analysis of meals out implies that at least some of the satisfactions of participation can be obtained when consuming services; that participation may be combined with the pursuit of other pleasures with considerable likelihood of enjoyment; and that an 'event' – the collection of people together for purposes of entertainment – is a highly effective contemporary source of the enjoyment of consumption. The creation of 'events', even for instance the fairs, fêtes and festivals invented by local tourist boards to attract visitors to their regions, is perhaps a way in which producers may avert the contraction of demand entailed by disappointment with consumer durables. By capitalising upon the capacity for events to bring people together in situations whose outcome may be partly uncertain (for, implicitly, we might miss something memorable if we were absent), and where they might expect to obtain the intrinsic satisfactions of participation, events' organisers may make a wide possible range of consumption activities attractive.

## Variety

The impression of the existence of an enormous volume of goods and services, and the belief that all consumers, by choosing freely among options, can broaden their experience, are major sources of the appeal and the legitimacy of consumer culture. The cultivation of these notions confers great value on breadth of experience, on variety. The impression of variety is functional for suppliers who can thereby differentiate their products from those of other producers, and it is functional for consumers because the options they select stand as signs of their individuality, their difference from other people. This symbiotic play on difference is part of the explanation of the fecundity of the consumer society. The impression of variety and difference has to be constructed and constantly reproduced. We seek to demonstrate how this impression is maintained, neither going so far as to agree with Wood that it is illusion, but on the other hand remaining very sceptical of many claims about the extent of variety.

Variety can be simulated by events. Each event is different, unique in its temporal location, potentially distinctive and memorable precisely because of its uniqueness. It is not that it must be very different from other events. Indeed, as with many instances of consumer goods, being too different smacks of idiosyncrasy and eccentricity, an effect which most consumers seek to avoid creating. An important feature of the 'event' is that it be structured without being entirely predictable. Reliable anticipation of what might transpire and what demands might be put on the participant is necessary to ensure that the event is sufficiently orderly so that it is not threatening because incomprehensible or dangerous. On the other hand it should not be exactly the same on each occasion, which might induce boredom. Small differences, so that one celebration can be distinguished from another, may be sufficient to sustain regular demand for the services which deliver events. The scale of difference required to instill an impression of variety may, as was shown in chapter 7, be minute. In order to explore this very general issue of the role of variety in consumer society we take our case study of meals out and enquire whether the differences in experience within and between the commercial and the communal modes of provision are significant bearers of cultural variety and if so, how.

Appadurai (1988: 9), talking of the emergence of a national cuisine in India, notes that 'eating permits a variety of registers, tied to particular contexts, so that what is done in a restaurant may be different from what is appropriate at home, and each of these might be different in the context of travel, where anonymity can sometimes be assured . . . The new cuisine permits the growing middle classes of Indian towns and cities to maintain a rich and context-sensitive repertoire of culinary postures'. Any estimate of the extent to which the habit of eating out adds to the range of cultural experience must be sensitive to registers and contexts. Social scientists who maintain that variety is illusory claim that many of the items advertised and sold as new and different appear, on closer scrutiny, to have much in common with other already available commodities. Wood, when adumbrating his critique of eating out, concentrates almost entirely upon food content, dismissing much of the appearance of variety because it is achieved through 'secondary features' of the practice, decor, fashion and so forth. We entirely agree that such features are a principal source of the appearance of variety, but question whether they are in any sense secondary. Rather, they appear very important, as accounts of the centrality of conviviality and companionship indicate. Moreover, nor do we entirely agree that the food is increasingly standardised!

The impression of variety in the commercial field is largely achieved through a process of specialisation. Competition requires that each outlet has some distinctive characteristic which will recommend it in comparison with closest competitors, but which does not make it so exceptional that its potential clientele shrinks to an unviable level. For the commercial producer, innovation involves presenting certain basic elements of the meal performance re-configured in different combinations. The basic elements for a commercial establishment are the ostensible requirements of its main clientele, the elaborateness of its cooking, the pedigree of the cuisine, the nature of the service and whether alcohol is sold. Using such criteria we distinguish between a Chinese restaurant and a motorway service station. Alternative restaurant regimes mostly have their origins in historical forms and often have domestic parallels. The appearance of innovation, a basis of fashion within the industry, is achieved by juggling the elements. New fashions include waiters acting as entertainers in theme restaurants; any number of different cuisines from across the globe; fast three courses and slow one course; Thai buffets and Turkish mezze; music and posters to give the impression of being in a far-off land. A small number of elements generate a vast number of permutations, the reason why someone like Wood is both right and wrong in perceiving processes of standardisation behind apparent diversity.

The impact of variety depends on how customers appreciate it. The existence of a range of commercial alternatives, just so differentiated, tells little about the way in which consumers make use of them. Their strategies seem to be numerous. From our evidence, variety seems to be expected, even though the experience of its true range is known to only a limited extent by most people. For some the contemporary market offers a pleasurable plethora of alternatives which can be used for particular purposes, for others much of the range is superfluous to their tastes or requirements. The strategy of 'omnivorousness' is one possible response to 'increasing variety', a search, for one reason or another, for as wide a range of experience as possible. In the process consumers may develop tastes for a wider range of items than previously, without it seeming necessary, or possible, or desirable to have favourites, to value one type of item over another. Other people seem content to return to the same types of venue, eating similar dishes and 'liking what they know'. Though surely the variety of options is increasing, there is nevertheless a tendency to exaggerate its extent, for much specialisation is based upon minute differentiation of mass-production techniques with interchangeable components packaged as differences. However, customers do consider those differences as of considerable significance. They discriminate. They have favourite pizza houses and Indian take-away shops. However, often it is small differences that are symbolically significant; witness our interviewee, Katrine, for whom a desired sense of variety was obtained by alternating the sauces served with steak.

With the advance of commodity culture, the consumer attitude becomes more entrenched, the value of consumer choice more vaunted, the value of that which is home-made more dubious. It is therefore perhaps revealing that the majority of respondents and interviewees valued domestic hospitality offered by a friend more highly than its commercial equivalent. This despite the fact that several features of the arrangement might in principle be unappealing. Obligation to reciprocate is incurred and that involves considerable labour; the value of the gift is not precisely measurable and the nature of the incurred obligation uncertain; it is not possible to complain or get another dish if the food is disliked for whatever reason; and there is no choice about what shall be eaten. So, most key features of the condition of consumer sovereignty are absent, yet people claim to be better pleased than in a restaurant. Private hospitality is a form of communal provisioning; it is highly valued for the intimations of intimacy attached to receiving invitations and the social commitment generated by acceptance. So although it is less laborious to treat guests in a restaurant the meaning is somewhat different and, prima facie, less prestigious.

We still know comparatively little about entertaining and the social relationships involved. Nevertheless, private hospitality is enjoyed more, people feel more relaxed and they particularly appreciate their companions, conversation and food. These attractions depend upon a particular 'definition of the situation' of the private host–guest relationship, including, above all, a norm of reciprocity shared by all. One very significant difference between the experiences of the commercial and the communal modes is the nature of the social relations and obligations. What is remarkable is that being a recipient of private hospitality is extraordinarily pleasurable despite the obligations to labour copiously in return at another date.

We also know that behaviour within the communal mode is itself very varied. What is eaten, with whom, when and under what circumstances is highly differentiated. One defining feature of behaviour in this mode is the capacity for different groups of people to improvise on common social templates to create very different occasions and effects. If the commercial source of variety is specialisation, the communal equivalent is improvisation.

A major line of sociological speculation concerns whether variety subverts standards and hierarchies. It is regularly argued that contemporary culture has become, relatively recently, pluralistic, though it is not exactly clear what this might mean. One interpretation of the claim, perhaps consistent with the early work of the Birmingham Centre for Contemporary Cultural Studies, might be that there were formerly hegemonic practices, ones that by no means everyone followed, which was why sub-cultures of resistance were interesting, but that either within classes, or across society as a whole, there were pre-eminent models of behaviour, expected codes of conduct and preferred readings of cultural symbols. This did not imply a genuine cultural pluralism since there were supervening legitimate modes of practice. While some legitimate arenas for dispute existed within the hegemonic culture, most people lived some negotiated version of that culture.

Aspects of our study suggest that behind the diversity of food practices there remain hegemonic understandings regarding the performance of meals. There are shared understandings, or social templates, governing the principal occasions for eating. Not only did we find strong vestiges of the notion of a proper family meal, but conventions governing occasions for eating out were widely acknowledged. People operated with a sense of how, ideally and properly, meals taken in restaurants or as a guest should be conducted. For example, the spectre of the formal middle-class dinner party lay behind discussions of entertaining. Of course, people did not necessarily, or regularly, perform in accordance with the social template. Rather the opposite, especially as regards entertaining. Yet even non-conformity by mutual consent, which characterised private hospitality in Preston, was more a matter of improvisation on the dominant model than its dismissal. The social rules governing primary eating events remain firmly embedded in popular consciousness and continue to offer guidance. There is a deep-lying set of thoroughly entrenched conventions associated with meal-taking which, though subject to improvisation, seems very difficult to shift and which, as we will suggest, has not been seriously challenged by the restaurant. Thus, change in food behaviour occurs as improvisation, slow and incremental development on hegemonic models regarding the proper meal, entertaining, the obligations and rules of companionship, etc. If the analysis focuses less on the content of what is consumed, and more on the underlying structure of social relations and social norms associated with meals, habits of eating seem resistant to change. Ultimately, there are few ways of doing the millions of eating events occurring daily.

If there are some bases of genuine variety of experience within and between the two modes of eating out, there are also some significant similarities. Though the principles of access, which determine who shall be entitled to what, differ, the same types of people tend to derive most benefit from each. It has usually been thought that the market mechanism augments, as well as reflects, social inequalities. Inequalities of income matter in commercial purchase simply because money is the medium of exchange. But as sociologists have generally pointed out, there is more to preferences than income and price and it will come as no surprise that other social factors also operate to determine how often, where and with whom people eat out. Age, ethnic origin, place of residence, occupational class often made a significant difference to frequency and style of eating out, as did practical constraints associated with the employment status of household members, size and composition of household and age of children. However, the social indicator which was often the most important discriminator in practice was the level of educational qualification. This corroborates the view that food practice, and especially eating out, is a field characterised by the circulation of cultural capital.

Though we cannot demonstrate the point conclusively on the basis of our study, since it is merely a snapshot of practices in the 1990s, there are grounds for thinking that informalisation is one of the most important trends in eating out. In comparison with earlier accounts, a good many features of the practice appear to have become less formal. Gender etiquette has changed. Women happily eat out in public and have no need of male company. The practices of staff appear to be less intrusive and less demeaning towards women, as judged by lack of complaint about such matters in our study. Informality probably eases frictions associated with rigid gender roles and, indeed, the adjustments in social relations between men and women in the last couple of decades may be one cause of informalisation. For all, there seems to be less harassment and unwelcome attention from waiting staff. Moreover, ritualised manners may be becoming less restrictive and less obligatory. In the past there was a code of formal behaviour, probably most widely honoured by the middle classes for whom it acted as an exclusionary device, so that while the working class could not be prohibited from eating in smart restaurants they could be dissuaded by being made to feel ill at ease. Some residues of this exclusion through manners probably explain the concentration of middle-class people in ethnic cuisine restaurants and at dinner parties, and it might be argued that the major shift in this sphere is a result of professional and managerial workers extending their repertoire of venues to more popular places, rather than lower classes widening their horizons.

It could equally be argued on the basis of our evidence that entertaining guests at dinner has also become a less formal affair. The evidence of improvisation around the social template certainly suggests so. Appropriate behaviour is increasingly a function of private negotiations endorsed through expectations shared by intimate, local circles of friends, acquaintances and wider kin. Many such events are, precisely, characterised by their relaxation of the rules of the dinner party. Forbearance stretches to the food; entertaining friends seemed to allow the preparation of a very wide range of dishes without need to abide by authoritative rules regarding food content or meal pattern.

Overall, we might say that not only service but also the content and structure of meals and the mannered rituals of the social performance of dining out have all become subject to informalisation. The same might be said of aspects of domestic provision too, where children's personal preferences are increasingly indulged and where meal times are less rigid.

A third similarity between the two modes is that neither the restaurant nor the communal meal fundamentally challenge the centrality of the structure of the domestic family meal. If anything they reinforce the social relations surrounding the mundane activity of preparing food for families. The commercial meal out is temporary respite for predominantly female providers, its exceptional occurrence merely underlining the normality of a gendered domestic division of labour. The communal version probably does this even more so, since the way the work is divided up when entertaining tends to replicate the distribution of labour within the household. So although we do not agree that the restaurant simply extrapolates from the domestic family meal to offer it in the form of the cooked dinner, we see the meal out as the exception that proves the rule about conventional domestic distribution of duties of care within families.

## The social consequences of eating out

Finally, we seek to estimate how the spread of restaurants has affected other aspects of food habits. To eat a main meal away from home, on an occasional basis, is now part of the experience of the vast majority of people in England. As such it is part of a long-term trend towards equalisation, for eating elaborate meals out was mostly restricted to the urban middle class, and was disproportionately a male activity, until at least the 1950s. But as yet it is still not a very common or frequent activity, and is still considered special. The proportion of household food expenditure devoted to food eaten away from home has increased steadily since 1960, having reached at the time of this study about one quarter. However, as a proportion of all household expenditure it has risen only a little since 1960, despite substantial increase in real incomes, suggesting that eating out on commercial premises may continue to command only a comparatively narrow share of total consumption. It is already a very important leisure activity and may yet become more routinely incorporated into outings for other leisure purposes. However, dining out for its own sake has yet to gather the esteem that it has in societies of, for instance, Chinese tradition (see Anderson, 1988). While there may well be more space for meals eaten for reasons of convenience, these are likely to be ones that are comparatively hurried and cheap (as in the USA), rather than ones associated with special occasions where food and companionship are celebrated – which is the current meaning of the practice for the urban population of England.

As yet, the restaurant has probably had limited effect on eating habits or the social relations of food consumption. While the spread of restaurants, in the context of wider cultural shifts, has probably had significant effect in changing the food content of dishes, it has had minor impact upon the other basic aspects of food practice. Restaurants have had their principal effect on *what* we eat. The dishes that our respondents reported as having eaten on their last visit to a commercial establishment ranged widely across the world's cuisines. More than anything, it is familiarity with dishes of foreign extraction, most obviously of curries, pasta and stir-fries, that has emanated from popular usage of restaurants. Burnett (1989: 312) records a widespread incapacity in 1976 to identify some of the more common meals reported in 1995 (in 1976 around 30 per cent knew of moussaka, 40 per cent of chilli con carne and 80 per cent of chow mein). Recipes slide from the restaurant table into domestic cookery books and versions of restaurant dishes have become domesticated.

It is not difficult to imagine that general familiarity with restaurants might have altered social practices radically. However, the catering trades as yet, rather than re-defining the elements of a meal, have mostly accommodated to its obligations. Indeed, the 'proper' meal may be better honoured when eating out than when at home. People associate eating out with an elaborate meal, of more than one course, sitting at the table, taking time, sharing company and conversation. So while the food content may be more varied than twenty years earlier, the restaurant has had comparatively little effect in other respects. In fact, the take-away shop may be a far more corrosive institution; foods purchased out of the house and brought home do seem to require less ritual than both those cooked at home and those eaten in a public dining room. Thus the restaurant has had limited effect on the structure of meals; indeed it has apparently imported the dominant domestic model of two or three courses to replace the gargantuan epics produced by hotels in the earlier part of the century (see Bowden, 1975).

Commercial providers colonise the rituals and social practices of companionship by trying to make the commercial setting appropriate for all kinds of social occasion associated with meals. For example, it is increasingly normal to mark a special occasion by buying a meal out, and a gift relation among the diners also operates when one person pays the bill for the whole company. But, socially, the mere purchasing of such a gift is insufficient; the person offering the gift must also participate among companions. Deep-set rules of companionship are the key or core values of the eating out experience; in many respects traditional survivals, they have an authority and inviolability which means that companionship incurs a certain set of obligations involving co-presence, communicative competence and some form of social commitment or investment. Joint participation creates the occasion, in the sense that the atmosphere both at individual tables and across the restaurant as a whole is a function not just of the ambience of the restaurant as designed by its management but of a form of social and collective self-servicing by the customers. This is not a process of conscious orchestration so much as an expression of the high level of self-discipline which the general social process of informalisation requires of individuals. It is the basic self-discipline of diners that gives them the power to improvise a meaningful social encounter on alien territory.

Finally, nor has the restaurant had much impact upon the kinds of companions with whom people eat. The presence of partners and kin around the commercial dinner table is frequent, though just possibly the degree of interaction with friends over meals has been augmented with the extension of the practice of eating out for pleasure.

Even if it has not undermined the dominant principles of the meal, eating out at restaurants probably has some significant consequences for social relations and social institutions. For example, it continues to operate as a field of distinction, marking boundaries of status through the display of taste. The survey demonstrated how different social groups frequented different types of outlet and offered presumptive evidence that some tastes are more prestigious than others, a tendency currently particularly pronounced with respect to establishments specialising in particular ethnic cuisines. Bryson (1996) identified a paradox, that while inequalities of income have increased over the last two decades, cultural differentiation has apparently diminished. One explanation is that there is now so much variety of choice that it is impossible to connect people's tastes to their social position. Thus taste becomes socially unimportant, distinction obsolete. However, class differences have not disappeared. The professional and managerial classes are thronging to ethnic cuisine restaurants, while poorer, working class, older, provincial people are not. Familiarity with ethnic cuisine is a mark of refinement.

Frequent eating out on commercial premises is associated positively with having high household income, being highly educated, being younger and being single, and negatively with being a housewife. Significantly, the same factors also operate, and even more strongly, in one sector of the communal mode, eating with friends. People with greater economic and cultural capital are most frequently invited to be a guest in someone else's home, while such characteristics are much less important in respect of kin. Happily, you don't have to be rich for mum to cook for you! Since there is a statistical association between restaurant going and entertaining, it is possible that the expansion of the former has encouraged the latter and even extended the habit of entertaining to a wider population than previously.

There is little evidence that the restaurant has had much effect on the gender relations of food preparation. There is no systematic use of commercial facilities to relieve women with the greatest burdens, nor indeed any redistribution of domestic tasks to deal with them. Hence, resort to pre-prepared 'convenience' foods at home is the most likely means to reduce pressure. For, while meals out reduce labour, they are mostly not a means of 'saving' time; they usually take longer and require as much advanced organisation as eating at home. Thus the principal competition to the expansion of the market share of the catering trades at the present is almost certainly the supermarket chains' capacity to produce packaged meals of acceptable quality and price. Not only has restaurant-going failed to reduce women's domestic obligations for food preparation but it may even have made the burden more onerous by raising expectations regarding quality and variety of dishes. On the other hand, a significant minority of men are reported as being involved in the core activities of food preparation and cooking, and their engagement, though almost always because they positively enjoy cooking, might possibly be accounted for by their greater familiarity with restaurants and the greater public visibility and reputation of professional chefs.

Eating out is a major and expanding conduit for sociable interaction. Few people go out to dine alone, and only a small proportion of eating out occasions are for purposes of business. Hence most people eat out in the company of family or friends, parties often containing both, thus increasing opportunities for social mixing. Overall, the practice of eating out provides a context for sociability and the maintenance of social networks of close relationships. In a world of geographic mobility, small households, smaller and unstable families, discontent with traditional divisions of labour, eating out is a rich source not of incivility, as Finkelstein maintained, but of conviviality and co-operation.

# Methodological appendix: data collection and analysis

The semi-structured interviews were conducted first because it was thought that in the absence of prior social scientific inquiry it would otherwise be difficult to construct informative questions for a survey instrument. For example, we were not sure whether people would be able to recall details of what they had eaten on their most recent excursions, something about which we were much reassured in the course of the interviews. Nor were we entirely confident that the themes and trends discussed in the popular media would intersect, never mind resonate, with the generality of ordinary experience. Thus, in the absence of previous scholarly investigation, we deemed it essential to pay great attention to the experiences and understandings of a cross-section of the population. Hence an accurate empirical description of practices and discourses, and their social distributions, was a major objective.

Semi-structured interviews – with thirty-three principal food provider(s) in thirty households in diverse circumstances living in Preston and the surrounding area, during the autumn of 1994 – each lasted between one and two hours.[1] To ensure variety, interviewees were volunteers contacted through various organisations, a leisure centre, a community association, a tennis club, an environmental group, a primary school, a trade union branch and, finally, a national DIY chain store.

Our sampling was modelled on DeVault (1991), and like her, we sought to speak to 'anyone, man or woman, who performed a substantial portion of the feeding work in the household' (22). Reflecting the prevailing gender division in domestic food work, twenty-eight women and five men were interviewed. Three men were interviewed on their own, and two were present in a joint interview with their partner.[2] We selected house-

---

[1] After the pilot stage, all interviews were conducted by Lydia Martens.

[2] One of the men interviewed alone, Steve, shared a house with a colleague and both depended to a considerable degree on the works canteen for their everyday meals. Amongst the joint interviews, David sat in and contributed to the discussion but could not be described as someone who did 'a substantial portion of the feeding work'. Peter did do some of the household's cooking and other food work.

holds with two or more people in them, but not necessarily households with children.[3] Nine of our households did not have children in them, seventeen households had dependent children, nine non-dependent children.[4] Of the thirty households in our sample, twenty-seven were 'white' and the other three were South Asian Muslims: one British–Indian, one British–Pakistani and one born in Pakistan.[5] These interviews suggested that the experiences of domestic eating as well as eating out, particularly for those who adhere to halal food rules, is different in many respects than for the 'white' sample, and we comment on these features where relevant. Eighteen of the women in our sample engaged in remunerated work, and equal numbers worked full- and part-time. Three of the nine full-time employed women had dependent children (and two of them were 'non-white' volunteers), whereas five of the nine part-time employed women had dependent children. Six women were housewives, and all but one had dependent children. Of the five men who were interviewed, four were full-time employed, and one worked part-time. Like DeVault, our sample contained households in different occupational and income categories. Our poorest households contained two students, two women who received disability benefit, two women who supported their households (containing an invalid husband and a retired husband respectively) with low-paid part-time work, and one housewife with an unemployed husband.

All interviewees were asked questions about aspects of eating at home and eating out. The interviews were semi-structured and discussion was wide-ranging around the key topics. Not all interviews addressed each topic in the same depth.

Preston is located in Lancashire, North-West England, at the north end of the nineteenth-century textile manufacturing belt. It had a population of 121,000 in 1991. Formerly, the principal source of employment was the cotton industry but since 1945 this has diversified, with British Aerospace and British Nuclear Fuels Ltd among the major employers. Preston is a major regional service centre, housing the administrative headquarters of Lancashire County Council, the large University of Central Lancashire and a range of state organisations commensurate with its size and function. About a third of all people in employment in 1991

---

[3] In this sense our sample differed from DeVault, whose volunteers all lived in households with children.

[4] Some of these households had both dependent and non-dependent children. We included amongst dependent children those aged fifteen and younger. Non-dependent children were sixteen and over and still living in the household. There were thirteen non-dependent children in our households, nine of whom were twenty or over. One of them was a single parent living with her mother.

[5] There were no Afro-Caribbean households in our sample.

were in the public administration, health and education sectors. Its occupational structure at the 1991 census was rather similar to the national pattern. Retailing was spatially concentrated in a compact central zone though it had in addition many catering outlets dispersed around the periphery. It had an unemployment rate one or two points above the national average for Great Britain during the 1990s, and contained pockets of social deprivation. Household disposable income per head for the county of Lancashire was about 90 per cent of the UK average in 1994 (Lancashire County Council, 1998: 122). Ten per cent of the population was classified as belonging to ethnic minority groups, the great majority Indian.

Analysis of our survey data suggested some interesting differences between the three cities, but these were not very marked and most of the distinctive characteristics were associated with London. Hence, we would not expect the qualitative interviews to be idiosyncratic on account of the location.

Preliminary analysis was undertaken in order to design a questionnaire for the second phase. Thereafter, the interviews were analysed in considerable detail,[6] focusing on shared understandings which defined eating events and differential orientations and attitudes towards eating out. As part of this, we analysed reasons for using eating out services, how often and with whom interviewees ate out, and likes and dislikes with respect to food, venues, time, etc. The procedure of analysis entailed coding all talk on specific questions[7] and themes[8] that interested us, and then examining these for sub-themes that revealed the complexity of meanings. Sometimes, the coding process was straightforward, for instance in answers to direct questions, sometimes complex, when themes occurred at different stages of the discussion. For example, judgements about food appeared throughout, in discussion of last meals, in specific questioning about attitudes towards novel and 'foreign' foods, but also in comments about appropriate quantities. Such evaluative talk on food was further analysed to isolate themes of 'good–bad foods' (and sub-themes like 'foreign', 'quality', 'quantity' and 'health'), 'novelty' (with further sub-themes of, for instance, 'adventurousness', 'variety' and ' traditional'), 'exotic', 'presen-

---

[6] All interviews were transcribed and the responses of twenty-six were coded using the NUD*IST package for the analysis of qualitative data.

[7] Specific questions asked and analysed related to the consumer's understanding of eating out, the reasons for eating out and engaging in a number of other eating events on the boundaries of eating out, and whether the interviewee would like to eat out more than he/she did at the time of interview.

[8] In relation to eating out, the text was scanned for talk on formality, pleasure, likes and dislikes, as well as for evaluative talk on food, venues, service, customers, company, decor, costs, time, and Preston as a place to eat out.

tation', 'drink', and differences between foods eaten in and out. Throughout, we examined the extent to which meanings varied between respondents on the basis of, for instance, class background, age and gender.

In Phase II, 1,001 people were surveyed using a questionnaire in three cities in England; London, Bristol and Preston were chosen to offer contrasts of socio-demographic composition and, putatively, cultural ambience.[9] The survey was undertaken in April 1995 and was administered to a quota sample which matched respondents to the overall population of diverse local sub-areas of the cities by age, sex, class and employment status. Interviews in the three cities were conducted in sub-divisions, identified by postcode, and selected for their spatial locations and their varied population mixes according to the 1991 small area Census. Ten sub-areas were sampled in each city.[10] Quotas were set for each sub-area and sub-division.[11] The final sample matched the socio-demographic features of the sub-areas reasonably satisfactorily.[12]

Quota samples are in certain respects problematic. Respondents are not selected randomly, those interviewed being ones readily accessible to the interviewers.[13] There is hence no means to estimate bias arising from selection or non-response and hence no justification for claiming that our results are generalisable to the populations of even the three cities. Consequently the precise frequencies recorded should not be given too much weight and the limitations of the data should be borne in mind when considering the interpretations laid upon our statistical analyses. However, we have no reason to believe that the general picture that we offer, with its intimations of systematically differentiated behaviour between social groups, is substantively flawed or misleading.

We used a variety of statistical techniques to analyse and interpret the

[9] The fieldwork was undertaken by Public Attitude Surveys (PAS).

[10] In Preston four sub-areas were selected within the postcode area PR1, another four in PR2 and two in PR5. In Bristol, two sub-areas were chosen in BS16 and one each in BS2, 4, 5, 8, 9, 11, 13, 14. Two London boroughs were covered, Islington (N1, 4, 5, 7, 19) in the inner city, and Ealing (W3, 5 [two sub-areas], 7, 13) an outer suburb to the west.

[11] Quotas were set in terms of gender, age (four groups 16–24, 25–39, 40–54, 55–64), class (ABC1, C2DE), ethnicity (white or other) and employment status (employed [full- or part-time] or not employed), based on the known profiles of each sub-division as recorded in the 1991 Census.

[12] Generally speaking the quotas set within each of the three cities were achieved, although some switching of priorities was required across the sub-divisions when inspection revealed significant differences in demographic make-up from the published profile. Table A1 indicates the quotas allocated and the final achieved.

[13] However, 'While interviewers had freedom of movement and thus selection within their sub-division, the allocation of quotas (in particular social class) ensured that they spread their interviews across the entire area, with the usual limitation of no more than one interview per household and the leaving of five households between successful interviews' (PAS, 1995:3).

Table A1 *The quota sample*

| | Preston | | Bristol | | Greater London Council | |
|---|---|---|---|---|---|---|
| | Allocated percentage | Achieved percentage | Allocated percentage | Achieved percentage | Allocated percentage | Achieved percentage |
| Gender | | | | | | |
| Male | 50 | 50 | 50 | 50 | 50 | 48 |
| Female | 50 | 50 | 50 | 50 | 50 | 52 |
| Age | | | | | | |
| 16–24 | 20 | 21 | 21 | 22 | 20 | 20 |
| 25–39 | 35 | 36 | 36 | 36 | 42 | 42 |
| 40–54 | 28 | 26 | 28 | 28 | 25 | 26 |
| 55–64 | 17 | 17 | 15 | 14 | 13 | 12 |
| Social class[a] | | | | | | |
| ABC1 | 51 | — | 54 | — | 63 | — |
| C2DE | 40 | — | 54 | — | 37 | — |
| Working status | | | | | | |
| full-time/part-time working | 62 | 62 | 59 | 60 | 63 | 61 |
| not working | 38 | 38 | 41 | 40 | 37 | 39 |
| Total (N =) | 340 | 337 | 340 | 334 | 340 | 330 |

*Note:*
[a] Social class (ABC1 and C2DE) was allocated as a quota based on the demographic profile of the region as a whole, i.e. North-West, South-West, Greater London Council. Census data is not available in these terms for the survey. We coded occupation in terms of socio-economic groups and the ABC1/C2DE categorisation was not coded.

survey data – means, cross-tabulation, factor analysis and multiple regression. Much of our analysis and interpretation could be sustained on the basis of the more elementary techniques and in most instances these are the results reported in the text. However, we did undertake factor analysis to explore the answers to some attitude questions about the experience of eating out, and used some logistic regression analysis to explore the primary bases of the social differentiation of practice.

Common sense, observation and market research tell us that the many kinds of eating out places are, to some extent, frequented by different sorts of people. The survey allows exploration in more detail, and with more incisive techniques than the cross-tabulations used previously. Such advanced methods are valuable because many socio-demographic variables like age, education, occupation and income are correlated with one another so that it is often unclear which features have greatest effect. For instance, is it the cultural learning process involved in obtaining a degree, or the occupational community of fellow professionals, or simply having greater than average salary which accounts for the clientele of French restaurants? More sophisticated statistical analysis compensates for their mutual dependence. Regression techniques estimate the importance of each explanatory variable on the assumption that there is no variation in any other variable. So, for example, when the relationship between education and familiarity with Indian cuisine is measured, income, age, class, gender and other factors are held constant. Because this technique involves automatic computation by strength of association, eliminating the more weakly correlated of any effects, there is a possibility of spuriously eliminating some important factors. It is therefore necessary to examine in a degree of detail which cannot be reported here (for the results are difficult to convey succinctly) the process or order in which variables have been eliminated and, where appropriate, to employ theoretical reasoning to prevent, or guide, elimination of factors postulated to be central. But this proved neither relevant nor necessary in this study.

# References

Abercrombie, N. (1994) 'Authority and consumer society' in R. Keat, N. Whiteley and N. Abercrombie (eds.) *The Authority of the Consumer* (London: Routledge), 43–57.

Abu-Lughod, J. (1991) 'Going beyond the global babble' in A. King (ed.), *Culture, Globalisation and the World System: contemporary conditions for the representation of identity* (London: Macmillan), 131–8.

Adorno, T. (1991) *The Culture Industry: selected essays on mass culture* (London: Routledge).

Allan, G. (1979) *A Sociology of Friendship and Kinship* (London George Allen and Unwin).

Anderson, Eugene N. (1988) *The Food of China* (New Haven: Yale University Press).

Appadurai, A. (1986) *The Social Life of Things: commodities in cultural perspective* (Cambridge: Cambridge University Press).

(1988) 'How to make a national cuisine: cookbooks in contemporary India', *Comparative Studies of Society and History*, 30(1), 3–24.

Atkinson, P. (1980) 'The symbolic significance of health foods' in M. Turner (ed.) *Nutrition and Lifestyles* (London: Applied Science Publishers), 79–89.

Bakhtin, M. (1968) *Rabelais and his World* (Cambridge, MA: MIT Press).

Ballaster, R., Beetham, M., Frazer, E. and Hebron, S. (1991) *Women's Worlds: ideology, femininity and the woman's magazine* (London: Macmillan).

Bataille, G. (1991) *The Accursed Share: an essay on general economy. Volume I: Consumption* (New York: Zone Books).

Baudrillard, J. (1981) *For a Critique of the Political Economy of the Sign* (St Louis, MO: Telos Press).

Bauman, Z. (1991) *Modernity and ambivalence* (Cambridge: Polity Press).

Beardsworth, A. and Keil, T. (1997) *Sociology on the Menu: an invitation to the study of food and society* (London: Routledge).

Beck, U. (1992) *Risk Society: towards a new modernity* (London: Sage).

Bell, D. and Valentine, G. (1997) *Consuming Geographies: we are where we eat* (London: Routledge).

Beyfus, D. (1992) *Modern Manners: the complete guide to contemporary etiquette* (London: Hamlyn).

Bishop, J. and Hoggett, P. (1986) *Organising around Enthusiasms* (London: Comedia).

Bogenhold, D., Petrowsky, W. and Tempel, G. (1997) 'Social inclusion and exclu-

234

sion of consumption', paper delivered to European Sociological Association Conference, Essex University, August.

Bordo, S. (1993) *Unbearable Weight: feminism, western culture and the body* (Berkeley: University of California Press).

Bourdieu, P. (1984) *Distinction: a social critique of the judgment of taste* (London: Routledge and Kegan Paul).

Bowden, G. H. (1975) *British Gastronomy: the rise of great restaurants* (London: Chatto and Windus).

Bowlby, R. (1985) *Just Looking: consumer culture in Dreiser, Gissing and Zola* (London: Methuen).

Brannen, J. (ed.) (1992) *Mixing Methods: qualitative and quantitative research* (Aldershot: Avebury).

Bryson, B. (1996) '"Anything but heavy metal": symbolic exclusion and musical dislikes', *American Sociological Review*, 61, 844–99.

Burgess, R. and Morrison, M. (1998) 'Chapatis and chips: encountering food use in primary school settings', *British Food Journal*, 100 (3), 141–6.

Burnett, J. (1989) *Plenty and Want: a social history of food from 1815 to the present day* (3rd edn) (London: Routledge).

*Business Monitor* (1996) *UK Service Sector: catering and allied trades* (London: HMSO).

Campbell, C. (1987) *The Romantic Ethic and the Spirit of Modern Consumerism* (Oxford: Blackwell).

—— (1995) 'The sociology of consumption' in D. Miller (ed.) *Acknowledging Consumption: a review of new studies* (London: Routledge), 96–126.

Campbell-Smith, M. (1967) *Marketing the Meal Experience: a fundamental approach* (Guildford: University of Surrey Press).

Caplan, P. (ed.) (1997) *Food, Identity and Health* (London: Routledge).

Charles, N. and Kerr, M. (1988) *Women, Food and Families* (Manchester: Manchester University Press).

Chivers T. (1973) 'The proletarianisation of a service worker', *Sociological Review*, 21 (4), 633–56.

Cockburn, C. and Ormrod, S. (1993) *Gender and Technology in the Making* (London: Sage).

Cook, I. and Crang, P. (1996) 'The world on a plate: culinary culture, displacement and geographical knowledges', *Journal of Material Culture*, 1, 131–54.

Crang, P. (1994) 'It's showtime: on the workplace geographies of display in a restaurant in southeast England', *Environment and Planning D: Society and Space*, 12, 675–704.

Cross, G. (1993) *Time and Money: the making of consumer culture* (London: Routledge).

Csikszentmihalyi, M. (1992) *Flow: the psychology of happiness* (London: Rider)

Csikszentmihalyi, M. and Rochberg-Halton, E. (1981) *The Meaning of Things: domestic symbols and the self* (Cambridge: Cambridge University Press).

Dennis, R., Henriques, F. and Slaughter, C. (1956) *Coal is our Life: an analysis of a Yorkshire mining community* (London: Eyre and Spottiswoode).

Dennis, N. and Erdos, G. (1993) *Families Without Fatherhood* (2nd edn) (London: Institute for Economic Affairs).

236    References

DeVault, M. (1990) 'Talking and listening from women's standpoint: feminist strategies for interviewing and analysis', *Social Problems*, 37 (1), 96-116.

(1991) *Feeding the Family : the social organisation of caring as gendered work* (Chicago: University of Chicago Press).

DiMaggio, P. (1987) 'Classification in art' *American Sociological Review*, 52, 440-55.

Douglas, M. (1975) 'Deciphering a meal', *Daedalus*, 101(1), 61-81.

(1996a) *Thought Styles* (London: Sage).

(1996b) 'On not being seen dead: shopping as protest' in *Thought Styles* (London: Sage), 77-105.

Douglas, M. and Nicod, M. (1974) 'Taking the biscuit: the structure of British meals', *New Society*, 19 (30 Dec.), 774.

Driver, C. (1983) *The British at Table, 1940-80* (London: Chatto and Windus).

Dunleavy, K. and Martens, L. (1997) 'Eating out is "special": the reproduction of sociality and the social construction of meals', paper delivered to European Sociological Association Conference, Essex University, August.

Erickson, B. H. (1991) 'What is good taste for?', *Canadian Review of Sociology and Anthropology*, 28(2), 255-78.

(1996) 'Culture, class and connections', *American Journal of Sociology*, 102(1), 217-51.

Euromonitor (1993) *Market Reports: Catering in the 1990s* (London: Euromonitor PLC).

Falk, P. (1994) *The Consuming Body* (London: Sage).

Falk, P. and Campbell, C. (eds.) (1997) *The Shopping Experience* (London: Sage).

Family Expenditure Surveys, Department of Employment (various years) (London: HMSO); after 1990 becomes Family Spending: a Report on the Family Expenditure Surveys (various years), (London: CSO).

Fantasia, R. (1995) 'Fast food in France', *Theory and Society*, 24, 201-43.

Fattorini, J. (1994) 'Food journalism: a medium for conflict?' *British Food Journal*, 96(10), 24-8.

Featherstone, M. (1991) *Consumer Culture and Postmodernism* (London: Sage).

Finch, J. and Mason, J. (1993) *Negotiating Family Responsibilities* (London: Routledge).

Fine, B. and Leopold, E. (1993) *The World of Consumption* (London: Routledge).

Fine, B., Heasman, M. and Wright, J. (1996) *Consumption in the Age of Affluence: the world of food* (London: Routledge).

Fine, G. (1995a) *Kitchens: the culture of restaurant work* (Berkeley: University of California Press).

(1995b) 'Wittgenstein's kitchen: sharing meaning in restaurant work', *Theory and Society*, 24, 245-69.

Finnegan, R. (1989) *The Hidden Musicians: making music in an English town* (Cambridge: Cambridge University Press).

Fischler, C. (1980) 'Food habits, social change and the nature/culture dilemma', *Social Science Information*, 19, 937-53.

Finkelstein, J. (1989) *Dining Out: a sociology of modern manners* (Oxford: Polity Press).

Gabaccia, D. (1998) *We Are What We Eat: ethnic food and the making of Americans* (Cambridge, MA: Harvard University Press).

Gabriel, Y. (1988) *Working Lives in Catering* (London: Routledge).

Gershuny, J. (1992) 'Change in the domestic division of labour in the UK: dependant labour versus adaptive partnership' in N. Abercrombie and A. Warde (eds.) *Social Change in Contemporary Britain* (Cambridge: Polity Press), 70–94.

Gershuny, J., Godwin, M. and Jones, S. (1994) 'The domestic labour revolution: a process of lagged adaptation' in M. Anderson, F. Bechhofer and J. Gershuny (eds.) *The Social and Political Economy of the Household* (Oxford: Oxford University Press), 151–97.

Giddens, A. (1991) *Modernity and Self-Identity* (Cambridge: Polity Press).

(1992) *The Transformation of Intimacy: sexuality, love and eroticism in modern societies* (Cambridge: Polity Press).

Gofton, L. (1990) 'Food fears and time famines: some aspects of choosing and using food', *British Nutrition Foundation Bulletin*, 15(1) 78–95.

(1995) 'Dollar rich and time poor?: some problems in interpreting changing food habits', *British Food Journal*, 97(10), 11–16.

(1996) 'Convenience and the moral status of consumer practices' in D. Marshall (ed.) *Food Choice and the Consumer,* (Glasgow: Blackie), 152–81.

(1998) 'British market research data on food: a note on their use for the academic study of food choice' in A. Murcott (ed.) *The Nation's Diet* (London: Longman).

Goody, J. (1982) *Cooking, Cuisine and Culture: a study in comparative sociology* (Cambridge: Cambridge University Press).

Gregson, N. and Lowe, M. (1993) 'Renegotiating the domestic division of labour?: a study of dual-career households in north-east and south-east England', *Sociological Review*, 41(3), 475–505.

Gregson, N. and Lowe, M. (1993) *Servicing the Middle Classes: class, gender and waged domestic labour in contemporary Britain* (London: Routledge).

Halkier, B. (1997) 'Environmental consideration in consumption: everyday experiences of young Danish consumers', paper delivered to European Sociological Association Conference, Essex University, August.

Hardyment, C. (1995) *Slice of Life: the British way of eating since 1945* (London: BBC Books).

Heal, F. (1990) *Hospitality in Early Modern England* (Oxford: Clarendon Press).

Health Education Authority (1996) *The National Catering Initiative: offering the consumer a choice. Findings from research into consumer attitudes to healthier eating out* (London: HEA).

Hermes, J. (1995) *Reading Women's Magazines* (Cambridge: Polity Press).

Hertz, R. (1992) 'Financial affairs: money and authority in dual-earner marriage' in S. Lewis et al. (eds.) *Dual-Earner Families: international perspectives* (London: Sage).

Hewitt, P. (1993) *About Time: the revolution in work and family life* (London: IPPR/Rivers Oram Press).

Hirsch, F. (1978) *Social Limits to Growth* (London: Routledge and Kegan Paul).

Hirschman, A. (1970) *Exit, Voice and Loyalty: reposonses to decline in firms, organizations and states* (Cambridge, MA: Harvard University Press).

(1982) *Shifting Involvements: private interest and public action* (Princeton, NJ: Princeton University Press).

238     References

Hochschild, A. (1983) *The Managed Heart: the commercialisation of human feeling* (Berkeley: University of California Press).
   (1989) *The Second Shift: working parents and the revolution at home* (London: Paithus).
Hoggart, R. (1958) *The Uses Of Literacy* (Harmondsworth: Penguin).
Holt, D. (1997a) 'Distinction in America?: recovering Bourdieu's theory of tastes from its critics', *Poetics*, 25, 93–120.
   (1997b) 'Poststructuralist lifestyle analysis: conceptualising the social patterning of consumption in postmodernity', *Journal of Consumer Research*, 23, 326–50.
James, A. (1990) 'The good, the bad and the delicious: the role of confectionery in British Society', *Sociological Review*, 38, 666–88.
Jerrome, D. (1984) 'Good company: the sociological implications of friendship', *Sociological Review*, 32(4), 696–718.
Keane, A. and Willetts, A. (1995) *Concepts of Healthy Eating: an anthropological investigation in south east London* (London: Goldsmiths' College, University of London).
Kempson, E. (1996) *Life on a Low Income* (York: J. Rowntree Foundation).
KeyNote (1996), *UK Catering Markets: 1996 market review* (London: Keynote).
   (1997) *Restaurants: 1997 market report* (London: Keynote).
Lamont, M. (1992) *Money, Morals and Manners: the culture of the French and American upper-middle class* (Chicago: Chicago University Press).
Lancashire County Council (1998) *Lancashire 1998: an economic situation report.*
Lane, R. E. (1991) *The Market Experience* (Cambridge: Cambridge University Press).
Lash, S. (1995) 'Reflexivity and its doubles: structure, aesthetics, community' in U. Beck, A. Giddens and S. Lash, *Reflexive Modernisation* (Cambridge: Polity Press), 110–73.
Leidner, R. (1993) *Fast Food, Fast Talk: service work and the rationalisation of everyday life* (Berkeley: University of California Press).
Levenstein, H. (1988) *Revolution at the Table: the transformation of the American diet* (Oxford: Oxford University Press).
   (1993) *The Paradox of Plenty: a social history of eating in modern America* (Oxford: Oxford University Press).
Levi-Strauss, C. (1966) 'The culinary triangle', *New Society*, December, 937–40.
Linder, S. B. (1970) *The Harried Leisure Class* (New York: Columbia University Press).
Lunt, P. and Livingstone, S. (1992) *Mass Consumption and Personal Identity* (Milton Keynes: Open University Press).
Lupton, D. (1996) *Food, the Body and the Self* (London: Sage).
Mack, J. and Lansley, S. (1985) *Poor Britain* (London: George, Allen and Unwin).
Marcuse, H. (1964) *One Dimensional Man: the ideology of industrial society* (Boston: Basic Books).
Mars, G. and Nicod, M. (1984) *The World of Waiters* (London: Allen and Unwin).
Marshall, D. (ed.) (1995a) *Food Choice and the Consumer* (London: Blackie).
   (1995b) 'Eating at home: meals and food choice' in D. Marshall (ed.), 264–91.
Marshall, G. (1986) 'The workplace culture of a licensed restaurant', *Theory, Culture & Society* 3(1) 33–48.

Martens, L. (1995) 'Gender and domestic decision-making processes around food consumption', paper presented at the Gender Perspectives on Household Issues Conference, Reading, April.

(1997) 'Gender and the eating out experience', *British Food Journal* 99(1), 20–6.

(1998) 'Juicy steaks in creamy sauces or salad sandwiches?: locating gender in the eating out experience', *Salford Working Papers in Sociology*, University of Salford.

Martens, L. and Warde, A. (1997) 'Urban pleasure?: on the meaning of eating out in a northern city' in P. Caplan (ed.) *Food, Identity and Health* (London: Routledge), 131–50.

(1998) 'The social and symbolic significance of ethnic cuisine in England: new cosmopolitanism and old xenophobia?', *Sociologisk Arbok*, 3(1), 111–46.

Mazurkiewicz, R. (1983) 'Gender and social consumption,' *Services Industries Journal*, 3(1), 49–62.

Medlik, S. (1972) *Profile of the Hotel and Catering Industry* (London: Heinemann).

Mennell, S. (1985) *All Manners of Food: eating and taste in England and France from the middle ages to the Present* (Oxford: Blackwell).

Mennell, S., Murcott, A., and Van Otterloo, A. (1992) *The Sociology of Food: eating, diet and culture* (London: Sage).

Miller, D. (1987) *Material Culture and Mass Consumption* (Oxford: Blackwell).

Miller, D. (ed.) (1995) *Acknowledging Consumption: a review of new studies* (London: Routledge).

Ministry of Agriculture, Fisheries and Food (MAFF) (1995) National Food Survey, 1994 (London: HMSO).

(1997) National Food Survey, 1995 (London: HMSO).

MINTEL (1994) *Special Report: Catering 1994* (London: MINTEL).

Mintz, S. (1985) *Sweetness and Power: the place of sugar in modern history* (Harmondsworth: Penguin).

Moorhouse, H. (1983) 'American automobiles and workers' dreams', *Sociological Review*, 31(3), 403–26.

(1991) *Driving Ambitions: an analysis of the American hotrod enthusiasm* (Manchester: Manchester University Press).

Morley, D. (1992) *Television, Audiences and Cultural Studies* (London: Routledge).

Morris, L. D. (1990) *The Workings of the Household* (Cambridge: Polity Press).

Morrison, M. (1996) 'Sharing food at home and school: perspectives on commensality', *Sociological Review*, 44(4), 648–75.

Murcott, A. (1982) 'On the social significance of the "cooked dinner" in South Wales', *Social Science Information*, 21, 677–95.

(1983a) 'Cooking and the cooked: a note on the domestic preparation of meals', in A. Murcott (ed.) *The Sociology of Food and Eating* (Aldershot: Gower), 178-85.

(1983b) '"It's a pleasure to cook for him": food, mealtimes and gender in some South Wales households' in E. Gamarnikow et al. (eds.) *The Public and the Private* (London: Heinemann).

(1988) 'Sociological and social anthropological approaches to food and eating', *World Review of Nutrition and Diet* 55, 1–40.

(1997) 'Family meals – a thing of the past?' in P.Caplan (ed.) *Food, Identity and Health* (London: Routledge), 32–49.

Narayan, U. (1995) 'Eating cultures: incorporation, identity and Indian food', *Social Identities*, 1, 63–86.

National Food Survey: annual report on food expenditure, consumption and nutrient intake, MAFF, various years (London: HMSO).

Nicod, M. (1980) 'Gastronomically speaking: food as a medium of communication' in M. Turner (ed.) *Nutrition and Lifestyles* (London: Applied Science Publishers), 53–66.

Oakley, A. (1974) *The Sociology of Housework* (London: Martin Robertson).

Olsen, W., Warde, A. and Martens, L. (1998) 'Social differentiation and the market for eating out in England', University of Bradford, Graduate School, Methodology Working Paper Series No. 3.

Pahl, J. (1989) *Money and Marriage* (London: Macmillan).
     (1990) 'Household spending, personal spending and the control of money in marriage', *Sociology*, 24(1), 119–38.

Pahl, R. (1984) *Divisions of Labour* (Oxford: Blackwell).

PAS (Public Attitude Surveys Ltd) (1995) *Eating Out and Eating In: a survey technical report* (High Wycombe: PAS).

Payne, M. and B. (1993) *Eating Out in the UK: market structure, consumer attitudes and prospects for the 1990s*, Economist Intelligence Unit Special Report No. 2169 (London: Economist Intelligence Unit and Business International).

Peterson, R. (1992) 'Understanding audience segmentation: from elite and mass to omnivore and univore', *Poetics*, 21, 243–58.

Peterson, R. and Kern, R. (1996) 'Changing highbrow taste: from snob to omnivore', *American Sociological Review*, 61, 900–7.

Pillsbury, R. (1990) *From Boarding House to Bistro: the American restaurant then and now* (London: Unwin Hyman).

Purcell, K. (1992) 'Women's employment and the management of food in households', *Food and Beverage Europe*.

Radner, H. (1995) *Shopping Around: feminine culture and the pursuit of pleasure* (New York: Routledge).

Reiter, E. (1991) *Making Fast Food: from the frying pan into the fryer* (Montreal and Kingston: McGill and Queen's University Press).

*The Restaurant* (1909) vol. 1 (no. 1).

Santich, B. (1996) *Looking for Flavour* (Adelaide: Wakefield Press).

Savage, M., Barlow, J., Dickens, P. and Fielding, T. (1992) *Property, Bureaucracy and Culture: middle-class formation in contemporary Britain* (London: Routledge).

Schama, S. (1987) *The Embarrassment of Riches: an interpretation of Dutch culture in the golden age* (London: Collins).

Scheff, T. (1988) 'Shame and conformity: the deference-emotion system', *American Sociological Review*, 53, 395–406.

Schor, J. (1992) *The Overworked American: the unexpected decline of leisure* (New York: Basic Books).

Schulze, G. (1992) *Die Erlebnisgesellschaft: Kultursoziologie der Gegenwart* (Frankfurt am Main: Suhrkamp).

Sen, A. (1981) *Poverty and Famines* (Oxford: Clarendon Press).

Sennett, R. (1976) *The Fall of Public Man* (Cambridge, Cambridge University Press).

Slater, D. (1997) 'Integrating consumption and leisure: "hobbies" and the structures of everyday life', paper to European Sociological Association Conference, Essex University, August.

Smith, D. (1987) *The Everyday World as Problematic: a feminist sociology* (Boston: Northeastern University Press).

Sombart, W. (1967 [1913]) *Luxury and Capitalism* (Ann Arbor: Michigan University Press).

Sosteric, M. (1996) 'Subjectivity in the labour process: a case study on the restaurant industry', *Work, Employment and Society,* 10(2), 297–318.

Symons, M. (1993) *The Shared Table: ideas for Australian cuisine* (Canberra: Office of Multicultural Affairs, Australian Government Publishing Service).

Synott, A. (1993) *The Body Social: symbolism, self and society* (London: Routledge)

Tomlinson, G. (1986) 'Thought for food: a study of written instructions', *Symbolic Interaction,* 9(2), 201–16.

Twigg, J. (1983) 'Vegetarianism and the meanings of meat' in A. Murcott (ed.), *The Sociology of Food and Eating* (Aldershot: Gower),18–30.

Urry, J. (1990) *The Tourist Gaze: leisure and travel in contemporary societies* (London: Sage).

Van der Berghe, P. (1984) 'Ethnic cuisine: culture in nature', *Ethnic and Racial Studies,* 7(3) 387–97.

Veblen, T. (1925 [1899]) *The Theory of the Leisure Class: an economic study of institutions* (London: George Allen and Unwin).

Visser, M. (1991) *The Rituals of Dinner: the origins, evolution, eccentricities and meaning of table manners* (Harmondsworth: Penguin).

Vogler, C. (1994) 'Money in the household' in M. Anderson, F. Bechhofer and J. Gershuny (eds.) *The Social and Political Economy of the Household* (Oxford: Oxford University Press), 225–66.

Vogler, C and Pahl, J. (1993) 'Social and economic change and the organization of money within marriage', *Work, Employment and Society,* 7(1): 71–95.

Warde, A. (1992) 'Notes on the relationship between production and consumption', in R. Burrows and C. Marsh (eds.) *Consumption and Class: divisions and change* (London: Macmillan, 1992), 15-31.

(1996a) 'Afterword: the future of the sociology of consumption', in S. Edgell, K. Hetherington and A. Warde (eds.) *Consumption Matters,* Sociological Review Monograph Series A, 302–12.

(1996b) 'Eating out and eating in: households and food choice', report to Economic and Social Research Council.

(1997) *Consumption, Food and Taste: culinary antinomies and commodity culture* (London: Sage).

(forthcoming)'Eating globally: cultural flows and the spread of ethnic restaurants' in D. Kalb, M. van der Land, R. Staring, B. van Steenbergen and N. Wilterdink (eds.) *The End of Globalization: Bringing society back in* (Boulder, CO: Rowman and Littlefield).

Warde, A. and Hetherington, K. (1993) 'A changing domestic division of labour?: issues of measurement and interpretation', *Work, Employment and Society,* 7(1), 23–45.

(1994) 'English households and routine food practices: a research note', *Sociological Review,* 42(4), 758–78.

Warde, A. and Martens, L. (1998) 'A sociological approach to food choice: the case of eating out', in A. Murcott (ed.) *The Nation's Diet* (London: Longman), 129–46.

Warde, A., Martens, L. and Olsen, W. (1999) 'Consumption and the problem of variety: cultural omnivorousness, social distinction and dining out', *Sociology* 33(1), 105–27.

Warde, A., Soothill, K., Shapiro, D. and Papantouakou, A. (1989) *Divisions of Labour in North West England* (Lancaster: Lancaster Regionalism Group Working Paper 38).

Warde, A. and Tomlinson, M. (1995) 'Taste among the British middle classes, 1968–88' in T. Butler and M. Savage (eds.) *Social Change and the Middle Classes* (London: UCL Press), 241–56.

Warren, G. (ed) (1958) *The Foods We Eat* (London: Cassell).

Weber, M. (1968) 'Class status and party' in H. Gerth and C.W. Mills (eds.) *From Max Weber: essays in sociology* (London: Routledge Kegan and Paul), 180–95.

Wheelock, J. (1990) *Husbands at Home* (London: Routledge).

Whitehead, A. (1976) 'Sexual antagonism in Herefordshire' in D. Leonard and S. Allen (eds.) *Dependence and Exploitation in Work and Marriage* (London: Longman), 169–203.

Whyte, W. H. (1948) *Human Relations in the Restaurant Industry* (New York: McGraw Hill).

Willmott, P. and Young, M. (1957) *Family and Kinship in East London* (Harmondsworth: Penguin).

Wilson, G. (1989) 'Family food systems, preventive health and dietary change: a policy to increase the health divide', *Journal of Social Policy*, 18, 167–85.

Wood, R. (1990) 'Sociology, gender, food consumption and the hospitality industry', *British Food Journal*, 92(6), 3–5.

(1992a) 'Dining out in the urban context', *British Food Journal*, 94(9), 3–5.

(1992b) *Working in Hotels and Catering* (London: Routledge).

(1994a) 'Dining out on sociological neglect', *British Food Journal*, 96(10), 10–14.

(1994b) 'Hotel culture and social control', *Annals of Tourism Research*, 21(1), 65–80.

(1995) *The Sociology of the Meal* (Edinburgh: Edinburgh University Press).

Wouters, C. (1986) 'Formalization and informalization: changing tension balances in civilising processes', *Theory, Culture* and *Society*, 3, 1–18.

Zelinsky, W. (1985) 'The roving palate: North America's ethnic restaurant cuisines', *Geoforum*, 16(1), 51–72.

Zubaida, S. and Tapper, R. (eds.) (1994) *Culinary Cultures of the Middle East* (London: I.B.Tauris Publishers).

# Index

Lightning Source UK Ltd.
Milton Keynes UK
UKOW041916141212

203696UK00001B/67/P